Using Netscape

Quick Start to Internet Success!

M000087664

The Netscape 2 Window

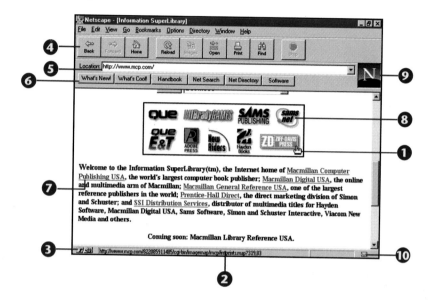

1. When the mouse pointer turns into a hand, it's pointing at a link.

2. Look at the status message for information such as the URL.

3. The broken key means that this is an insecure document.

4. The toolbar provides quick access to common commands.

5. Type a URL (Web address) here, and press Enter to go to that page.

6. Click on a button here to go to a useful document.

7. Underlined and colored words are links; click to see another document.

8. Pictures and logos are often links; click on them to see other documents.

9. This icon shows you when Netscape is working; the meteors move across the sky.

10. Click here to open the Mail window.

QUE® 201 W. 103rd Street • Indianapolis, IN 46290 • (317) 581-3500
Copyright© 1995 Que Corporation

All About URLs

A URL (Uniform Resource Locator) is a Web "address." Here's what one looks like:

```
http://home.mcom.com/newsref/news/index.html
   ❶        ❷              ❸         ❹
```

❶ This is the type of URL, the "protocol" used to use the resource.

❷ This is the host name of the computer containing the file referenced by the URL.

❸ This is the directory path to the file.

❹ This is the name of the file. (It's not always required.)

You can use a URL by clicking on a link (the URL is inside the link), or by typing the URL into the Location text box and pressing Enter.

To go to the Rolling Stones Web site, type this:
http://www.stones.com/

To go to the Win95 archive at the popular Winsite shareware site, type this:
ftp://winsite.com/

To go to the famous Wiretap Gopher site, type this:
gopher://wiretap.spies.com/

To read the alt.binaries.pictures.clip-art newsgroup, type this:
news:alt.binaries.clip-art

URL Types

Here are the different types of URLs:

URL Type	Purpose
http://	HyperText Transfer Protocol—points to a Web document.
https://	Points to a Web document on a secure server.
file:///	References a file on your hard disk.
ftp://	File Transfer Protocol—points to an FTP site where you can transfer files.
gopher://	Enables you to go to a Gopher site.
telnet://	Launches whatever Telnet program you've configured and starts a Telnet session.
tn3270://	Launches your tn3270 program (similar to Telnet).
wais://	Wide Area Information Server—opens a WAIS database. (You can use this only if your system administrator has set up a WAIS proxy.)
mailto:	Starts the Netscape Mail program so you can send an e-mail message.
news:	Opens the Netscape News program and displays a newsgroup.
snews:	Opens the Netscape News program and displays a newsgroup at a secure news server.
about:	Provides information about the program (and some weird stuff). Try the following: **about:plugins, about:security, about:mozilla, and about:jwz.**

The Newsgroup Window

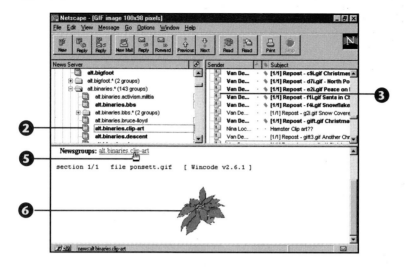

2 *Double-click on a newsgroup to retrieve messages.*

3 *Click on a message to view the contents.*

5 *Newsgroup messages may contain links; click on the link to display the referenced newsgroup or Web page.*

6 *If the message contains a MIME or UUENCODED picture, Netscape displays the picture.*

 New
Opens the Message Composition window so you can send a message to the newsgroup.

 Post Reply
Lets you send reply to the selected message to the newsgroup.

 Post and Reply
Lets you reply to the selected message, and send the reply to the author of the original message via e-mail.

 New Mail
Click here to write an e-mail message to anyone (not just to a newsgroup).

 Reply
Click here to reply to the author of the selected message via e-mail.

 Forward
This lets you forward a message to someone else.

 Previous Message
Displays the previous unread message.

 Next Message
Displays the next unread message.

 Mark Thread Read
Marks all the messages in the thread (conversation) as read, so you won't see them next time you view this newsgroup.

 Mark All Read
Marks all displayed messages.

 Print
Prints the selected messages.

 Stop
Tells Netscape to stop transferring the message.

The Toolbar buttons

 Back
Click on this button to see the previous Web document.

 Forward
Click on this button to see the next Web document—the one you left by clicking the back button.

 Home
Click on this button to return to the home page.

 Reload
Click on this button to reload the currently displayed document from the Web.

 Images
If you are viewing Web pages with inline images turned off, you can quickly retrieve the missing images from the current document by clicking on this button.

 Open
Click on this button to display the Open Location dialog box, into which you can type the URL of a document you want to view.

 Print
Click here to print the currently displayed document.

 Find
Click here to open a Find dialog box to search the current document for a particular word or phrase.

 Stop
Click on this button to stop the current procedure—to stop transferring the Web document or file.

 Status Indicator
As long as the meteors are shooting across the sky, Netscape is busy doing something: retrieving a document, trying to connect to a Web server, or transferring a file. You also can click here to return to the Netscape home page.

Security Indicators
There are three different indicators, which show you the type of document you are viewing:

 The broken key indicates that this is not a secure document. Either it's on a Web server capable of security but not set up to use the security features, or it's on a Web server that uses a security system that Netscape cannot work with.

 The key with one tooth indicates that the document is using "medium-grade" security.

 The key with two teeth indicates that the document is using "high-grade" security.

Using

Netscape™ 2
for
Windows® 95

Using

Netscape™ 2 for Windows® 95

Peter Kent

Using Netscape 2 for Windows 95

Copyright© 1996 by Que® Corporation.

All rights reserved. Printed in the United States of America. No part of this book may be used or reproduced in any form or by any means, or stored in a database or retrieval system, without prior written permission of the publisher except in the case of brief quotations embodied in critical articles and reviews. Making copies of any part of this book for any purpose other than your own personal use is a violation of United States copyright laws. For information, address Que Corporation, 201 W. 103rd Street, Indianapolis, IN 46290. You may reach Que's direct sales line by calling 1-800-428-5331.

Library of Congress Catalog No.: 96-72567

ISBN: 0-7897-0728-4

This book is sold as is, without warranty of any kind, either express or implied, respecting the contents of this book, including but not limited to implied warranties for the book's quality, performance, merchantability, or fitness for any particular purpose. Neither Que Corporation nor its dealers or distributors shall be liable to the purchaser or any other person or entity with respect to any liability, loss, or damage caused or alleged to have been caused directly or indirectly by this book.

98 97 96   6   5   4   3   2   1

Interpretation of the printing code: the rightmost double-digit number is the year of the book's printing; the rightmost single-digit number, the number of the book's printing. For example, a printing code of 96-1 shows that the first printing of the book occurred in 1996.

All terms mentioned in this book that are known to be trademarks or service marks have been appropriately capitalized. Que cannot attest to the accuracy of this information. Use of a term in this book should not be regarded as affecting the validity of any trademark or service mark.

Screen reproductions in this book were created with Collage Complete from Inner Media, Inc., Hollis, NH.

Composed in *ITC Century*, *ITC Highlander* and *MCPdigital* by Que Corporation

Credits

President and Publisher
Roland Elgey

Associate Publisher
Stacy Hiquet

Editorial Services Director
Elizabeth Keaffaber

Managing Editor
Sandy Doell

Director of Marketing
Lynn E. Zingraf

Senior Series Editor
Chris Nelson

Publishing Manager
Jim Minatel

Acquisitions Manager
Cheryl D. Willoughby

Product Director
Mark Cierzniak

Senior Editor
Nancy E. Sixsmith

Editors
Thomas C. Cirtin
Noelle Gasco
Chuck Hutchinson

Assistant Product Marketing Manager
Kim Margolius

Technical Editor
Brian-Kent Proffitt

Acquisitions Coordinator
Ruth Slates

Operations Coordinator
Patricia J. Brooks

Editorial Assistant
Andrea Duvall

Book Designer
Ruth Harvey

Cover Designer
Ruth Harvey

Production Team
Steve Adams
Brian Buschkill
Jason Carr
Anne Dickerson
Bryan Flores
DiMonique Ford
Jason Hand
Damon Jordan
Clint Lahnen
Glenn Larsen
Stephanie Layton
Michelle Lee
Laura Robbins
Bobbi Satterfield
Kelly Warner
Jody York
Karen York

Indexers
Craig Small
Tina Trettin

To Debbie.

About the Author

Peter Kent lives in Lakewood, Colorado. He's been training computer users, documenting software, and designing user interfaces for the last fourteen years. Working as an independent consultant for the last nine years, Peter has worked for companies such as MasterCard, Amgen, Data General, and Dvorak Development and Publishing. Much of his consulting work has been in the telecommunications business.

Peter is the author of *Using Microsoft Network* (Que) and *Using Microsoft Internet Explorer* (Que), and the best-selling *The Complete Idiot's Guide to the Internet* (Que). He's also written another seven Internet-related books—including *The Complete Idiot's Guide to the Internet for Windows 95* and *The Complete Idiot's Guide to the World Wide Web*—and a variety of other works, such as *The Technical Writer's Freelancing Guide*, and books on Windows NT and Windows 3.1. His articles have appeared in many periodicals, including *Internet World*, *Dr. Dobb's Journal*, *Windows Magazine*, *The Dallas Times Herald*, and *Computerworld*. Peter can be reached via CompuServe at 71601,1266 and the Internet at **pkent@lab-press.com.**

Acknowledgments

Thanks very much to everyone who helped with this book. At Netscape Communications, I'd like to thank Christopher Lamey for finding the time to answer my questions while trying to get his real job done at the same time.

Over at Que, I'd like to thank everyone in the editorial team—Doshia Stewart, Mark Cierzniak, Nancy Sixsmith, Chuck Hutchinson, Noelle Gasco, and Tom Cirtin. I'd also like to thank Brian-Kent Proffitt, the technical editor.

Thanks also to the other couple of dozen people at Que who have a role in creating a book from its electronic form.

We'd Like to Hear from You!

As part of our continuing effort to produce books of the highest possible quality, Que would like to hear your comments. To stay competitive, we *really* want you, as a computer book reader and user, to let us know what you like or dislike most about this book or other Que products.

You can mail comments, ideas, or suggestions for improving future editions to the address below, or send us a fax at (317) 581-4663. For the online inclined, Macmillan Computer Publishing has a forum on CompuServe (type **GO QUEBOOKS** at any prompt) through which our staff and authors are available for questions and comments. The address of our Internet site is **http://www.mcp.com** (World Wide Web).

In addition to exploring our forum, please feel free to contact me personally to discuss your opinions of this book: I'm **mcierzniak@que.mcp.com** on the Internet.

Thanks in advance—your comments will help us to continue publishing the best books available on computer topics in today's market.

Mark Cierzniak
Product Development Specialist
Que Corporation
201 W. 103rd Street
Indianapolis, Indiana 46290
USA

Contents at a Glance

Table of Contents

8 Saving Stuff from the Web 129

Part III: Traveling the Internet

11 Not By Web Alone—FTP and More   189

12 Throw Away Your E-Mail Programs!   203

Part IV: Netscape's Advanced Features

Introduction

Everyone and his dog seems to be using Netscape these days. A little over a year or so ago, almost nobody had heard of it. Now it's *the* most popular Web browser. Of course, a little over two years ago, nobody had heard of the Internet either, and now you can hardly pick up a paper or turn on the TV without hearing something about it. That's the way the Internet works, at warp speed. Changes that might take a couple of years in most types of software—in the world of word processing, spreadsheets, or graphics—happen in a few months on the Internet.

While most program updates are released every year and a half or longer, the leading Internet programs are released every few months. Here we are, little more than a year into Netscape's life; we've seen several versions, and we're already looking at version 2, a version with dramatic improvements and additions.

In the middle of 1994, the word on the Web was that *the* best browser was Mosaic. It wasn't true at that point (there were other easier-to-use, more capable browsers), but people's perceptions take time to catch up. Then came Netscape, and within a matter of months, Mosaic was out and Netscape was in. For a short while, it looked like InternetWorks might beat Netscape, but when America Online bought out the company that produced InternetWorks, the program was killed, Netscape retained its preeminence, and now nobody's heard of InternetWorks.

Right now, Netscape is still on top (though it's being given a real run for its money by Internet Explorer, Microsoft's Windows 95 browser). Netscape's publisher, Netscape Communications, has gone public in a blast of publicity and hype; the founders instantly made multimillions—billions, in fact!

All this fuss—thanks to a computer program, **Netscape Navigator**, or simply **Netscape** for short. Perhaps the best (certainly *one* of the best) Web browsers available for Microsoft Windows. Definitely the most popular— more people use this browser than all others combined.

But none of this really matters if you are using Netscape. What counts is how to use the program effectively and efficiently. That's what this book is all about. I'm going to explain how you can make the most of Netscape, how you can surf the Web at high speed and mess around in other areas of the Internet, how to search FTP sites, how to dig around in Gopher sites, how to read newsgroup messages, how to search WAIS databases, and plenty more.

What makes this book different?

This book explains how to work with Netscape, from the basics (installing it and moving around in Webspace), to more advanced stuff (FTP sessions, using newsgroups, working with Java applets, using frames, and working with plug-ins).

You can use Netscape without my help; you'll quickly figure out how to click on links to move around, even how to enter URLs to jump directly to a Web site. But will you understand what the cache is all about (and the dangers that the cache can pose to your career!)? Will you understand the how and why of drag-and-drop bookmark entries; how to manage newsgroup messages; or why another Netscape window just opened, even though you did nothing to make it do so? Will you be able to figure out why your friend swears there's an inline video at a particular page, yet Netscape just shows a static image? Will you understand how to create your own Web pages (or even *why* you should bother)?

By the time you finish this book, you'll know more about working on the World Wide Web than 99% of all Web users. You'll be able to use Netscape quickly and efficiently, and to find what you need when you need it.

You don't have to be a power user to work with this book. I'm assuming that you have a few Windows basics down—how to use a mouse, how to open menus and work in dialog boxes—but I won't give you abbreviated instructions that only a computer geek could understand. I'll tell you clearly what you need to do to get the job done. This is a book for people who want to understand how to use Netscape right now—with a minimum of fuss and a maximum of benefit.

How do I use this book?

You can dip into this book at the point you need help—you don't have to read from page one to the end if you don't want to. I've put plenty of cross references in, so if you reach a point where you need some background information that I've covered earlier, you'll know where to go.

There are a number of ways for you to find information, too. There's a detailed Table Of Contents—in most cases, you'll be able to skim through this and find exactly where to go. There's an index at the back of course, to help you jump directly to a page. We've also included an Action Index, just before the normal index. Quickly read through the Action Index sometime— you'll find that it's essentially a list of procedures and things you want to do with Netscape, with the number of the page you need to go to for the instructions.

It's a good idea to spend a few minutes just leafing through the book, finding out what's here. That way, when you run into a problem, you'll have an idea of where to go to find the directions you need.

How this book is put together

I've divided this book into several parts, according to the different functions and procedures. Part I provides a quick explanation of the Internet and the Web, and explains how to find and install Netscape. Part II describes working on the World Wide Web. Part III explains how to use Netscape to work with non-Web Internet systems (newsgroups, FTP, e-mail, and so on). Part IV explains Netscape's advanced features—security, Java applets and JavaScript, frames, and targeted windows. Part V explains how to use the Netscape Navigator Gold version to create your own home page, and even publish on the Web.

Part I: Before We Surf

In chapter 1, I explain what the Internet and Web actually are, to make sure we start off with a clear understanding. I'm not going into a great deal of detail, though; by now, a couple of years into the Internet boom, you've probably heard the basics before. In chapter 2, I describe where you can find Netscape, the different versions that are available, and how you can install it.

Part II: Caught in the Web

Part II of this book is dedicated to the Web proper. Chapter 3 explains how to begin moving around on the Web—the basic point-and-click moves. In chapter 4, I explain the more advanced navigation techniques, such as entering URLs. I also explain the purpose and use of the cache.

Chapter 5 describes what you'll find as you move "further into the Web:" some of the less common Web-page components, such as forms, tables, frames, Java applets, and more. Chapter 6 describes the two systems you can use to make finding your way around much easier—the history list and bookmarks—and how to create desktop shortcuts to your favorite Web pages.

In chapter 7, I'll explain how to search for information on the Web—how to use the special directories and "search engines" that help you find the information you need. Chapter 8 tells you how to save what you find; how you can save documents, pictures, and URLs for future use.

In chapter 9, we'll get to the really fancy stuff. This chapter explains how to install the special viewers you'll need to hear music, view videos, read non-Web hypertext documents, and so on. I'll explain plug-ins, too, which are programs that bring multimedia support right into Netscape. Then, in chapter 10, I'll describe specific viewers that you may want to install, and where to find them.

Part III: Traveling the Internet

There's plenty more on the Internet *outside* the Web, and in this part of the book I explain how you can use Netscape to work with other parts of the Internet. In chapter 11, I'll explain the different types of addresses that point out of the Web—such as ftp://, gopher://, and mailto: URLs. I'll also show you how to use Netscape to work at FTP sites, so you can transfer things from the Internet's vast file libraries. You can grab programs, sounds, clip art, documents, and more.

Chapter 12 discusses Netscape's e-mail system: how you can send and receive e-mail with Netscape Mail, the e-mail program that's built into Netscape. Chapter 13 describes what happens when you click on a news link—a link to an Internet newsgroup. You'll learn how you can go directly to a newsgroup using Netscape's special newsreader. And chapter 14 explains a few more non-Web systems that you can access through Netscape: Gopher, finger, Telnet, chat, and WAIS.

Part IV: Netscape's Advanced Features

This part of the book describes Netscape's more advanced features that you may not run into often quite yet, but which point in the direction that the Web is moving. In chapter 15, I'll explain how to use Netscape's security features to make sure your online transactions are safe.

Chapter 16 describes an exciting new feature, built-in Java support. (Java applets are little programs that run in an associated Web document.) It also describes JavaScript, a simplified version of Java that even non-programmers can use to bring their Web pages alive.

Chapter 17 is all about the way that Netscape handles frames, another new feature that improves the Web hypertext format by allowing documents to contain multiple, interactive, panes.

Part V: Creating Web Pages with Navigator Gold

In this part of the book, I'll explain a subject that you may not have considered quite yet: Web authoring. In chapters 18 and 19, you'll learn how to create your own home page (it's really quite easy), and even how to set up your own Web site so other people can view your words of wisdom. If you have the Navigator Gold version, you'll find built-in editing tools that make creating Web pages easy; you'll learn how to do it in only a few minutes.

Information that's easy to understand

This book uses a number of special elements and conventions to help you find information quickly—or to skip things you don't want to read.

Web addresses (URLs) and newsgroups are all in **bold type** like this: **rec.food.sourdough** and **http://www.netscape.com**, as is text that I'm instructing you to type, and new terms. Messages that appear in message boxes and status bars are in *italic*, as is link text (that is, the text in a Web document which, when clicked on, takes you to another document or file). Items that can be selected from drop-down list boxes are also in *italic*.

Program or HTML text is in `this special font`.

Throughout this book, we use a comma to separate the parts of a menu command. For example, to start a new document, you choose File, Open File. That means "Open the File menu, and choose Open File from the list."

If you see two keys separated by a plus sign, such as Ctrl+X, that means to press and hold the first key, press the second key, and then release both keys.

TIP   **Tips either point out information easily overlooked or help you** use your software more efficiently, such as through a shortcut. Tips may help you solve or avoid problems.

CAUTION   **Cautions warn you about potentially dangerous results. If you** don't heed them, you could unknowingly do something harmful.

Q&A   ***What are Q&A notes?***

Q&A notes appear as questions and answers. We try to anticipate user questions that might come up and provide answers to you here.

   Plain English, please!

Plain English, please! notes define technical terms or computer jargon.

Sidebars are interesting nuggets of information

Sidebars include information that's relevant to the topic at hand, but not essential. You might want to read them when you're not online.

Here, you may find more technical details or interesting background information.

Part I: Before We Surf

The Internet and the Web—a Quick Intro

● **In this chapter:**

Just in case you missed all the hype over the last two years, here's a quick introduction to the Internet and the World Wide Web. . . . . ▸

If you are reading this book, you are using—or plan to use—the most recent version of the world's most popular World Wide Web browser, Netscape Navigator 2.0 (about 75% of all Web users work with Navigator.) You may even be planning to use Netscape Navigator Gold, the special version that includes editing tools. (In chapters 18 and 19, you'll see how easy the Gold version makes it to create your own Web pages.) You can publish your own work or simply create Web pages to keep on your computer's hard disk—pages that quickly take you to the Web sites you work with most frequently.

Either way, we've got a lot to cover in this book. Netscape has plenty of features to describe, and I have a limited amount of paper to fill. So, in this chapter we'll start with a quick summary of the Internet and the Web, so we'll be ready to get started with Navigator in the next chapter.

What's the Internet, anyway?

The **Internet** is a network of networks. A **computer network** is a group of computers connected so that they can communicate with each other. The computers send messages to each other and share information in the form of computer files. The Internet connects tens of thousands of these networks, with more being added constantly. And on these networks are millions of computers.

No doubt, you've noticed all the Information Superhighway hype over the last couple of years. Thanks to heavy media coverage, the Internet is growing rapidly. Though few people had even heard of it three years ago, now almost everyone's heard of the Internet (even if not everyone really knows what it is).

The networks that make up the Internet belong to government bodies, universities, businesses, local/community library systems, and even some elementary and high schools. Most are in the United States, but many are overseas.

Who owns the Internet?

I use this analogy: the Internet is like a phone system. A phone system has lots of different "switches," owned by different organizations, all connected together. When someone in Denver tries to phone someone in New York, he doesn't need to know how the call gets through—which states and cities the call passes through. The telephone network handles it all for him. These private companies have decided the mechanics—the electronics—of the process, and it doesn't matter one whit to the average caller how it's done. The Internet works in much the same way. Just as there's no single telephone company, there's no single Internet company.

Nobody "owns" the Internet. Who owns the world's telephone network? Nobody. Each component is owned by someone, but the network as a whole is not owned by anyone. The Internet is a system that hangs together through mutual interest. The world's telephone companies get together and decide the best way the "network" should function. They decide which country gets what country code, how to bill for international calls, who pays for transoceanic cables, and the technical details of how one country's lines connect to another.

The Internet is very similar. It began in the early '70s with various government computer networks, and it has grown as different organizations realized the advantages of being connected. The origins of the Internet can be traced back to ARPANET, a Department of Defense computer system that was used to link a variety of research centers together. But the Internet has grown tremendously since its birth. All sorts of organizations connected their networks, each having its own particular configuration of hardware and software.

 TIP **In the past, the Internet was a non-commercial system; business** was even frowned upon. In spite of that, the largest growth of the Internet has been in the last two years as the system has become commercialized. This commercialization has brought millions of dollars into the Internet, allowing development of new software, new connections, online businesses, and so on.

So what's available?

Why would you want to use the Internet? Let's get a little more specific, and look at the services available to you on the Internet (see table 1.1):

Table 1.1 Internet services

Service	Description
E-mail and mailing lists	Send e-mail messages to anyone in the world (well, assuming that person has an Internet E-mail account). You can also subscribe to discussion groups.
Newsgroups	Thousands of discussion groups, on almost any subject you can think of.
The World Wide Web	A giant hypertext system. While you are viewing a document, you can click a link, and another document appears. Travel around the world by pointing and clicking. Sound, pictures, video, even 3-D images enrich the World Wide Web and make it *the* hot Internet tool. The WWW is a primary concern of this book, of course, as Netscape is a Web **browser**, a program used to view Web documents.
Gopher	A menu system that lets you wander through computers on the Internet, searching for documents. Until early 1994, it really seemed like the Gopher system would play a critical role in the future of the Internet. Now you hardly hear about Gopher; everyone's more interested in the World Wide Web.
FTP	Stands for **File Transfer Protocol**; a system that lets you transfer files from computers all over the world back to your computer. It's like a giant software library—millions of files—that contains programs, sound clips, music, pictures, video, and documents.
Telnet	A system that lets you log in to someone else's computer and run programs on it. Some people actually invite the public into their computers; you might get to play chess, view a government job listing, or search a NASA database.
WAIS	Stands for **Wide Area Information Servers**. You don't hear a lot about these servers right now; again, the Web is all that seems to interest people. Still, WAIS provides a handy system for searching databases for information, and you can often use it from the World Wide Web.
finger	A service originally based on the UNIX finger command. It lets you request information about a particular user's account. You may get basic stuff such as the user's name and the last time he was logged into his account. Or you might get some information that the user wants to distribute—weather or earthquake reports, book reviews, sports results, or whatever.
IRC	Stands for **Internet Relay Chat.** A giant, worldwide **chat** system. You type messages that other people can read and respond to immediately. It's a real-time form of messaging.

Plain English, please!

Hypertext is the term given to electronic documents that have links to other documents. As you are reading the document, you see some form of link: a picture or underlined text. Clicking the link takes you to a different document. **99**

Fig. 1.1
An example of what awaits you on the Web: the World of Coasters Web document at **http://tmb.extern.ucsd.edu/woc/**.

This list is not all-inclusive. You can use other services, such as programs that let you talk to other Internet users, either by typing messages or by speaking into a microphone connected to your sound board. But this list covers the basics, the most common and popular services.

If you already know a little about the Internet, you may be surprised to hear that we'll be covering several of these services in this book. No, this book isn't about the Internet; it's about Netscape, which runs on the World Wide Web. But Netscape can also run FTP and Gopher sessions and launch Telnet sessions. In Part III of this book, "Traveling the Internet," we're going to jump from the World Wide Web proper into some of the other Internet services you can use from Netscape.

All about the World Wide Web

This book is about a World Wide Web browser, not the Internet in its entirety. You should probably understand a few basics about the Web before we jump straight in. What is the Web? How does it all fit together?

As you've already learned, the Web is a hypertext system of documents linked together electronically. The Web lets you "navigate" between documents by clicking links between those documents. And it lets you go directly to a document by providing your browser (your Web program, Netscape) with the document's address.

To understand the workings of the World Wide Web, let's start with its basic building blocks.

HTML—Web bricks

The primary building material on the Web is the **HTML** document. (HTML means **HyperText Markup Language**. HTML documents are computer files containing ASCII text—just plain ol' text.

But the text contains special codes, or **tags.** The codes are created using the normal ASCII-text characters, but they are codes nonetheless. They are not there for *you* to read; they are there for recognition by Web browsers.

A **browser** is a program that helps you read HTML documents. When your browser opens an HTML document, it looks closely at the codes. The codes, or tags, tell the browser what to do with each part of the text—"these few words are a link to another document, this line is a heading, this is the document title," and so on.

After the browser has read the codes (which happens very quickly, by the way), it then displays the text on your computer screen. It strips out the codes and formats the text according to the code's instructions. What do you see? A document, much like a word processing document, is displayed within the content area of the browser.

 TIP **You really don't need to know what these HTML codes are, unless** you want to publish your own Web documents—and even then you can use Navigator Gold to publish without knowing much. (You learn more about Navigator Gold in chapters 18 and 19.)

For now, take a quick look at figures 1.2 and 1.3. Figure 1.2 shows a document displayed in Netscape, after the browser has formatted the HTML document. Figure 1.3 is the same document displayed in Netscape's special source window, which shows you what the actual HTML document looks like, codes and all.

Fig. 1.2

Here's what the Netscape Store document looks like in Netscape.

Fig. 1.3

Here's the document from figure 1.2, shown in Netscape's source window.

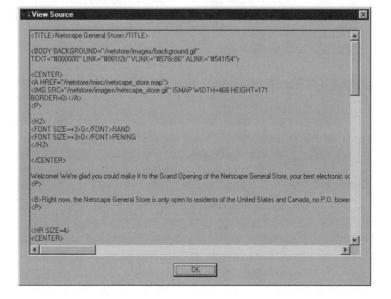

Where is all this? The Web server

So where, physically, are these documents stored? On computer systems throughout the world. How do you get to them? A Web **server** makes them available. The server is a computer, running a program, that receives requests from your browser and transmits the Web documents back to you. What term should we use for the actual information stored on the computer? Each individual HTML file is known as a **document** or **page**. You'll also often hear the term **site**, to mean a collection of documents about a particular subject, stored on a particular computer. This term is also sometimes used to refer to a computer that contains a number of documents or pages.

Smaller bricks—other media

The Web is based on text, but plenty more is out there, too. Just about any form of Internet tool or computer file can be linked to the Web. You'll find pictures, sounds, video, FTP sites, Gopher sites, WAIS database searches, finger sites, 3-D images, and more.

You'll usually start by reading a document and then jump from that document to something else. And many documents have **inline graphics**, which are pictures that are linked into the documents and appear when you display the document (you can see a picture in fig. 1.1, for instance). How can these pictures be linked to an ASCII document? A special HTML tag tells the browser where the picture is (generally in the same directory as the HTML document), and the browser grabs the picture and inserts it in the correct position.

Your HTML "player"—browsers

If you want to listen to a music CD, you need a CD player. If you want to listen to an LP, you need a record player. If you want to see a word processing document, you need a word processor. And if you want to see an HTML file, you need a browser, such as Netscape.

Plain English, please!

Browsers are sometimes also known as Web **clients**. A Web **server** is a system that contains Web **documents** and lets people in to view those documents. A client is the program that is serviced by the server; it's the program that displays the Web documents. The term browser, however, is more commonly used.

Browsers can be very simple, letting you view nothing but the text in Web documents, letting you move between documents, but little else. Or they can be very sophisticated, letting you save information, play sounds and video, and create bookmarks so you can find your way back. Netscape is one of the best browsers available, providing many neat features.

How does the browser get the data?

When you want to view a Web document, Netscape has to transfer the document from a site—in Austria, Albany, or Australia—back to your computer. How's that done?

The Internet has all sorts of **transfer protocols**, systems used for transferring different forms of data across the Internet. They include **SMTP**, the Simple Mail Transfer Protocol (used for sending e-mail); **NNTP**, Network News Transfer Protocol (used for transmitting newsgroup messages all over the place); and **HTTP**, HyperText Transfer Protocol.

HTTP is the system used by the Web to transfer data to and fro. That's really all you need to know, and the only reason I'm telling you is that

you'll run across the term **HTTP** now and again. I'm not going to explain how HTTP works in this book, just what it can do for you!

By the way, like many writers and Web users, I refer to the Web as if you were traveling around on it. I (and others) say "go to the such and such site," "navigate to something or other," and so on. Strictly speaking, of course, you are not going anywhere. (Your chair will remain firmly attached to your floor.) Rather, documents are being sent from the Web server computers to your computer. But in many ways the "travel" analogy works well. You are getting documents, pictures, and sounds from all over the world. Although you physically remain in one spot, intellectually you are on a journey.

URLs—the Web address

Everything on the Internet needs some kind of address—otherwise, how would you find anything? The Web's no different. Each resource on the Web has an address, a **URL—Uniform Resource Locator**. Here's an example:

> **http://www.iuma.com/IUMA-2.0/pages/registration/**
> **registration.html**

The URL starts with **http://**. This indicates the site is a normal HTTP (HyperText Transfer Protocol) site; you are going to an HTML document. Sometimes the URL starts with something different. If it starts with **ftp://**, for instance, you are on your way to an FTP site. As you'll see in chapters 11 though 14, Web browsers can access other Internet systems, not just HTTP.

Next comes the address of the host computer (the address of the computer that has the Web server you are contacting), in this case **www.iuma.com**. Following that is the address of the file directory containing the resource—**/IUMA-2.0/pages/registration/**.

 TIP In the world of Windows and DOS, directories are indicated with backslashes (\). In the UNIX world, however, they are indicated with forward slashes (/). Most Internet Web sites are running on UNIX computers (though that may change because Windows NT seems to be taking off), so the forward slash has become the standard for URLs.

Finally, you have the resource itself—**registration.html**. In this case, you can tell that it's an HTML document. The .html extension makes that clear. (If the document is on a Windows computer, it may have an .htm extension instead.)

Sometimes, the URL doesn't have a file name at the end. That's not necessarily a mistake. For instance, if you want to go to the Macmillan Publishing Web site you'll use the following URL: **http://www.mcp.com/**. This specifies the host, but no directory or document. That's okay; the Web server is set up to show you the document they want you to see.

What can you do with it?

What are you going to do with a URL? Well, you can get almost anywhere on the Web by simply following links in documents. But you may spend several weeks trying to get where you want to go. The URL is a shortcut. You can tell Web browsers to go to a particular URL. I'll show you how to get Netscape to go where you want it to go in chapters 3 and 4.

> **TIP**   **You may read something like** `Point your Web browser to...` .
> This direction simply means to use your browser's URL command to go directly to the document.

You'll find URLs all over the place. They're in *Newsweek*'s regular Cyberscope column, in various directories of resources on the Net, in newsgroup messages, and throughout this book.

Tools to simplify life

We've pretty much covered the basics of the Web itself, but before we move on, let's consider some of the ways that Netscape can make traveling the Web easier for you.

First, it's nice to be able to save the document you are viewing. Netscape lets you do so in a number of ways: you can save a text file directly to disk, copy text to the Clipboard, and even drag text from the browser to another program. (I'll describe all this in chapter 8.) And you can let Netscape save documents in its **cache**, so the next time you want to view the document you can retrieve it very quickly. (You learn about the cache in chapter 4.)

Then how about downloading files? Lots of files on the Web are "pointed to" by links in text documents. Netscape lets you transfer these files back to your computer. In fact, you can even carry out FTP sessions to grab files—not just from Web sites but from File Transfer Protocol sites, libraries of programs, sounds, documents, and plenty more. You'll learn more about this in chapters 8 and 11.

The home page

Here's an argument I'm not going to win—"What is a **home page**?" It's a greatly misused term, that's what it is! You'll often hear this term used to refer to a particular Web site's main page. "Hey, dude, check out the Rolling Stones' home page," you might hear someone say. (It's not a home page, dude, but nonetheless it's at **http://www.stones.com/**.) It would be more correct to call it the Rolling Stones' **Web site** or **page** or **document**.

Fig. 1.4
Welcome to The
Rolling Stones'
Web site.

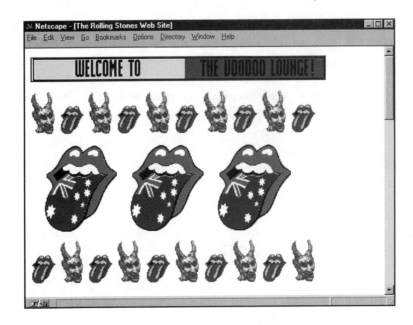

Home page is actually a browser term, not a Web site term. The home page appears when you first open your Web browser. For example, a company can set up a document for all its employees. When the employees start their browsers, they see this home page, with all the links they would normally need. Or a service provider can set up a home page so that when any subscriber started a browser it displayed that page. And you can even create your own home page, with links to all the sites you commonly use (see chapter 18).

The home page is a sort of starting point, and most browsers have a command or button that takes you directly back to the home page from wherever you happen to be on the Web. (If every document on the Web is a home page, what sense does having a Home Page button make? *Which* home page should it take you to?)

Anyway, I've pretty much lost this argument. Many HTML authors are creating what they are terming "home pages," so the term now has, in effect, two meanings.

Where have I been?—the history list

Some kind of **history list** is useful. It is simply a list of the documents you've viewed in the current session. A history list lets you quickly select a document and return to that document.

You can find different forms of history lists. Some show all the documents you've viewed in the current session; others show documents from previous sessions, sometimes going back weeks or months. Netscape currently has a very basic history list, which keeps track of only the current session but doesn't show *all* the documents from the session, as you'll learn in chapter 6.

Where did I go yesterday?—bookmarks

A **bookmark** system lets you save the URLs and the titles of documents to which you think you'll want to return. It's easy to get lost on the Web. Spend an hour online, close your browser, and then try to repeat your path through the Web—impossible. Just remember poor old Hansel and Gretel trying to find their way through the woods. And you are traveling across the world!

By using bookmarks, you can create a list of this useful stuff and then use the list to go directly back to one of the sites. Netscape comes with a good basic bookmark system, but you can add **SmartMarks**, a program that turns your bookmarks system into a "personal agent." SmartMarks automatically checks Web pages to see if they've changed and searches the Web to find new pages related to your interests (you learn all about it in chapters 6 and 7).

Finding and Installing Netscape

● **In this chapter:**

Several versions of Netscape are available. Here's how to find and install the one you need. . . . . ▶

Where can you get Netscape? A variety of places. Perhaps you've been given a copy by your company. Many companies are now buying site licenses that allow everyone, it seems, to use Netscape— from the CEO to the cafeteria staff. (I recently heard that one major company in the Denver area bought a site license for several thousand copies of Netscape; I doubt if anybody did a cost-benefit analysis of having so many people surfing around the Web!)

Perhaps you bought some software, and got Netscape with it; I've seen the browser bundled with other Internet programs. Or maybe nobody's given you a copy, so you want to go get one. I'll explain where you can find it. First, though, note that we're interested in the 2.*x* versions only. You can probably find earlier versions lying around, but this book is about 2.0 and later. And we're interested only in the Windows versions; versions for a variety of operating systems are available, and all are very similar. But the focus of this book is on the Windows-compatible programs (Windows 3.1, Windows 95, and Windows NT).

 Plain English, please!

The Netscape Navigator browser is generally known as **Netscape**, even though Netscape is the company name (Netscape Communications). Originally, the company name was Mosaic Communications, and the browser was called Netscape Mosaic. The browser's name was, therefore, shortened to simply **Netscape**, and that's how it became known. (Tell people you're working with **Navigator**, and they won't know what you're talking about.)

Netscape versions

Several different flavors of Netscape 2.0 are available:

- **Netscape Navigator 2.0 for Windows 3.1.** This is the 16-bit version of the basic Netscape program. You can download this version from the Netscape Web or FTP sites (see *"Finding Netscape,"* later in this chapter). You can download a review copy and register it if you like it.

- **Netscape Navigator 2.0 for Windows 95 and Windows NT.** This is the 32-bit version for Windows 95 and Windows NT. Again, you can download a review copy of this version from the Netscape Web or FTP sites.

- **Netscape Navigator Gold 2.0 for Windows 3.1.** This version is the same as Netscape 2.0, *plus* it has special HTML editing software that allows you to create your own Web pages (see chapter 18). This 16-bit version works with Windows 3.1. At the time of writing, it wasn't clear how this version would be available, but you'll probably be able to download a review copy.

- **Netscape Navigator Gold 2.0 for Windows 95 and Windows NT.** This is the 32-bit version of Navigator Gold. Same as above, but for Windows 95 and NT.

- **Netscape Navigator 2.0 Personal Edition for Windows 3.1.** This version should be available early in 1996. It's a retail version of Netscape—you have to buy it outright, you can't just download, try it, and pay for it if you like it. It comes with the Netscape 2.0 software, *plus* the TCP/IP software you need to set up an Internet connection. It will probably be available for download through the Netscape store.

- **Netscape Navigator 2.0 Personal Edition for Windows 95 and NT.** As listed previously, only this is the 32-bit version.

- **Netscape Navigator 2.0 Gold Personal Edition for Windows 3.1.** Again, this version will probably be available early in 1996, and for retail sale only—no review. It's the same as the Netscape Navigator 2.0 Gold, with the TCP/IP connection software.

- **Netscape Navigator 2.0 Gold Personal Edition for Windows 95 and NT.** As listed previously, only this is the 32-bit version.

TIP **There's a special program provided by Microsoft—Win32s—that** allows you to run 32-bit programs in Windows 3.1 (a 16-bit operating system). However, note that even if you install Win32s, you still won't be able to run the 32-bit version of Netscape. If you're using Windows 3.1, you must use the 16-bit version of Netscape, even if you've installed Win32s.

Is that enough flavors for you? Note, however, that when you get down to it, there are really only two versions of Netscape Navigator 2.0. There's plain old Netscape Navigator 2.0 and there's Netscape Navigator 2.0 Gold, which has the added HTML editing stuff. All the rest are simply different ways to run or bundle the software. So, for instance, the retail version (Netscape Navigator 2.0 Personal Edition) has exactly the same features as the shareware version. It simply comes with software to help you set up a TCP/IP connection (more about these connections in a moment).

Q&A **What's the Netscape Navigator LAN Edition?**

This is simply another name for Netscape Navigator 2.0. Netscape Communications have sometimes used the term **LAN Edition** to differentiate the software from the Personal Edition. The Personal Edition comes with the dial-in TCP/IP software; the LAN Edition doesn't. To use the LAN Edition, you must either be working on a LAN (local area network), or you must find some other dial-in TCP/IP software.

Netscape is free—*not!*

You might have heard the rumor going around that Netscape is free software. In most cases, it's not. You can download Netscape and use it for free in two cases: if you are (to quote from the license agreement) "a student, faculty member or staff member of an educational institution (K–12, junior college, college or library) or an employee of a charitable non-profit organization; or your use of the Software is for the purpose of evaluating whether to purchase an ongoing license to the Software. The evaluation period for use by or on behalf of a commercial entity is limited to 90 days; evaluation use by others is not subject to this restriction."

So, if you're not covered by the educational, charitable, or non-profit umbrella, once you've decided you like and want to continue using Netscape, you should register it; you can choose Help, Registration Information within Netscape for more details. The registration price is currently $39 (Navigator Gold will probably be $79).

Your TCP/IP connection

To use Netscape, you need a **TCP/IP** connection to the Internet. What's this? It's a **Transmission Control Protocol/Internet Protocol** connection, which is the "protocol" that computers on the Internet use to communicate with each other.

Two basic kinds of TCP/IP connections exist: LAN and dial-in connections. A **LAN connection** is one from a local area network to the Internet. Your company may already connect its network to the Internet. As long as you have access to the Internet from your computer, using the LAN's TCP/IP connection, you can use Netscape.

A **dial-in connection** is one that is made over telephone lines; you use your modem to dial a special number, and then your software sets up the TCP/IP connection. You may have heard this referred to as a SLIP, CSLIP, or PPP connection—they are simply different types of TCP/IP connections designed for use over phone lines.

This book does *not* explain how to set up TCP/IP connections. If you want to use Netscape at work, talk to the LAN system administrator. If you want to set up a TCP/IP connection at home, you need to contact a service provider (a local provider, or one of the major online systems such as CompuServe). These days, most service providers will help you set up a connection. You can also get *The Complete Idiot's Guide to the Internet for Windows 95* (Que), which describes in some detail how to use the Windows 95 Dial-Up Networking software to set up a TCP/IP connection. From here on, I'm assuming that you already have your TCP/IP connection and are ready to install and run Netscape.

 TIP **If you're using the 32-bit version of Netscape on Windows 95 or** Windows NT, you must also use 32-bit TCP/IP software. You can't use a 16-bit version of Trumpet Winsock, for instance, because Netscape won't run. Both Windows 95 and Windows NT have built-in 32-bit TCP/IP software.

The Holy Grail—finding Netscape

You can download a copy of Netscape directly from the Internet, from a variety of Web and FTP sites. If you already have Web access, start by going to the **http://home.netscape.com/** Web page; you'll find information there about how to download Netscape. You can download a version that you can use to evaluate the software, without charge. Or you can go to the Netscape store and buy a fully supported version immediately.

If you can't get through to the Netscape site (you probably will be able to, but it may be too busy or not functioning), try this site: **http://mistral.enst.fr/netscape/**.

If you have FTP access, try **ftp://ftp.netscape.com**. This site is often very busy, though; if you can't get through, try one of these "mirror" sites:

> **ftp://ftp.netscape.com**
>
> **ftp://ftp2.netscape.com**
>
> **ftp://ftp8.netscape.com**
>
> **ftp://ftp.pu-toyama.ac.jp/pub/net/WWW/netscape**
>
> **ftp://ftp.eos.hokudai.ac.jp/pub/WWW/Netscape**
>
> **ftp://ftp.nc.nihon-u.ac.jp:/pub/network/WWW/client/netscape**
>
> **ftp://ftp.leo.chubu.ac.jp/pub/WWW/netscape**
>
> **ftp://ftp.tohoku.ac.jp/pub/network/www/Netscape**
>
> **ftp://ftp.cs.umn.edu/packages/X11/contrib/netscape/**
>
> **ftp://server.berkeley.edu/pub/netscape/**

Plain English, please!

A **mirror site** is a site that contains the same files as the site it is mirroring. Thus, Netscape's mirror sites should contain the same software as the main Netscape sites, so you can download software from a mirror site when you can't get into the main site.

Installing the program

If you have one of the Personal Editions of Netscape, follow the instructions that come with the program. If you are downloading the program from the Internet, follow these instructions:

1 Place the program file in a directory you have created for it.

2 Open Windows Explorer and double-click the file name. Because it is a compressed archive file, when it runs it will extract a series of files into the directory.

3 After all the files have been extracted, double-click the file named SETUP.EXE. Clicking this file name starts the Netscape installation program.

4 Follow the instructions on your screen.

 TIP **The Netscape installation program may take a long time to** appear—so long that you may think it's not going to start. But if you hear your hard disk churning, just wait a little while and the program will start eventually.

Once Netscape has been installed, you can go back to Windows Explorer and delete the files in the installation directory that you created (the files that were extracted from the file you downloaded). You may want to keep the original file that you downloaded, though, in case you have to reinstall for some reason.

The HTML association

When you install Netscape, it automatically changes your Windows 95 HTML **association**. The Windows file association system allows you to link data files to program types. For instance, the .TXT file extension is associated with the Notepad text editor. Double-click .TXT in Windows Explorer (the Windows 95 file-management program), and Notepad opens and displays the file.

Netscape, then, associates itself with the .HTML and .HTM file extensions, the file extensions used for Web documents. This means that if you see a Web document in Windows Explorer, you can double-click it to open Netscape and view the document.

You should note, however, that another program may have been associated with .HTML and .HTM previously. For instance, if you've been using Internet Explorer, the Windows 95 Web browser, Netscape will remove the association between these files and Explorer. The next time you open Explorer, it will discover what has happened and get a little peeved. You'll see a message saying that it knows what has happened, and asking if you want to "restore it [Explorer] as your default browser." In fact, every time you try to use Explorer, you'll see the same message, and, thanks to the way that Microsoft created Explorer's bookmark system (the Favorites), bookmarks won't work in Explorer all the time. That's fine if you don't plan to use Explorer any more, irritating if you do.

TIP **Netscape doesn't currently modify any another associations. For** instance, when you install Internet Explorer, it associates itself with the .GIF, .XBM, .JPG, .JPE, and .JPEG graphics formats and the .AIF, .AIFF, .AIFC, .AU, and .SND sound formats. The only associations that Netscape currently modifies are the .HTM and .HTML associations.

If you want to remove the Netscape association for some reason, open Windows Explorer and choose View, Options. In the Options dialog box, click the File Types tab. You then see a list of registered (associated) file types. When you click one, you'll see the association information below the list. Click the item you want to change (Netscape Hypertext Document), and then click the Edit button. Change the Description of Type, then click the Edit button, and change the Application Used to Perform Action. See your Windows 95 documentation for more information.

In Windows 3.1, you change file associations in File Manager. Click a file name with the .HTM association (in Windows 3.1, you can't use .HTML associations because Windows 3.1 allows only three-digit file extensions). Choose File, Associate, and then click on the Browse button to choose the application with which you want to associate the program.

TIP **If you want to revert to Internet Explorer, the quickest way to** reassociate is to open Explorer and click the Yes button when prompted.

If you remove Netscape's HTML association, certain procedures won't work. You won't be able to double-click on an .HTM or .HTML file in Windows Explorer to open it in Netscape, and you won't be able to use the Start, Run command to open Netscape and go to a Web document (see chapter 3).

Setting up the Auto-Dial feature

If you are using Windows 95, you can use its built-in TCP/IP software, Dial-In Networking. I don't have space in this book to explain this process in detail (I describe it in detail in *The Complete Idiot's Guide to the Internet for Windows 95*.) If you do install this software, you may find a special Auto-Dial feature. (The Auto-Dial feature is not available with the plain vanilla Dial-Up Networking provided by Windows 95. Rather, it's included with the software in the MS Plus! add-on package, and the Internet Jumpstart kit that can be downloaded from various online sites.)

When Netscape starts, it calls up Dial-Up Networking. All you do is click the Connect button, and Dial-Up Networking dials into your service provider and makes the connection so that Netscape can get to work. Check the Auto-Dial settings before you start, to ensure that they are set the way you want them:

1 Open the Start menu and choose Settings, Control Panel. The Control Panel folder opens.

2 Double-click the Internet icon. The Internet Properties dialog box then opens (see fig. 2.1).

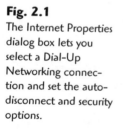

Fig. 2.1
The Internet Properties dialog box lets you select a Dial-Up Networking connection and set the auto-disconnect and security options.

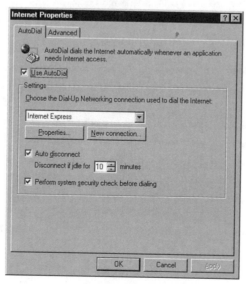

3 Make sure that the Use AutoDial check box is selected. If it *isn't*, you'll have to start your TCP/IP connection before you use Netscape; Netscape won't be able to "call" it automatically.

4 Select the Dial-Up Network connection you want to use from the drop-down list box.

5 Notice the Auto Disconnect check box. This option saves you money by automatically logging off if your Internet programs are inactive for the time specified in the Disconnect if Idle For...Minutes incrementer box. For instance, if you have this option set, you can leave Netscape Navigator downloading a file from the Web, and Dial-Up Networking will log off automatically for you a few minutes after the download has finished (the number of minutes in the incrementer).

6 Notice the Perform System Security Check Before Dialing check box. If you are the only person using your computer, you'll probably want to leave this option turned off. It's useful if others use your computer, because this feature will check to make sure file sharing is not turned on before you connect to the Internet.

Selecting this check box tells Auto-Dial to check to see if file sharing is turned on before it connects to the Internet. (If you start your connection directly from Dial-Up Networking rather than let Netscape call Dial-Up Networking through the Auto-Dial, it won't check for file sharing.) If Dial-Up Networking finds that your computer has file sharing turned *on*, you'll see a warning dialog box. You can then click No to continue with your connection to the Internet, or Yes to turn off file sharing and reboot your computer.

CAUTION **Windows 95's networking features allow you to share the files on** your hard disk with other network users. If you have file sharing turned on when you install the TCP/IP Dial–Up Networking software, the Setup program warns you. But what happens if you or someone else turns on file sharing later, after the Internet software's installed? If you connect to the Internet with file sharing turned on, other people on the Internet may be able to get to your files. (Unlikely, but possible.)

7 Finally, notice the Advanced tab. This area enables you to set up a **proxy server**, which is a special network connection to the Internet through a local area network. If you're connecting to the Internet through your company's Internet connection, for example, your system administrator may have set up a proxy server.

8 After you finish with this dialog box, click the OK button to save your settings.

Firewalls, proxies, and SOCKS

If you are using a LAN/Internet connection, you may need to set up **proxies**. They are special "gateways" out of the LAN. Rather than provide a connection directly onto the Internet—like omitting a wall when building a house—system administrators can set up **firewalls**, which block the Internet (the outside world). Of course, doing so defeats the purpose of having an Internet connection, so they then set up **proxies** and **SOCKS**, which are special doorways onto the Internet.

The SOCKS program and the proxy servers take requests from your software, send the request out through the firewall, wait for a response, and then send it back to you. (After the SOCKS and proxies are set up, this process is all invisible to you; you just use your software normally, and the network handles the rest.) Using a system like this provides a way to control communications between the LAN and the Internet, a way to keep intruders out (and sometimes to keep people on the LAN from using Internet services that the bosses have deemed a waste of time).

If you have to set up proxies and SOCKS, you'll be told what to do, or, perhaps more likely, the system administrator will set it up for you. Talk with your system administrator if you need more information.

Que dijiste?—those wacky language modules

Here's a subject I'm *not* going to be able to tell you much about. At the time of writing, Netscape Communications was adding some functions designed for foreign markets—the capability to load different language modules. You can get to this information by opening Netscape (see chapter 3); choosing Options, General Preferences; and clicking on the Languages tab. You'll find a list of languages from which you can select, a text box in which you can define another language, and an Accept List, into which you can enter the modules that you want to work with.

The purpose of this is to work with multi-language Web documents. You'll soon be seeing documents on the Web in several languages. When you retrieve such a document, the browser will take a look at the available languages, and pick the most suitable for you. The languages stuff in Netscape is where you will be able to select the language you want to use, along with alternatives if your preferred language is not available. You'll also be able to prioritize the languages, so if two of your chosen languages are available, Netscape picks the highest on the list.

Exactly how will all this work? That's not currently clear; the language functions had not been fully integrated at the time of writing.

Part II: Caught in the Web

3

The Opening Moves

● **In this chapter:**

● **Starting Netscape**

● **The Netscape Window**

● **What the Web document contains**

● **Moving around the Web**

● **Clicking links**

● **Status messages**

● **How do I find my way back?**

● **Changing Netscape's appearance**

Now we are ready to begin navigating around the Web . . .

Let's get moving. I assume that you already have your connection to the Internet (you need a TCP/IP—SLIP or PPP—connection) and Netscape Navigator installed. I'm going to explain how to start Netscape Navigator and get it running on the Internet (there are several ways), and show you what to do once you are online—how to move around on the Web.

Starting Netscape Navigator

Depending on how you have configured your software, there are several ways to start Netscape Navigator. Use these methods to start:

- Start your TCP/IP connection. If you use Windows 95 software, open the Dial-Up Networking Connect To dialog box; choose Start, Programs, Accessories, Dial-Up Networking, double-click on the connection icon; then click on Connect to start your TCP/IP connection. Start Netscape Navigator by double-clicking on the Netscape icon on your desktop.

Netscape
Navigator

- Before you start your TCP/IP connection, double-click on the Netscape Navigator icon on your desktop. Netscape Navigator opens. The Windows 95 Auto-Dial program (see chapter 2) will open the Dial-Up Networking Connect To dialog box, so that you can connect to your service provider.

- You can also open Netscape—before or after you've made your TCP/IP connection—by choosing Start, Programs, Netscape, Netscape Navigator.

- Open an .HTM or .HTML file by double-clicking on it in Windows Explorer (Windows 95's file-management program), or by "running" it from the Start menu's Run command; Netscape Navigator will open and load the file so you can read it. (This assumes that the .HTM and .HTML extensions are associated with Netscape, as they are by default; see chapter 2.)

- Double-click on a desktop shortcut that references a Web page (you learn about shortcuts in chapter 6). Netscape will start and open the referenced Web page.

You don't *have* to be connected...

To move around on the Web, you have to be connected through a TCP/IP connection. That's true, but…you don't have to be connected in order to use Netscape. You can open Netscape and view documents on your hard drive without being connected to the Internet.

You'll have to open Netscape and set it up correctly first. Choose Options, General Preferences, click on the Appearance tab, then select the Start With Blank Page option button and click on the OK button. Now, each time you start Netscape it opens, but doesn't display the Netscape home page. You can then choose File, Open File to open an HTML document on your hard disk. Some Web authors use this technique to take a look at Web documents they've created before putting them on the Web.

There's something that Netscape *can't* do. Most browsers—Netscape included—have something called the **cache** (discussed in chapter 4). The cache is a place on your hard disk where the browser stores copies of Web documents that are already transferred from the Web. In other words, when you ask the browser to retrieve a document from the Web, it not only displays it in the Web browser, but also places a copy in the cache. Then, if you want to view the document again later, instead of grabbing it from the Web it can grab it from the cache, saving a lot of time.

CAUTION   **Unfortunately, Netscape only uses the cache if you are online.** Unlike other browsers, you can't start Netscape and work your way back to previously viewed documents without being online. Even if the document you need is in the cache, Netscape expects you to log onto the Web first.

The home page

You should have Netscape Navigator open by now…and you see what's known as the **home page**. This is the page that Netscape opens when you first start the program. What does the home page look like? At the time of writing, it looked like the page shown in figure 3.1. This page is stored on the Netscape Communications host computer, and adds and removes announcements as necessary.

Fig. 3.1
Here's what the
Netscape Navigator
home page looks like.
Don't worry—it'll
change.

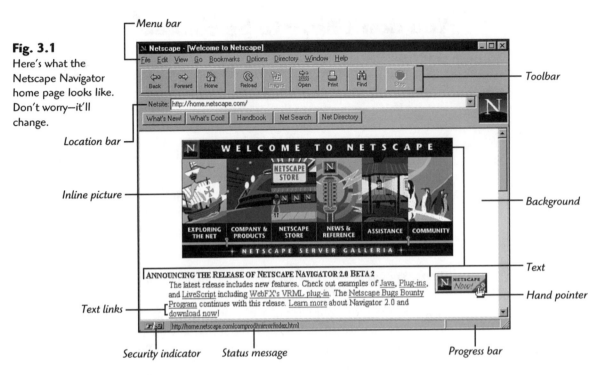

Menu bar

Toolbar

Location bar

Inline picture

Background

Text

Text links

Hand pointer

Security indicator   Status message   Progress bar

How can I define another home page?

Choose Options, General Preferences, then click on the Appearances tab.
Then type the URL of the document you want to use into the Start With
text box.

To use a document on your hard disk, begin by using Netscape's File, Open
File command to open the document. Copy the document's URL from the
Location text box at the top of Netscape (highlight it, and then press
Ctrl+C). Then choose Options, General Preferences, click on the Appear-
ances tab, and paste the text into the Start With text box (highlight the
current text, and press Ctrl+V).

Let's take a look at the components of the Web document itself:

- **Background.** The background may be the default color of gray. But
  Web authors can create special background textures, patterns, and
  colors that are used instead of the browser's default color. And you can
  modify the background, too. (See "You can change Netscape's appearance," later in this chapter.)

- **Text.** A Web document usually contains text. Not all the text you can see is true text, though. The text at the bottom of the document is true text, but the text near the top of the document is part of the inline picture.

- **Inline picture.** Web authors can place inline images or pictures into their documents. Such pictures are, in some cases, links to other documents. Notice the small hand pointer in figure 3.1: it indicates that the image it's pointing to is a link to another document.

- **Text links.** Web documents can contain special text that, when clicked on, cause the browser to display another document. This text is usually underlined and colored blue. The underlined words near the bottom of the screen are links.

Here are other important Netscape components: command

 Back. Click to see the previous Web document.

 Forward. Click to see the next Web document—the one you left by clicking the back button.

 Home. Click to return to the home page.

 Reload. Click to reload the currently displayed document from the Web again.

 Images. If you view Web pages with inline images turned off (you cleared the Options, Auto Load Images menu option), click to retrieve the missing images from the current document.

 Open. Click to display the Open Location dialog box, where you can type the URL of a document you want to view.

 Print. Click to print the currently displayed document.

 Find. Click to open a Find dialog box, so you can search the current document for a particular word or phrase.

 Stop. Click to stop the current procedure—to stop transferring the Web document or file.

 What's New! Click to open the **whats-new.html** document at the Netscape site, where you'll find information about new Web sites.

What's Cool! Click to open the **whats-cool.html** document, which lists more interesting sites.

Handbook. Click to display the Netscape Handbook document, the online user manual.

Net Search. Click to see the **internet-search.html** document, which helps you use several Search systems to find the information you need on the Web. (See chapter 7.)

Net Directory. Click to see the **internet-directory.html** document, which helps you use the Yahoo Internet directory, and others. (See chapter 7.)

Status Indicator. As long as the meteors are shooting across the sky, Netscape is busy doing something; retrieving a document, trying to connect to a Web server, or transferring a file. Also, you can click on the indicator to return to the Netscape home page.

Security Indicator. Shows you the type of document you are viewing. There are three different indicators (see chapter 15 for detailed information about security):

The broken key indicates that this is not a secure document (that is, either it's on a Web server capable of security but has not been set up to use the security features, or it's on a Web server that uses a security system that Netscape cannot work with).

The key with one tooth indicates that the document uses "medium-grade" security.

The key with two teeth indicates that the document uses "high-grade" security.

Hand pointer. When the mouse pointer changes to a small pointing hand, it's over a link. When it's a normal arrow pointer, it's over an "inactive" part of the document.

Title bar. Shows the title of the currently displayed document. (Web authors can—and usually do—provide each document with a title, which is not necessarily the same as the heading you see at the top of a document.)

Menu bar. Select most of the Netscape commands here.

Toolbar. A few basic commands can also be found here. Click on a button to carry out an action.

Progress bar. Shows the progress of a data transmission; when Netscape is receiving a Web page, you'll see a dark band move along this bar, left to right, to indicate how much of the document, or how much of an external image, has been received. (An **external image** is simply a picture that isn't embedded inside a document; you find out about these in chapter 9.)

Status message. Shows what's going on while a document is being transferred—when the Web server has been contacted, the percentage of the document that's been sent, and so on. Once Netscape finishes getting a document, it shows information about the link or missing inline image you are pointing to with the mouse.

Location bar. Contains a box that shows the URL (the Web "address") of the document currently displayed (see chapter 4 for more on using URLs). The bar's label changes. If it says `Netsite`, the current document is on a Netscape server; if it says `Location`, the document is on a non-Netscape server. And when you start typing a URL into the box—so you can go to a specific document—the label changes to `Go to` (press Enter to go to the document).

Scroll bars. These are typical Windows scroll bars; use them to move around in the current document.

Q&A *What's this blue bar?*

When you open some Web documents, you see a blue bar across the top of the page, immediately below the directory buttons. This shows that you are viewing a "secure" document. (You learn more about security in chapter 15.

What does a Web document contain?

Before we start moving around, let's take a closer look at the contents of a Web page. Remember that a Web document is really a simple ASCII text document that contains two basic components:

- Text that the author of the document wants your browser to display so you can read it

- Text that provides instructions to the browser, telling it *how* to display the document

You learn more about these special instructions in chapters 18 and 19, when we talk about creating your own Web documents. For now, take a quick look at the following:

```
<HTML>
<head><title>Information SuperLibrary</title></head>
<BODY bgcolor="#FFFFFF">
<P ALIGN=CENTER><A HREF = "/698759910031/cgi-bin/imagemap/
➥general/graphics/new/super.map"  >
<IMG ALT="" BORDER=0 SRC="super.gif"ISMAP></A><P>
<CENTER>View our <A HREF = "/698759910031/general/map/
➥index.html"  >text only</A> version.<P>
<H2>Browse One of Our Subjects...</H2>
<FORM method = "POST" action = "/698759910031/cgi-bin/find-
➥books.cgi"  >
<input type=submit value="Go to">
```

This is from the current main page at the Macmillan Publishing Web site (**http://www.mcp.com**), which you can see in figure 3.2. All the text between the angle brackets (between < and >) are instructions. The rest of the text is text that you see on your screen.

Fig. 3.2
Here's what our sample HTML actually looks like in Netscape.

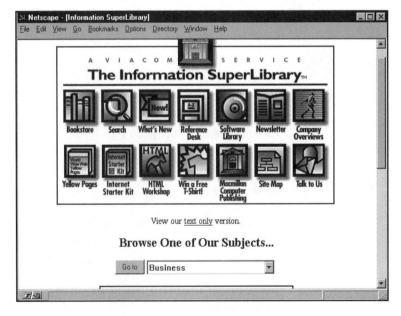

So, when a Web server sends a document to Netscape, Netscape reads this text and **renders** the document. In other words, it looks at all the special commands inside the document, strips the codes out of the document, and then displays the text on your screen in the manner instructed by these commands. But what about the pictures, I can hear you ask? How do they get there? In the preceding example, you see a line like this:

```
<IMG ALT="" BORDER=0 SRC="super.gif"ISMAP></A>
```

This special instruction says "get the image file called SUPER.GIF, and place it right here."

Each Web document has its own address, a **URL** (Uniform Resource Locator). You can see it in the Location bar, immediately below the toolbar. The URL may look complicated, but it's really not; you learn what all the parts mean in chapter 1.

Finally, a Web document contains two basic forms of information. First, some stuff—the text and pictures—that just sits there, for you to read or view. But the document also contains **links**, things that are **active**. Both text and pictures can be active. When you click one of these links, something happens. Generally, clicking one of these links sends a message to a Web server asking for another document. However, it may also ask for an **external picture**, a picture file that is not embedded inside a document. Or it might ask for the Web server to transfer a file—a shareware program, perhaps—or some kind of unusual file format (a sound or video file, for instance).

How, then, do you know where these links are? In figure 3.3, you can see several links. Links in text are shown with underlining and, at first, colored blue. (As you'll learn in "Your links will change color," later in this chapter, after you've used a link, it changes to purple, though you can tell Netscape not to use underlining, and to change the default color.)

Links on pictures are not so easily identified. Some have a blue border around them. This border appears in cases in which the Web author has turned the entire picture into a link by using the same technique that he or she might use to convert a word or sentence into a link.

Fig. 3.3
Text links are under-
lined and colored. You
can identify picture
links by pointing to the
picture and looking for
the hand pointer.
Notice also the status
message at the bottom
of the window.

To make
more room,
I've removed
the bars at
the top using
the <u>O</u>ptions
menu.

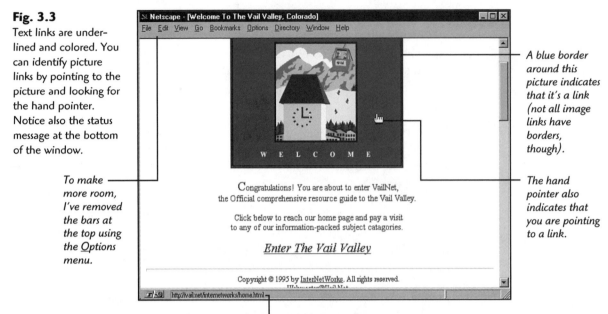

A blue border
around this
picture indicates
that it's a link
(not all image
links have
borders,
though).

The hand
pointer also
indicates that
you are pointing
to a link.

The status message shows the URL of the document referenced by the link you are pointing to.

Other image links don't use this method, so they don't have the blue border
around them. Point to a picture using the mouse, though, and see if the
mouse pointer changes to a hand pointer. If it does, you are pointing to a link.
If it doesn't change, move the pointer around a little; some parts of a picture
may contain a link, whereas others don't. (I hate to complicate the issue, but
in some cases, the mouse pointer *won't* change to a hand pointer when you
point at a link on an image. Some image links are created in a special way, so
that Netscape can't tell what will actually happen until you click on the
image.)

Also, notice the status message at the bottom of the window. While you point
to a link, information about that link is shown in the status message. Point to
a simple link, and you see the URL of the document or file that the link
"points to," the document or file that will be transferred when you click the
link. Point to a **hypergraphic** (also known as an **imagemap**), a picture with
multiple hotspots (areas containing links), and you'll see the URL of the
image itself, plus some numbers indicating the area of the image to which
you are pointing.

Your first clicks

What's Cool Let's begin with a few clicks. Here's a good place to start. First, click the What's Cool button on the Directory Button bar. (If this bar isn't displayed—it's below the Location bar—choose Options, Show Directory Buttons.)

A list of interesting locations on the Web then opens. You can now begin clicking links, to go to any site that tickles your fancy. Simply move around, clicking link after link, to see what happens. Note that when you click a link, the link changes color for a moment (it changes to red). The color changes so that you can tell for sure that you got a good click on the link and that Netscape knows what you want to do.

TIP **For now, I want to stick with simple Web documents. You may** click a link that displays a picture by itself or perhaps causes a sound to play; that's fine. But if you click a link and see a dialog box asking you to save a file or asking how to handle some kind of strange file format, cancel out of the dialog box and try some other link. (These subjects are covered in chapters 8 to 10).

Watch the status messages

When you click a link, you may want to watch the status messages in the status bar at the bottom of the window. You'll see a variety of messages, such as these:

- `Reading file.` Netscape is grabbing the document out of the document cache rather than from the World Wide Web itself. See chapter 4 for information about the cache.

- `Connect: Looking up host: www.mcp.com.` This message tells you that Netscape is looking up the host address part of the URL to try to find the Web server specified by the link you clicked.

- `Unable to locate host www.ieee.com.` If the link you click has a bad host address, you'll see a message saying that Netscape can't find the host. You'll also see a dialog box saying that `The server does not have a DNS entry`. This means that when Netscape contacted DNS (Domain Name Service, the Internet system that keeps track of all the host addresses), it was told that the host address did not exist.

Q&A   *I know the URL is correct—why did Netscape tell me that the server doesn't have a DNS entry?*

Netscape is not always correct about the host not having a DNS entry. I've noticed a little bug in which Netscape can sometimes get stuck and keep telling you that there's no DNS entry for its own server (**home.netscape.com**). This problem happened to me when I was offline, though, and Netscape didn't call the Dial-Up Networking program properly. Also, there may be a problem getting through to the host at that particular time; try again later.

- `Connect: Contacting host: www.mcp.com.` Netscape has sent a message to the server and is waiting for an acknowledgment that the server received the message.

- `Interrupt the current transfer.` Hold on, something's gone wrong. Wait a moment and maybe Netscape will be able to get things moving again.

- `Connect: Host Contacted: Waiting for reply.` Netscape has sent a message to the Web server and is waiting for it to respond.

- `Transferring data.` The server has begun sending the document to Netscape.

- `45% of 80k.` A message, similar to this one, indicates how much of the document has been transferred and the size of the document. If the document contains inline images, you may see several of these messages, for the text itself and each image. In some cases, you'll also see information about how fast the data is being transferred and an estimate of how much longer it will take. Watch the progress bar to the right of the status messages, too, to see a graphical representation of the amount that's been transferred.

- `Document: Done.` That's it, Netscape's got the entire document.

TIP   **If you begin a transfer and decide that you want to stop** (perhaps it's taking too long, or you realize you clicked the wrong link), click the Stop button or press the Esc key.

Don't wait—start working right away

In the olden days on the Web—okay, a bit more than a year ago—when you clicked a link, the document would start transferring, and you'd have to stare at a blank screen for a while, twiddling your thumbs. After all the information had been transferred, your browser would then display it on the screen.

That's all changed. Now, as soon as Netscape receives some text, it displays it on your screen. You can start scrolling around in the document, reading the text, while Netscape continues getting the rest of the text and then gets the pictures. For instance, figure 3.4 shows a document with missing pictures: Netscape has transferred the text, put "placeholders" in the document to show where the pictures will go, and is now transferring the pictures.

Fig. 3.4
Netscape is still transferring the pictures, though it has all the text (this page is from the Rolling Stones Web site, at **http:// www.stones.com**).

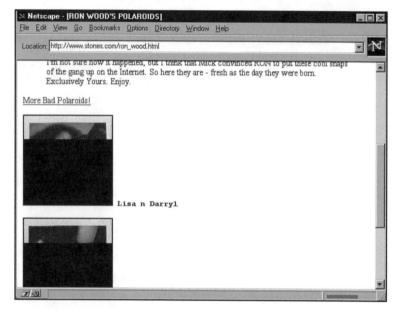

But there's more. Two types of special images, designed to be used as inline pictures, transfer to Netscape very quickly: interlaced GIF and progressive JPEG. You can recognize interlaced GIFs by the fact that you see all the image very quickly, but it's very fuzzy. Then, as more of the image is transferred, it gets sharper. The progressive JPEG image simply loads very quickly and smoothly. Of course, not everyone is using these special formats. If a Web author uses simple .GIF, .JPEG (or .JPG), or .XBM images, they transfer a little more slowly. (These three image types can be used for inline images; .XBM is a UNIX format that you don't run into very often these days.)

TIP   **You can tell Netscape not to display pictures piece by piece, but** to display an entire picture once it has transferred the entire thing. Choose Options, General Preferences, click on the Images tab, then choose the Display Images After Loading option button.

So, what are you going to do while Netscape is transferring all the text and pictures? You can read the document and view the images that have already arrived. And if you find a link you want to use, don't wait. Simply click the link. Netscape will stop transferring the current document and start working on the document referenced by the link you clicked.

 TIP   **Click on the bottom of the vertical scroll bar to move down the** document while the images are being transferred. Sometimes the text doesn't show up until you move the page a little.

Moving around the document

You can move a document around so that you can view it all. Web documents have no set length: some are visible in entirety in the window; others may be hundreds of lines long, most of which will be off-screen.

You can use the window's scroll bars to move up and down, of course, and side to side. You can also use these keys:

- **Up and down arrows**. Move up and down a line or two at a time.
- **Page Up and Page Down**. Move up and down about a screenful at a time.
- **Spacebar**. Move down about a screenful at a time.
- **Ctrl+Home**. Move to the top of the document.
- **Ctrl+End**. Move to the bottom of the document.

 TIP   **These keystrokes work only if the "focus" is in the content area.** If you try to use the keys and they don't work, click inside the Netscape window and then try again. Also, note that if the focus is on the Location bar or Directory Button bar, these keystrokes may cause Netscape to select another document.

Your links will change color

You may notice as you move around that links change color. At first, all the links are blue, and then some of them become purple. The purple links are links to documents you've already seen. Not just links you've clicked, but links to documents that you've already visited. For example, suppose that you are in document A, and you click a link that takes you to document B. Later, while in document C, you see a purple link, one you've never clicked before (because you've never been in document C). You point to the link, then look at the status messages, and see that the link points at document B. Netscape figures out these links when it transfers the document, and it changes the color accordingly.

How long will these links remain colored purple (or whatever other color you choose as the "followed-link" color)? By default, they stay that way for 30 days. However, you can tell Netscape to use a different time period or tell it to use the followed-link color forever.

Choose Options, General Preferences, then click on the Appearance tab in the Preferences dialog box. At the bottom of the box, you see the Followed Links option buttons; click on Never Expire if you want to use the special color forever, or use the Expire After option button and the Days text box to define how long Netscape should mark the links. Or you can click the Expire Now button to remove the color from all links immediately.

Lost yet? Finding your way back

Eventually, you'll reach a place in which you are stuck. You can't find a way forward—no more links you can click. Or maybe you simply don't want to go forward; you want to return to where you've just been. So let's look at a few ways to return.

Click the Back button to go to the previous document (or press Alt+left arrow). This takes you back through the history list, which we'll look at in chapter 6.

Click the Forward button to go forward through the history list to the document from which you've just come back. (Or press Alt+right arrow.)

Click the Home button to view the Netscape home page.

continues

Click the status indicator to view the home page.

Click the little triangle at the end of the Location drop-down text box, select a URL, and then press Enter to go to that document.

Open the <u>G</u>o menu and select a document from the list. (This is the history list.) Right-click and choose Back or Forward. (We'll cover the right-click menu in more detail in chapter 5.)

That's all the navigating we're going to be doing in this chapter. I'll explain a few more techniques in the following chapters, though. Before we move on, let's look at a few things you may notice as you travel around the Web.

Special text, special backgrounds

Now and again, you may run across Web pages in which all the colors seem wrong. The text color is not the color you are used to, the links—are they links?—are different colors, the background is completely different, and so on.

Netscape has a series of default colors, but Web authors can override these colors if they want. They can make a particular word or paragraph a different color, or they can use a different color background—or even a special pattern. In figure 3.5, for instance, you can see that the document background is black with white dots, not the normal gray. And, although you can't see it in this black-and-white book, the links are green. And even if I use a link, when I come back, the link is still green; it doesn't change to the "followed-link" color. This author has defined a background and picked his or her own text colors.

You can override the author's overriding if you want! You can tell Netscape that you don't want to allow an author to pick backgrounds and text colors. You'll do this in the Colors area of the Preferences dialog box. Choose <u>O</u>ptions, <u>G</u>eneral Preferences, then click on the Colors tab. Then select the Always Use My Colors, Overriding Document check box. (You can even define your own background, for use in *all* documents; click on the <u>I</u>mage File option button, then use the Browse button to pick the file you want to use.

For an example of how you can override the author's wishes, see figure 3.6. Notice that the background has gone. The text has now changed back to the normal colors, and some new text has even appeared. The black text at the bottom of the screen had previously been obscured by the black background. (Well, actually it's not quite the normal colors; by default, Netscape has a gray background. I'm using a white background in most illustrations to make them clearer.)

Fig. 3.5
The **http:// www.kpig.com/** document shows an example of how an author may choose to pick a special background and text color.

Fig. 3.6
We've overridden the author's overriding! Now we have default colors and have removed the background. Notice the black text now visible at the bottom, formerly covered by the background.

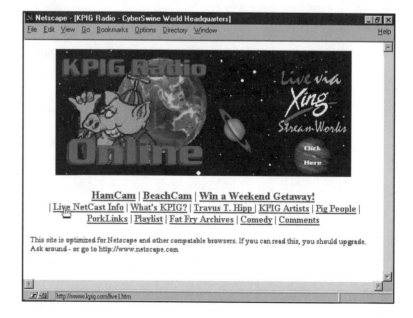

You can change Netscape's appearance

You can modify Netscape's appearance in lots of ways. You can remove the Location bar, toolbar, and Directory buttons; change the size of the toolbar buttons; change the background color and link colors; and so on.

Choose Options, General Preferences, then view the information under the Appearances and Colors tabs. Note that you can also use the Show commands on the Options menu to remove or add the toolbar, Location bar, and Directory bar.

Fonts and Document Encoding

Netscape uses a document-encoding system that allows it to display documents that have been created using different character sets. For instance, most documents are currently created using the Western (Latin 1) character set, but documents may be created using the Central European (Latin 2) set, or a variety of Japanese and Chinese character sets.

You can select which character set should be used by choosing Options, Document Encoding; you'll see a drop-down menu with a list of options. At the time of writing, it was *very* uncommon for it to be necessary to use these options; so uncommon that few people at Netscape Communications knew what they were for.

You can also define which fonts you want to use in documents displayed by Netscape. Choose Options, General Preferences, then click on the Fonts tab. You'll find a drop-down list box, with Latin 1 selected, the default; you don't need to select another Encoding option from this box unless you are using other character sets. However, you can click on the Choose Font buttons to choose the font type you want to use for the selected Encoding. You have two font types; the Proportional Font (representing most of the text in Web documents) and the Fixed Font (used only when an author has defined text as fixed text).

Plain English, please!

A **proportional font** is one in which different characters may have different sizes; the letter "i" takes up less room than the letter "w." A **fixed font** is one in which all the letters are the same width. **99**

Changing your video mode

Netscape's appearance is, to some extent, dependent on how you've set up your video monitor. If you're using a 16-color video mode, many images you see on the Web will appear rather murky. A 256-color mode is better. (Some, but not many, images use more than 256 colors.) Also, you may find that the Netscape window is rather cluttered. Because I have to shoot my screen snapshots down so much to get them to the correct size to be laid out in a book, I use VGA resolution: 640 by 480. These numbers refer to the number of pixels (the smallest part of the video image that can be displayed on your screen) across the screen and down the screen. But 640 by 480 isn't really very convenient because everything's very large using this resolution. If I used 800 by 600, or even 1024 by 768, Netscape would be able to display more of each document inside the content area of the window.

The problem with using a higher resolution, however, is that a high resolution "squeezes" things. The text and pictures in the document will become smaller. (How do you think it gets more into the content area?) So there's a trade-off. The larger your screen, the higher resolution you can use comfortably; the smaller your screen, the more difficult high resolutions will be to work with. Also, the higher the screen resolution you use, the more work your video board has to do. At very high resolutions, you may find that things work more slowly. And you may also find that you can no longer use a 256-color mode.

So, experiment a little. Try all the different resolutions you can, while still keeping 256 colors. In Windows 95, you can modify your video modes using the Display Properties dialog box. Right-click the Windows desktop and then choose Properties. When the dialog box opens, click the Settings tab—you'll find the color and resolution settings.

You can also tell Netscape what to do with an image in a document if your system displays fewer colors than contained in the image. Choose Options, General Preferences, then click on the Images tab. Notice the following Choosing Color options buttons:

- **Automatic.** Let Netscape figure out what to do.

- **Dither.** Tell Netscape to **dither** the colors; that is, if there's a color in the picture that your monitor can't display, mix dots of the colors that it *can* display to get close to the actual color.

- **Substitute Colors.** Tell Netscape to substitute rather than dither; that is, replace the color that can't be displayed with another color (hopefully, one that is close to the original).

4

Advanced Navigation

● In this chapter:

Now you are walking. Let's learn to run. . . . .

Now that you know how to use the basic Netscape navigation commands, we can move on to the more advanced moves. In this chapter, I'll explain how to work a little faster, how to run multiple Web sessions at the same time, how to go directly to a Web page, and so on. You need to know these advanced moves to really work efficiently on the Web.

Speeding things up—removing objects

The Web is a very colorful place. Web authors really get into their work. They include wonderful art in their works, photographs of themselves or their dogs, and fancy "buttons" and "toolbars." But all this colorful stuff is a double-edged sword. Sure, it makes the Web an interesting place to visit, but for many of us, it also makes visiting the Web a very *slow* journey. Many people, perhaps most, are now working on dial-in lines, using modems to transfer the information from the Web back to their computers. And the really fancy stuff that's found on the Web can move very slowly, even with a fast modem.

After working on the Web for awhile, when all these pictures are no longer a novelty, you may want to speed things up a bit by *removing* the pictures. You can then move very quickly through pages in which you have little interest and view the pictures only in the pages in which you want (or need) to view the pictures. You'll find you move around on the Web much more quickly.

Simply choose Options, Auto Load Images, removing the check mark from this menu option. The next time you go to a Web page, you won't see the pictures. Well, that's not quite true; if the page is in the cache, and if the page was originally retrieved with Auto Load Images turned *on*, then you'll see the pictures. However, when you go to a Web page that is *not* in the cache, Netscape will not retrieve the pictures.

You'll discover, however, that not only do you sometimes *want* to view a missing picture, but sometimes you *have* to. Because so many Web pages these days contain images that are essential, you'll soon reach sites that you can't move through without viewing a picture first. See the example shown in figure 4.1. This page has been retrieved with Auto Load Images turned off, and you can see the little icons that Netscape uses to replace missing images.

This page has no text links, so if you want to navigate "through" this page, you have to view these pictures.

Fig. 4.1
I retrieved this Web page with Auto Load Images turned off. Notice the right-click pop-up menu.

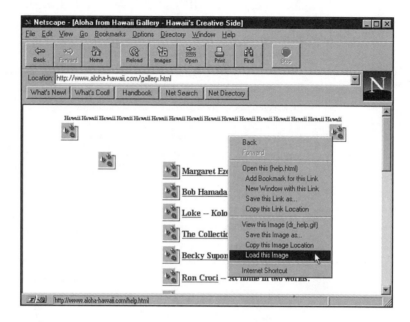

TIP **After you've selected options from the Options menu, you can** then choose Options, Save Options to make sure Netscape uses the same options the next time you open the program.

Notice the pop-up menu on the Web page. You can display this menu by right-clicking the picture. Notice that the menu has a Load this Image option. If you select this menu option, Netscape retrieves the missing image for you. (Note the View this Image option with the name of the image file in parentheses. This option displays the image by itself in the Netscape window; you can't use any links contained by the image if you use this option. (See chapter 8 for more information.)

But this Web page has several missing images, so you might want to use another method—click the Images toolbar button. You'll see that when the Auto Load Images option is turned *off*, this button is turned *on*—it's enabled. Click this button to tell Netscape to retrieve all the missing images in the current Web page.

Traveling directly to Web pages with URLs

Now and then, you may find a URL—a Uniform Resource Locator, or Web "address"—in a newspaper or magazine. Or perhaps you'll run across one in a newsgroup message, or a friend e-mails you something he's just found.

Now you need to know how to go directly from here to there. You don't want to follow links to this document; you want to go directly to it. There are several ways to get there:

- Click inside the text box in the Location bar (remember, the Location bar is labeled Netsite if the current document is on a Netscape server); then type the URL. (When you click in the text box, the current URL is highlighted. When you type, the URL is replaced with the new one.) Then press Enter. For instance, type http://www.mcp.com/, and then press Enter to go to the Macmillan Publishing Web site.

 TIP **You can omit the http:// bit if you want; when you press Enter,** Netscape will add it for you. In this example, type www.mcp.com/, and press Enter.

- Copy a URL into the Windows Clipboard from another application. Then paste it into Netscape's Location bar, and press Enter. (You also can press Ctrl+V, or choose Edit, Paste.)

 - Click the Open button, or choose File, Open Location. The Open Location box then appears. Type the URL and choose OK. (This dialog box is simply an alternative to the Location bar, in case you choose to remove the Location bar from the screen by choosing Options, Show Location.)

 TIP **Sometimes you'll find that a URL doesn't work, perhaps simply** due to a typo. Try this approach: remove the rightmost portion and try again. For instance, if you try **http://www.mcp.com/author/pkent**, and it doesn't work, try **http://www.mcp.com/author/**. If that still doesn't work, try **http://www.mcp.com/**. (The first URL wouldn't work because there's a typo; it should be authors, not author. You can actually get to my Web page by using **http://www.mcp.com/authors/pkent**.)

Don't want to keep switching from the mouse to the keyboard? Here's a quick way to enter a URL. Simply press Ctrl+L to open the Open Location box, type the URL, and press Enter.

Now, what was that URL?

Let's say you entered a URL a few days ago. Now you want to return to the same document, but you don't remember the URL. You can use a bookmark (if you created one for the document you want to view). You'll learn more about bookmarks in chapter 6. But there's a quicker way. Notice the small down-pointing triangle at the end of the Location text box.

Click this triangle, or click inside the text box and press F4. The URL list opens up, as you can see in figure 4.2. This list shows the URLs you've entered in the past; just click the one you want, and Netscape loads that document. (You can also use the down arrow to move through the list, though Netscape will attempt to load each document in turn as it is highlighted.)

Fig. 4.2
Select a URL that you've used earlier by opening the Location list.

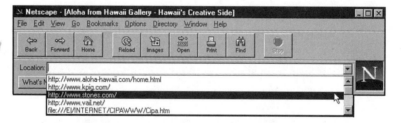

TIP **The problem with selecting from the URL list is that you may not** recognize the URLs; they often are not very descriptive. If you can't remember the URL, and you haven't placed the document in the bookmark list, you may be able to use the history list if you are returning to a document you've seen in the current session. The history list uses the document titles—which are much more descriptive and easier to remember. See chapter 6.

Note that only URLs that were entered into the Location text box—not the Open Location dialog box—are stored in the drop-down list box.

How can I share URLs?

You may want to share URLs that you've found. You can copy them from Explorer and paste them into letters, memos, e-mail, and so on. Here's how.

If you want to copy the URL of the page you are currently viewing, click in the Location text box. The entire text is then highlighted. Then press Ctrl+C, or choose Edit, Copy. This copies the text to the Windows Clipboard. Then you can change to another application and paste the text.

If you want to copy a URL from a link—in other words, you haven't gone to the Web document, so the URL isn't in the Location text box—point to the link and right-click it. When the pop-up menu opens, choose Copy this Link Location. The URL referenced by the link is copied to the Clipboard. You can then copy the link into an e-mail message—you'll learn about that in chapter 12.

Running two (or more) Web sessions

Netscape allows you to run more than one Web session at the same time. You can read Dilbert cartoons in one window while you wait for information to transfer into the other window (see fig. 4.3). Or maybe you need to find information at another Web site, but don't want to "lose your place" at the current one.

Fig. 4.3
You can open two (or more) windows, so you can run multiple Web sessions.

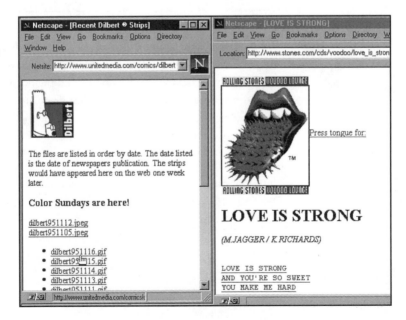

You can start new sessions in a couple of ways. You can point to the link and right-click it. A pop-up menu then opens. Choose New Window With This Link. A new Netscape window opens, and the referenced document opens in that window. You end up with two windows open, each displaying a different document.

The other method is to choose File, New Web Browser. Another Netscape window opens, displaying the first Web document that you viewed in the current session. This is the home page, unless you set up the General Preferences to display a blank page when Netscape opens, in which case it's the first document you went to after starting Netscape. You can then begin navigating through the window in a different "direction," so you have two sessions running at once.

TIP **It might be more convenient if the File, New WebBrowser** command opened a window and displayed the current document, not the home page. However, you can quickly open the current document in the new window by choosing Go, 0 to select the previous entry in the history list. (You cannot use the Back button to do this.)

Q&A *A second window opened automatically; what happened?*

Netscape allows Web authors to open "secondary" or "targeted" windows for you. You click on a link, and the referenced document opens in the new window. See chapter 17 for more information.

Opening files on your hard disk

Eventually, in your exploration of the Web, you may end up with .HTM or .HTML files on your hard disk. You'll have them in your cache (which we'll discuss next), you may save documents using the File, Save As command (see chapter 8), or perhaps you'll even create your own (see chapters 18 and 19). Netscape provides a way to open these files.

Choose File, Open File. The Open box then opens. Use this dialog box to find the .HTM or .HTML file you want to open. Click the file name, and then click the Open button. Netscape then displays that document.

Q&A *Why can't I see any .HTM or .HTML documents?*

Take a look at the Files of Type drop-down list box. The selected file type may be something other than Source (*.htm, *.html). If you've installed a plug-in (see chapter 9), that plug-in's file type may be displayed, for instance. Choose the Source (*.htm, *.html) option.

You can open other items, too. Choose All Files (*.*) if you want to find and open .GIF, .XBM, .JPG, and .JPEG files (which are graphics files.) You can also select Text (*.txt) to open text files. In fact, you can open any file type for which you have configured a viewer or helper (see chapter 9).

TIP **Here's a geek trick for you. If you know the exact path to the file** you want to open, and if you can type quickly, click in the Address text box. Then type file:/// followed by the path. For instance, you might type file:///C:/Program Files/Netscape/Navigator/about.html to open a document called about.html in your Navigator directory. (Note that you can type the forward or backslash; for instance, if you type file:///C:\Program Files\Netscape\Navigator\about.html, Netscape will still grab the correct document, even though Web URLs generally use the forward slash.)

Here's another way to open an .HTM or .HTML file that you have saved on your hard disk. You can open Windows Explorer, find the file you want to open, and then double-click the file name. When you installed Netscape, it **associated** itself with the .HTM and .HTML extensions, so when you double-click one of these file names, Windows Explorer knows just what to do: open Netscape and display the file. You can also position Windows Explorer and Netscape so you can see both windows, then drag an .HTM or .HTML file from Explorer and drop it onto Netscape.

And now...the cache

Now you're ready to learn about the cache and the Reload command. I've mentioned it a few times already, because it seems to touch on so many areas. So let's learn about it in detail.

When you go back to a Web document that you've previously viewed, you may notice that it's displayed much more quickly. That's because Netscape isn't taking it from the Internet; it's getting it from the **cache**, an area on your hard disk or in your computer's RAM (memory) in which it saves pages. This capability greatly speeds up working time on the Web.

By default, Netscape is set up to use 600K of computer memory and 10,000K (almost 10M) of disk space as the cache. The memory stores the most recent documents. Older ones can be found in the hard disk cache, which by default is the `C:\Program Files\Netscape\Navigator\Cache` directory.

This cache can get very big—as big as you allow it. Choose Options, Network Preferences to see the Preferences dialog box, and then click the Cache tab. You'll see the information shown in figure 4.4. Note that the Disk Cache Directory line shows which directory is being used as the cache. You can enter a different directory if you want. For instance, if your C: drive doesn't have much space, but your D: drive does, you may want to place the cache on that drive. First, open Windows Explorer and create a directory for the cache. Then return to Netscape's Preferences dialog box, and type the path to the directory you just created.

Fig. 4.4
The Preferences dialog box lets you determine the size of your cache.

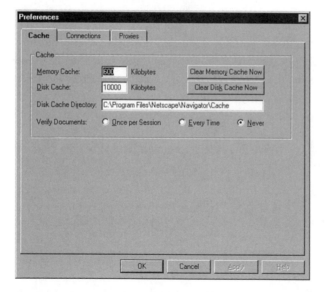

> ## 66 *Plain English, please!*
>
> In Windows 95, directories on your hard drive are often known as folders. I've been using PCs too long to get used to the idea, though, so I still call them directories. (I know I'm not alone!—Netscape's programmers are still using the term directory, too.) 99

You can also configure the cache size by entering numbers into the Memory Cache and Disk Cache text boxes. How large should these numbers be? Well, the larger the numbers, the better—though, as with everything involved with computers, there's a trade-off. The memory cache holds recent documents, so when you return to those documents—using the Back button or history list, for instance—Netscape can display them more quickly. The larger the memory cache, the more documents it can store.

If the document Netscape needs isn't in the memory cache, it looks in the hard disk cache. So the larger the hard disk cache, the more likely a document is to be there. If your hard disk cache is big enough, you can store documents for weeks or even months.

Note, however, that you are not reserving an area of your hard disk for the cache. For instance, if you have a 30,000K (almost 30M) disk cache, Netscape doesn't create a 30,000K file, so other programs can't use that disk space. Rather, it simply means that Netscape can use that much disk space for the cache, *if available*.

So what's the catch? Why not make your cache as large as possible? Because if you do so, you'll be using up resources that other applications may need. Fill up your hard disk cache, and that much less disk space will be available to save files from other programs. Reserve a large area of memory, and other programs can't use the memory. Also, Netscape Communications says that a very large disk cache may cause Netscape to close slowly.

 Q&A *Why is Netscape putting files in the TEMP directory?*

Netscape doesn't use the cache for everything. If it transfers files that it cannot display, it has to pass them onto a viewer (you'll learn about viewers in chapter 9). These files are not placed into the cache. Rather, they are placed into your WINDOWS\TEMP directory. For instance, when you transfer .AU sound files, Netscape places them in the WINDOWS\TEMP directory before starting its internal sound program to play them.

Notice also that the Preferences dialog box has Clear Memory Cache Now and Clear Disk Cache Now buttons. Click these buttons to remove all the data from the respective caches. In the case of the disk cache, this button literally deletes all the files from your hard disk. Before you do that, though, read on, because in chapter 8, I'm going to explain how to grab information from the Web—the cache can provide a storehouse from which you can extract information, even after you've logged off the Internet.

CAUTION   **Be careful with that cache—it's a record of everything you've** done! Let's say, for instance, that you like to sit in your cubicle at work and use Netscape to cruise around the naughty bits of the Web: the Hustler, Playboy, and Penthouse Web sites, for instance. Well, each time you view a picture of Candy or Bonita, that picture is placed in your hard disk cache. That evening—or the next day, or next week, or next month, if the cache is large enough—your boss or coworkers can look through the cache and find out exactly what you've been up to! I would never advise that you spend time at these naughty sites—but if you do, practice safe sex; click the Clear Dis̲k Cache Now button afterward.

Netscape verifies the cache for you

In some cases, Netscape tries to verify the page for you, to see if the document on the Web has changed since the last time a copy of it was placed in the cache. That is, it sends a message to the Web server from which the document originally came, asking if the document has changed. If the Web server responds that the document *has* changed, then Netscape asks the server to send a new copy; if it hasn't changed, Netscape simply retrieves it from the cache.

When does Netscape send this verification-request message? That depends on what you've selected in the Preferences dialog box.

The dialog box contains three Verify Documents option buttons: O̲nce Per Session, E̲very Time, and N̲ever. If you choose the O̲nce Per Session option button, Netscape will ask for verification the first time you view a document. If you go to the document later in the same session, Netscape doesn't bother verifying the document; it assumes that the document hasn't changed during the session. For instance, let's say you visited the Dow Jones page (**http://www.dowjones.com/**) yesterday. Today, you open your browser and go back to the Dow Jones page. Does Netscape ask the Web server if the page has changed? Yes, if O̲nce Per Session is turned on. And if Netscape finds that the page has changed, it retrieves a new copy and places that page in the cache.

If you leave the Dow Jones page and return to it later, Netscape retrieves the document from the cache—it doesn't bother reverifying the document.

Then there's the E̲very Time option button. This button tells Netscape to always verify the document, to see if any changes have been made, regardless of how many times you have viewed the document during the session.

Finally, you have the Never option button, which tells Netscape not to bother verifying documents; as long as the document is in the cache, Netscape will use that document. It will never check to see if a document has changed, so it will never automatically update the document. Documents will change in only two circumstances: if the document "falls out" of the cache (because the cache filled up and Netscape removed old documents to make room for new ones), or if you use the Reload command (as discussed later in this chapter).

Which of the cache options should you use? I prefer Never because it makes my Web sessions *much* quicker. Whenever I tell Netscape to go to a Web page that's already in the cache, Netscape loads the page from the hard disk right away, without sending a verification message to the server first. On the other hand, I have to remember to keep using the Reload command to make sure I'm viewing the latest version of the Web pages. Some people may prefer to use the Once Per Session option so that they can be sure of always looking at the latest page.

When is a page verified?

Now that you've got the verification set up, you should be aware that the verification message is also dependent on *how* you access a page. Assuming you've turned on verification, Netscape will verify a document if you reach that document by clicking a link, choosing a bookmark, entering a URL into the Location text box, or clicking the Reload button. However, when you use the Back command or select an item from the history list (see chapter 6), Netscape does *not* bother to verify the document. It simply grabs it from the cache (under the assumption that you are requesting a previously viewed page, anyway).

What's reload all about?

Reload is a "cure" for the cache. What happens if you return to a Web document that's stored in the cache? Netscape gets it from the cache, right? However, that means you are not getting the latest document. Now, getting the most recent document doesn't always matter, but in a few cases, it *does*.

For instance, let's say you want to return to a site you visited several weeks ago. If you have a very large cache, that document may still be available. If you have the Never option button selected in the Preferences dialog box, you'll be seeing the *old* document, though the corresponding document stored on the Web may have changed in the last few weeks. Or perhaps you are viewing a Web document that changes rapidly, such as a stock-quote page. Even if you viewed the page only a few minutes ago, it could already be out of date.

The cure for old stale Web pages is to reload them. Click the Reload button, or choose View, Reload. Netscape overwrites the current document in the cache, replacing it with the latest version.

Two more related commands are also available. First, there's View, Reload Cell. You use this command to update the contents of a table. We'll look at tables in more detail in chapter 5. And there's View, Refresh. This command gets a new copy of the current document from the memory cache, *not* from the Web itself. Using this command is simply a way to "clean up" the document; if your computer is having some kind of video problem and displaying pictures or text incorrectly, this command "repaints" the screen.

Searching within documents

Some Web pages are pretty big. In fact, some are *very* big—dozens of pages long—with links from the top of the document to "sections" lower down. Many Web authors prefer to create one large page, rather than lots of small linked ones because once the page has been transferred to your browser, you can use links to move to different parts of the page very quickly.

So Netscape helps you search long documents. Click the Find button, or choose Edit, Find. The Find dialog box then opens (see fig. 4.5). Type the word or words you are looking for, choose Match Case (if necessary), and then choose one of the direction buttons: Up or Down. Choose Find Next, and Netscape moves the document so that the first line containing the word or words you are searching for is at the top of the window.

Fig. 4.5
Use the Find dialog
box to search large
Web documents.

If the first occurrence of the word isn't what you want, you can click Find
Next again. Or you may want to close the dialog box and read what Netscape
found for you. Then choose Edit, Find Again (or press Ctrl+G) to quickly
continue the search. (The Edit, Find Again command wasn't working at the
time of writing; perhaps it will be by the time you read this.)

 TIP   **Don't forget the Find command. It can come in very handy for**
searching long Gopher menus and WAIS directories (see chapter 14),
FTP file listings (see chapter 11), and large Web documents.

Remember to right-click

Remember to use the right-click pop-up menu. Point at something in the
Netscape window's content area, and then press the right mouse button. Up
pops the menu, as you can see in figure 4.6. This menu provides shortcuts to
a number of commands, some of which are duplicates of menu and toolbar
commands, but some are only available through the pop-up menu. You won't
see all of the menu commands in some cases; for instance, if you click in a
blank area of the content area, you'll only see three options, while if you click
on a picture, you'll see 12.

We've already looked at the pop-up menu a couple of times, but let's quickly
see what the other options on this menu can do for you.

Fig. 4.6
The right-click menu
provides shortcuts to
several commands.

Back	Returns you to the previous document.
Forward	Takes you to the document you've just come back from.
Add Bookmark for this Link	Adds the Web document referenced by the link you are clicking on to your bookmarks (see chapter 6).
New Window with this Link	Opens another Netscape window, and then opens the document referenced by the link in that window.
Save this Link as	Saves the document referenced by the link you are clicking on to your hard disk (see chapter 8).
Copy this Link Location	Copies the URL referenced by the link to the Windows Clipboard.
View this Image	Removes the current document and displays just the picture you are clicking on (see chapter 8).
Save this Image as	Saves the image you are clicking on to your hard disk (see chapter 8).
Copy this Image Location	Copies the URL of the image you are clicking on to the Windows Clipboard.
Load this Image	If you are clicking on an icon "placeholder" for a missing image, this tells Netscape to retrieve the image.
Internet Shortcut	Creates a Windows 95 desktop shortcut that references this document (see chapter 6).

Moving Further into the Web

● **In this chapter:**

● **What are tables and forms?**

● **Secure sites and password protection**

● **Frames—multiple panes in your Netscape window**

● **Java, JavaScript, multimedia, and live objects**

● **Features that Netscape *can't* use**

● **Viewing a document's info**

You know how to move around the Web by now…but what are these strange things you keep running into? You'll learn about Web pages that do things, pages divided into sections, and more. . . . . ⊘

We've seen all the basics by now, the Web documents, links, pictures, and so on. But there are a variety of other items you'll find spread around the Web. In fact, if you haven't looked closely at the Web for just a few months, you may be surprised at the things you'll find. Things like these:

- Tables

- Forms

- Secure sites

- Password-protected sites

- "Secondary" or "targeted" windows

- Frames

- Java applets

- JavaScript

- Multimedia

- Push and pull commands

We'll look at each of these in turn.

Working with tables

A **table** is...well, you know, a table. It's a set of columns and rows in which text—and sometimes pictures—has been organized. You can see an example in figure 5.1. (While Netscape can display tables, a number of other browsers *cannot*.) Often a table is simply used to format information in a document in a different way. But sometimes, the cells in the table contain information that is updated periodically; you can use the View, Reload Cell command.

Fig. 5.1
Unlike some other browsers, Netscape can display documents containing tables.

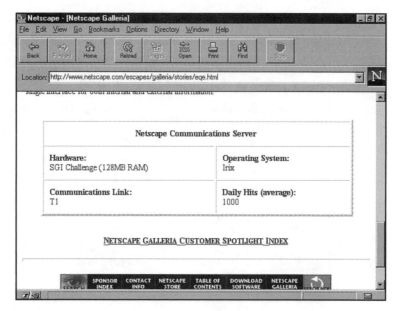

Interactive Web pages—using forms

A **form** is a special *interactive* Web document. It contains the sorts of components that we've become familiar with while working in today's graphical user interfaces: text boxes, option buttons, command buttons, check boxes, list boxes, drop-down list boxes, and so on.

Figure 5.2 shows part of the form used to take information from you when you buy something online; in fact, I found this particular form at the Netscape Store (**http://merchant.netscape.com/netstore/**). Want a Netscape T-shirt? A Mozilla mug? Better still, some Mozilla boxer shorts?

66 *Plain, English, please*

 Mozilla? He's the Netscape mascot, a little green, uh, lizard. (Yes, I checked; he's not a dragon or a dinosaur, he's a lizard.) 99

This form contains drop-down list boxes (click on the little down triangles and a list of choices will appear), a text box, into which you type your credit-card number, and a couple of command buttons, which are used to clear or submit the form.

Fig. 5.2
Forms allow you to
send information back
to the Web server—so
you can buy important
things, for instance.

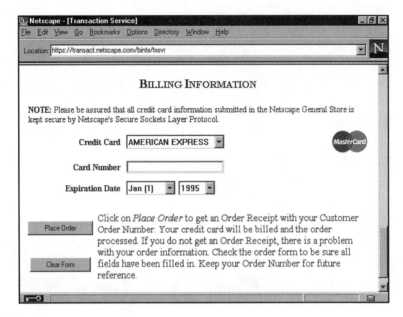

Oh, what happens when you click on a button? Well, you may see a message
saying that you are sending insecure information…which we'll get to right
now.

Playing it safe—secure sites

When you enter information into a form and send that information back to
the Web server, what happens to the information between here and there? It
could be intercepted by someone and read (actually it's not very *likely* that
it'll be intercepted, but that's another story, which I'll get to when we cover
security in detail in chapter 15). If you've just transmitted your credit card
number or other information you don't want some snooper to see, you're in
trouble.

Netscape provides a special way to send information *securely*. If the form
you are viewing comes from a special **https://** server (a Netscape secure
server), it's encrypted when the information is sent back from the form to the
server. When the server receives the information, it then decrypts the information. In-between your computer and the server, the information is useless;
anyone intercepting the information will end up with a load of garbled
rubbish. I'll explain more about how this all works in chapter 15.

How do I get into password-protected sites?

There's another form of security we should discuss: the **password**, which has nothing to do with encryption. It's simply a feature that allows Web authors to deny access to users unless they enter the correct password. For instance, you may have noticed by now that there are a number of, ahem, sexually-oriented Web sites. Some of these contain "teasers," just a little bit of smut available to anyone who cares to view. But to get to the real stuff, you have to register, and once registered, you are given a password. You can then enter the "private parts" of the site using this password.

Well, okay, it's not *just* the sex sites using this system, there are other by-subscription-only sites, too. Companies can use this system to create Web sites for their customers and reserve a special area for access by registered customers only, for instance. Anyone who wants to set up a "pay-per-view" site can use a password system to do so.

How do you use a password? Well, when you click on a link that a Web author has set up to provide access to a restricted area, you'll see a dialog box similar to the one shown in figure 5.3.

Fig. 5.3
Enter your user ID and password to get into a password-restricted site. You can see that this site has both Members and Non-Members areas.

What are "secondary," or "targeted" windows?

Netscape now allows Web authors to open what might be termed **secondary windows**. I've used that term because it's an existing hypertext term that some readers may already be familiar with, and I'm not sure I like the term given to this feature by Netscape Communications; they've called it **targeted windows**. This feature allows a Web author to automatically open another

Netscape window for you. In other words, when you click on a link, another window opens and displays another document. You now have two windows open: the first one, in which you clicked on the link, and the second one, displaying the document referenced by the link.

Panes (frames)

Netscape now allows multiple panes within a Web document; in "Netscape-speak," these are known as **frames**. Figure 5.4 shows three frames: the top frame contains a sort of document title, the left frame contains a picture of the eye, and the right frame contains text. Click on one of the callouts in the eye diagram, and the associated text in the right frame changes.

Fig. 5.4
How We See, a great example of the way frames can make the Web look more like a CD encyclopedia.

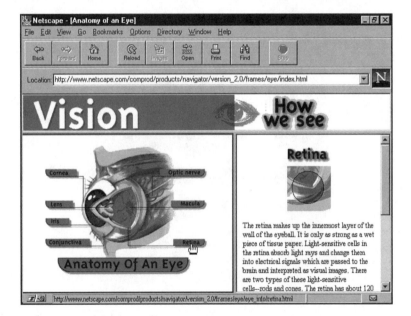

Right now, you won't find many Web documents containing frames, so I'm relegating this subject to the "Netscape's Advanced Features" section of the book, where I'll explain more; see chapter 17.

Web pages come alive—Java applets

This is a neat one. **Java applets** are special little programs that are associated with a Web document and created by using Sun Java, a new programming language from Sun Microsystems. Java applets can provide Web documents with animation; interaction with the readers; and regular, automatic information updates. For instance, figure 5.5 shows a demo site, at which stock quotes continually scroll across the Web page. We'll look at Java applets in chapter 16.

Fig. 5.5
Java at work. The banner at the top scrolls across the screen, showing stock quotes. The charts are updated every few seconds, too.

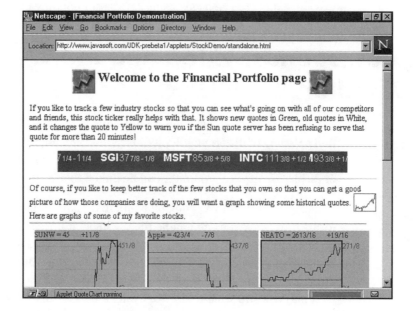

JavaScript

Here's another new feature: **JavaScript**. It's sort of a macro language for your Netscape browser (it's actually a simplified version of Java). A Web author can create simple scripts that link certain components together: Java applets, the Web document itself, inline **plug-ins** (special programs that help Netscape play various file formats—see chapter 9), and **user events** (mouse-clicking, document opening, tabbing into a field in a form, and so on).

For instance, authors can use JavaScript to make their forms a bit smarter—when you try to submit a form, a JavaScript script can check the information you enter into the form to make sure that it makes sense. It can check to see that your credit card number is in the correct format, or that you've entered all the information required.

Scripts can also be used to display or play special introductory information—perhaps music—when you first open a document, or play some kind of goodbye statement when you leave the document. At the time of writing, this was all very new—it was difficult to find sites actually using JavaScript. But you can expect to see pages using JavaScript popping up all over the place.

Pictures, sounds, video and more— multimedia

You'll find all sorts of different file formats on the World Wide Web. You'll find a variety of different still pictures, video and animations, sounds, electronic documents, 3-D images, and so on. Any file format that can be played or displayed on your computer can be linked to a Web page.

What happens when you click on a link that takes you to one of these file formats? If Netscape can handle the file itself, it does so—it displays the document or picture in the window in the normal way. But if the file is a format that Netscape can't handle, it has two options. It may send the file directly to a program that *can* handle it (known as a **viewer** or **helper app**). Or it may ask you what to do. We'll take a look at this subject in chapter 9.

 Plain English, please!

There's a special form of multimedia object called a **live object**. This is a small data file or program that is automatically transferred to your computer along with the Web page. For instance, a live object may play a background sound, or display a picture in a special high-resolution format. We'll learn more about these objects in chapter 9.

Pushing and pulling

Pretty soon, you may notice that Web pages start to do things by themselves. Rather than information arriving at your screen because you've directly requested it—by clicking on a link or entering a URL—Web pages will soon be using **server push** and **client pull**.

Server push occurs when the Web server continues sending information, even though you haven't requested it. For instance, you might click on a link to display a Web page. Then, a few minutes later, the Web page changes; you haven't requested more information, but the server has sent updated information. And the server continues periodic updates until you close the page.

Client pull is similar, except that the request for updates comes from Netscape. For instance, suppose that you open a page. At the same time that the server sends the page, it sends a special program (you don't see this; it all happens in the "background"). This program tells Netscape when to request updates. After the defined interval, Netscape sends a request to the server asking for the information. Again, this will continue until you leave the page.

These systems appear very similar to each other—you usually won't know which method is being used. They are very useful for any information that changes rapidly, such as stock quotes, weather reports, news headlines, or auctions.

The Microsoft versus Netscape war

There's a war going on between Microsoft and Netscape Communications. You see, when Netscape was founded, not so many months ago, the company set out to create the very best Web browser that it could. But in order to make the browser really neat, they decided they'd also have to create new HTML codes. (You'll remember that in chapter 1, I explained how the source HTML document contains special codes—tags—that a browser reads in order to figure out how to format the document.) Well, the original idea behind the Web was that everyone would play by the same set of rules: that a governing body would publish a set of HTML codes that everybody could incorporate into their browsers if they wished.

But Netscape Communications changed the equation by creating its own special HTML codes, designed to work with Netscape. That didn't stop other browser publishers from adding support for Netscape features, of course, but it did give Netscape a lead, and very soon Netscape was the most popular Web browser in the world. And all over the place little signs were appearing in Web documents, saying things like *Optimized for Netscape*, or *This document looks better in Netscape*, or whatever.

Microsoft wanted a bit of the Web pie, so it released Internet Explorer along with Windows 95, to give Netscape a real run for its money. Microsoft began creating its own HTML tags, and then encouraging people to design their Web pages using these neat features, and to put up little signs in its Web pages, saying *Optimized for Internet Explorer*.

Not all browsers can do all things, however. There are some things that Internet Explorer cannot do—for example, the current version can't use frames or Java applets. Nor can it display blinking text (a Netscape feature that causes text to flash on and off).

But there are also features that Netscape cannot work with. Here are a few Internet Explorer features that, at the time of writing, Netscape can't handle:

- **Non-scrolling backgrounds.** This feature creates a background that doesn't scroll as you move down the document. Rather, the text simply scrolls over the top of the static background. If you find a document with this feature, you may not know it; Netscape simply treats it as a normal background.

- **Colored table cells.** Background colors can be added to table cells; Netscape simply ignores the colors.

- **Background sound.** A sound plays automatically when you display the document—it may play once, or may play over and over again as long as you are viewing the page. Netscape simply doesn't play the sound.

- **Marquee.** This is a piece of text that moves across a document, like text on electronic signs you see in airports and sports arenas. The text moves across the page, right to left. Netscape displays marquees as static text.

- **Inline video.** This is a small movie that sits inside the Web document and runs automatically. If Netscape sees one, it may display the video as a static picture, or it may display a placeholder frame, showing where the video *should* be.

Of course, both Microsoft and Netscape are playing catch-up, trying to incorporate each other's features. Internet Explorer does use many of the basic formatting features—such as colored text—and recently added security. I wouldn't be surprised if it works with frames and Java soon. Netscape may well add marquees, background sounds, inline videos, and other Internet Explorer features.

TIP   If you want to see if the version of Netscape you are using can now work with these features, go to **http://www.microsoft.com/windows/ie/ie20html.htm** or **http://www.microsoft.com/windows/ie/iexplorer.htm**, where you can find examples.

Q&A   *Netscape seems to be able to use Explorer features at some sites, but not at others. Why?*

Just to complicate the picture, it's possible that a Java applet is being used to perform a procedure. For instance, although Netscape currently can't play background sounds, a site might use a Java applet to play a sound. Netscape can't play an Internet Explorer inline video, yet a Java applet can place a video inside a document. These are two different ways to play the sound or video, though you may not be able to tell the difference.

Viewing document information

Before we move on, let's take a look at a special feature that provides information about a document. Choose View, Document Info; another Netscape window will open (if it doesn't, the Document Info window may already be open; use Alt+Tab to switch to it). You can see an example in figure 5.6; this is exactly the same as a normal Netscape window, though I've removed the toolbar, document-button bar, and Location bar so you can see as much of the information as possible.

Fig. 5.6
The Document info window shows useful information about the document you've been viewing.

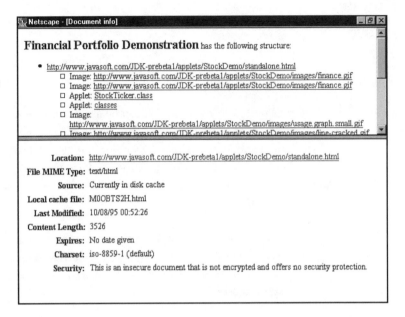

This window uses two frames. You can move the middle bar up and down, to provide more room in either frame. Here's the information you will find:

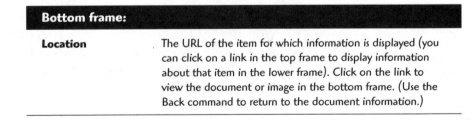

Top frame:	
Document title	The title of the document you were viewing.
Document structure	The URL of the document, and the URLs of the objects (inline images, Java applets, and so on) inside the document. You can click on any item to see that item's information in the bottom frame. If the document contains a form, you'll also see information about the form.

Bottom frame:	
Location	The URL of the item for which information is displayed (you can click on a link in the top frame to display information about that item in the lower frame). Click on the link to view the document or image in the bottom frame. (Use the Back command to return to the document information.)

Bottom frame:	
File/MIME type	Shows the file type of the current item. Initially, it will show *text/html*, but if you click on one of the links in the top frame, this will change, to *image/gif*, for instance. You'll learn more about MIME in chapter 9.
Source	This shows whether the document is currently in the cache. It usually is, unless the cache is turned off (set to 0Kbytes).
Local cache file	If the file's in the cache, you'll see the name of the cache file (when Netscape places a document or image in the cache, it renames it by giving it an "M" name, such as M008NOQB.gif).
Last modified	The date the cache file was last modified.
Content length	The length of the document.
Expires	A Web author can add an expiration date to his documents using the <META HTTP-EQUIV="EXPIRES"> tag (though few do); perhaps the Web document contains information that will be irrelevant or incorrect after a certain date. If there's an expiration date associated with the document, it's displayed here.
Charset	This is the character set that was used when the document was created. If you find a document with strange-looking text, look in the document info and see what character set is used. Most documents use *iso-8859-1*. If the document you are viewing is using something else, it may be that your computer doesn't have that character set installed. For instance, documents in Japanese or Chinese will use a different character set.
Security	This tells you whether the document is secure or not, or whether Netscape knows about its security. If the document *is* secure, you'll be told what security level it has.
Certificate	If the document you were viewing is a secure document, you'll also see information about the site certificate (see chapter 9).

TIP   **If you open the Document info window, then use the links within** the Document info to navigate, or even use the Back button to return to the document, you can continue wandering around the Web using the Document info window. However, if you select Document info again, you'll find that the information is displayed in that window—you won't get another Document info window—and you may not get the full structure information.

Bookmarks, SmartMarks, and Shortcuts

● In this chapter:

- **Using the history list**

- **How can I create bookmarks?**

- **Exporting and importing bookmarks**

- **Using SmartMarks**

- **What can I do with drag-and-drop?**

- **Creating Windows 95 desktop shortcuts**

Don't get lost. Use the history list, and create bookmarks and shortcuts to find your way around. . . . . ➤

Hypertext has been around for a long time; it was invented years before the Web appeared on the scene. And it's long been known that one of the most serious problems with hypertext is that people tend to get lost. It's hard to get lost in a book; you read from the front to the back, or maybe dip into the book in the middle. The book has a direction, from page 1 through to page 300 or 400 or whatever. But hypertext has no direction. Or rather, it has many directions.

There are literally billions of different paths that can be taken through the World Wide Web. To make it worse, the paths are constantly changing. New ones appear every minute, and some that were there yesterday are gone today. Play around on the Web for a while and you'll soon find that you can get lost, that you're not exactly sure where or how you found that interesting document about aliens and UFOs at Groom Lake (try **http://www.cris.com/ ~psyspy/area51/index.shtml**), or how to get back to the page explaining how Bill Gates had the author beaten up (**http://www.halcyon.com/ redrose/joan.html**).

Netscape can help you out. It has a couple of essential features that will assist you in your travels around the Web: the history list and bookmarks. We'll start with the history list.

Where've you been?—using the history list

A **history list** is, quite simply, a list of documents you've viewed during the current Web session. The history list is created automatically. Each time you view a document, that document is added to the history list.

TIP **At the time of writing, Netscape has a rather weak history-list** system. It only lists documents from the current session, not previous sessions. And it doesn't even list *all* the documents from the current session. This may change, though, because many browsers now maintain very large history lists that can go back days or even weeks. With luck, Netscape Communications will improve its history list soon.

There are a few ways to use the history list. The quickest and easiest is to use the Back and Forward buttons. They move you back and forward through the list. Back to the previous document, back to the one before that, forward to the one you've just come from, and so on.

TIP You can also choose <u>G</u>o, <u>B</u>ack or <u>G</u>o, <u>F</u>orward; or use Alt+left arrow or Alt+right arrow. And if you right-click inside a document, you'll find Back and Forward commands on the pop-up menu.

The other way to use the history list is to open the <u>G</u>o menu and select a page from the bottom. You'll find a list of documents that you've viewed recently. Simply click on one to display that document.

Not *all* the documents!

I stated that the history list is a list of documents viewed during the current session. But it's not a list of *all* of the documents you've viewed, unfortunately. Here's how it works. Let's say you are in document A, and click on a link to go to document B, then go to C, then to D, then to E. Now you use the history list to return to document B. In document B, you select another link that takes you to, say, document 1. Now take a look in the history list. You'll find that documents C, D, and E are no longer there; they've been thrown out of the list.

This is a little confusing, because the history list doesn't take you back in an exact line, and you can't view a list of all the documents you've seen in the current session. The history list truncates your short excursions, and only maintains a list of the current route.

TIP You can also view the History window. Choose <u>W</u>indow, <u>H</u>istory. This window shows a list of the documents in your history list.

Remember the Location bar?

Remember that there's another form of history list: the Location bar's drop-down list box. This shows you a list of URLs that you have entered into the Location text box. This goes back to prior sessions, by the way. Its main problem, though, is that it only shows URLs, not document titles, so it can be a little difficult to use sometimes. And it only shows URLs that you've typed into the Location bar, not those typed into the Open Location dialog box.

The bookmark system

Though Netscape's history list is a little weak, the bookmark system is much more helpful. **Bookmarks** are just what they sound like; they are markers on Web pages. Just as you might place bookmarks inside a paper book to find your way back to a particular page, Netscape's bookmarks allow you to quickly return to a Web page. (You are not literally adding a bookmark to a Web page, of course; rather, you are creating a list of URLs and Web addresses, and using that list to help you find your way back to the pages.) Bookmarks stay until you remove them; they are not limited to the current session, you'll be able to use them weeks or months later.

There are a variety of bookmark procedures. You can add bookmarks, select a bookmark from the Bookmarks menu, open the Bookmarks window and select a bookmark from there, create a hierarchy of bookmark folders, and create bookmark files.

Adding a bookmark

This is the simplest procedure. If you find a Web page that you think you'll want to return to later, simply choose Bookmarks, Add Bookmark. That's it, the bookmark has been added. If you now open the Bookmarks menu, you'll see that the document title has been added to the bottom of the menu. You'll be able to return to the document at a later date by simply opening the menu and clicking on the entry.

 TIP   **You can add a bookmark to a document you haven't viewed yet.** Right-click on a link and choose Add Bookmark for This Link to create a bookmark to the document referenced by the link.

Or add a bookmark for a document you viewed earlier in the session. Choose Window, History, click on the document in the history list, then click on the Create Bookmark button.

There are a few problems with the menu entry, though. You may not want to use the document title. Some are too vague or verbose, and it's nice to be able to modify them. Also, the list in the menu is not in alphabetical order, making it hard to find things after a while. And all the bookmarks are lumped together, with no kind of hierarchy. Don't worry, though, we can solve all these problems in the Bookmarks window.

Modifying your bookmarks

Open the Bookmarks window by choosing <u>B</u>ookmarks, <u>G</u>o to Bookmarks
(or <u>W</u>indow, <u>B</u>ookmarks). You'll see something like the window in figure 6.1
(assuming you've added a few bookmarks). As you can see, all the bookmarks have been placed into a single "folder." We're going to create a hierarchy of folders, though, so we can organize the bookmarks more efficiently.

Fig. 6.1

The Bookmarks
window allows you to
create bookmark
hierarchies.

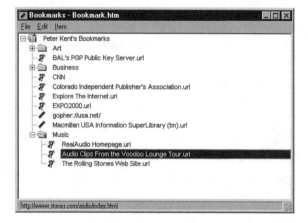

Choose <u>I</u>tem, Insert <u>F</u>older to open the Bookmark Properties dialog box.
Type a title for your new folder into the Name text box: Sports, Politics,
Aliens, Conspiracies, Business, Shopping, or whatever other kind of category
you care to create. You can also enter a Description, a few words explaining
what the category is intended to hold (press Enter at the end of each line so
all the text fits within the box). Click on the OK button and your new folder
will appear inside the Bookmarks window.

Now you can move bookmarks into the folder. Click on a bookmark, hold the
mouse button down for a moment, then, still holding the button down, drag
the bookmark onto the folder and release the button. You can move several
bookmarks at once. Hold Ctrl while you click on each one that you want to
move, then point at one and drag that single bookmark into the folder—the
rest will be moved, too. You can also select a contiguous block of bookmarks
by clicking on the first in the block, holding the Shift key down, and clicking
on the last in the block.

TIP   **You can also move bookmarks using the menu commands. Select** them and then choose <u>E</u>dit, <u>C</u>ut. Then click on the folder into which you want to place them and choose <u>E</u>dit, <u>P</u>aste.

Create as many folders as you wish. Note, by the way, that when you create a folder within your Bookmarks window, you are automatically modifying the <u>B</u>ookmarks menu, too. When you open the menu, you see that each folder is represented by a cascading menu. The folder name appears in the menu with a small triangle to the right; click on the entry and you'll see another menu open, displaying the contents of the folder.

More bookmark operations

Once you've created a bookmark hierarchy, you may want to modify your bookmarks further. Here's what you can do:

- **Rename a bookmark.** Click on the bookmark, choose <u>I</u>tem, <u>P</u>roperties, then type a new Name. You can also modify the URL and add a description. (See fig. 6.2.)

- **Copy a bookmark to another folder.** Click on the bookmark, choose <u>E</u>dit, <u>C</u>opy, click in the folder you want to copy to, and choose <u>E</u>dit, <u>P</u>aste. (Or try dragging the bookmark while holding the Ctrl key down— this *might* work.)

- **Delete a bookmark.** Click on it, and press Delete.

- **Find a bookmark.** Choose <u>E</u>dit, <u>F</u>ind, type a word (part of the bookmark title or the URL), and press Enter. This will even find bookmarks in closed folders.

- **Open or close a folder.** Double-click on it, or click once on the + icon to the left of it.

- **Insert a menu separator.** To place a separator line on the Bookmarks menu between items (remember, the menu reflects the Bookmark window's format), click on the entry after which the line should appear and choose <u>I</u>tem, Insert <u>S</u>eparator.

- **Add a bookmark manually.** Click where you want to place the bookmark, then choose <u>I</u>tem, Insert <u>B</u>ookmark. Type a Name, the URL, and a Description if you wish.

- **Sort the bookmarks.** Click on the folder at the top of the Bookmarks window, then choose <u>I</u>tem, <u>S</u>ort Bookmarks to sort the bookmarks and folders alphabetically.

Fig. 6.2
The Properties dialog box, where you can change an item's name and URL, and add a description.

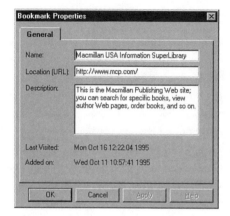

 TIP **You can also open the Properties dialog box by right-clicking on** the bookmark and choosing Properties.

Using the bookmarks

How do you actually use your bookmarks? You've seen how you can select a bookmark from the <u>B</u>ookmarks menu. To go to a bookmarked document from the Bookmarks window, you can use several methods: double-click on the entry; click once and press Enter; right-click and choose Goto Bookmark; or click once and choose <u>I</u>tem, <u>G</u>o to Bookmark.

 TIP **When you go to a bookmark from the Bookmarks window, the** window remains displayed; you won't automatically switch back to the Netscape window. Click on the window below to return to it.

Creating bookmark files

You can create and import bookmark files. This provides several benefits. It allows another hierarchical level; for example, you might have one bookmark file for business-related Web sessions, one for your personal interests, one for each member of the family, or one for each co-worker using the computer.

It also provides a convenient way to share bookmarks: create a bookmark file, put it on a floppy disk and take it home to load into your personal copy of Netscape, or give it to a friend or colleague. And it allows you to import other lists of links, perhaps from other programs, and use them as bookmarks.

TIP **If you've been using Internet Explorer, you can quickly import its** history list and use it in Netscape. Explorer creates a hidden file called GLOBHIST.HTM, which it places in the history folder (look in the Explorer Options dialog box to see where this is). Use Netscape's File, Import command to import this file, and Netscape will create a bookmark for each history entry. Although I haven't yet figured out a quick and easy way to import the Favorites list from Internet Explorer, many, if not all, of the Favorites may be in the history list already. You can also go to each item in the Favorites list, add it to the history list again, and then import the GLOBHIST.HTM file. (This is a lot of work!)

There are three basic procedures (one of which may sound a bit strange, but that's the way the software's currently working):

- **Create a bookmark file.** Choose File, Save As to create an HTML document containing all of your bookmarks.

- **Import a bookmark file,** To add the contents of a bookmark file to your current bookmarks, choose File, Import.

- **Open a bookmark file.** To *replace* the current bookmarks with another set, first choose File, Save As and save the current set (use a name other than BOOKMARK.HTM, which is the default bookmark set). Then select all the entries in the list of bookmarks (except the top-level folder), and press Delete to remove them all. Then choose File, Import to open the other list of bookmarks.

CAUTION **Netscape's Open, Import, and Save dialog boxes have what is** sometimes termed a "bug-like feature." That is, they don't work properly!

Take a look at the Files of Type drop-down list box at the bottom of the dialog box. You'll probably see that the file type is inappropriate for the operation you are trying to carry out (it may show the file extension for the last plug-in you installed—see chapter 9). Select the correct file extension—in the current example, you would select *Source (*.htm;*.html).*

Dragging-and-dropping bookmarks

Not only can you drag-and-drop bookmarks within the Bookmarks window, but you can drag-and-drop between windows, too. If you drag a bookmark from the Bookmarks window onto Netscape, Netscape will load the document referenced by the bookmark. If you drag a bookmark to, say, a WordPad or Word for Windows window, the URL will be copied into the word processing document. You can also drag a bookmark onto the Windows 95 desktop to create a desktop shortcut (which we'll look at under "Creating desktop shortcuts," later in this chapter). And if you have Netscape Navigator Gold, you can drag bookmarks onto a Web document that you are creating in order to quickly make links—see chapter 18.

You can go the other way, too: highlight a URL in Word for Windows, drag it onto the Bookmarks window, and drop it. A new bookmark will be created. It won't have a real title (it will use the URL as the title), but you can quickly right-click on the new entry and type a title.

 Plain English, please!

Note that you can only drag-and-drop between OLE applications. **OLE** stands for **Object Linking and Embedding**, which is a special system used by Windows for sharing data between programs. WordPad and Word for Windows, for instance, are OLE programs; Notepad is not. WordPad is what's known as an OLE **client**, a program that can accept data from an OLE **server**. Notepad is not.

Smart Bookmarks

Wouldn't it be nice if there was an easy way to know when your favorite Web pages have changed? Or when there's more information added to a page, when a new song is available at a music site, or when new shareware is added to a shareware site? and so on. Well, there is.

Choose File, What's New? and you'll see the What's New? dialog box (see fig. 6.3). You can click on the <u>A</u>ll Bookmarks option button (to tell the system to check all of your bookmarks), or on the <u>S</u>elected Bookmarks (to check just those bookmarks that you clicked on). Then click on the <u>S</u>tart Checking button. The bookmarks system will send a request to each Web server that contains the documents you want to check, asking for information about the

Web document. If it finds that documents have been changed, it shows you
by adding a special icon (see fig. 6.3).

Fig. 6.3
You can ask the
bookmark system to
search for changes; it
marks the bookmarks
that reference the
changed documents.
(And no, the icon isn't
blue, at least at the
time of writing; it's
yellow with a blue
stripe.)

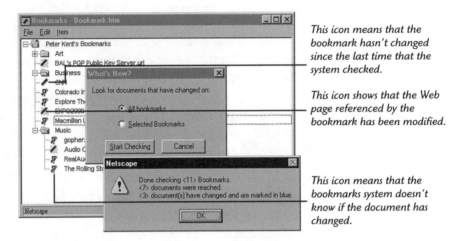

*This icon means that the
bookmark hasn't changed
since the last time that the
system checked.*

*This icon shows that the Web
page referenced by the
bookmark has been modified.*

*This icon means that the
bookmarks system doesn't
know if the document has
changed.*

As useful as this feature may be, it's not as advanced as the Netscape add-on
bookmarks system called SmartMarks, which we'll look at next.

Using SmartMarks

SmartMarks is a special add-on program you can download and try for
free—its registration price is currently $24.95. SmartMarks has two basic
functions; to help you search the Internet (we'll look at this in chapter 7), and
to help you organize your bookmarks and keep them up-to-date. It also has a
nice little directory of interesting Web sites, from the Associated Press to
Zarf's List of Interactive Games.

TIP **At the time of writing, it was hard to find at the Netscape home**
page—it could be purchased through the Netscape Store, but was close to
impossible to track down, otherwise. However, it was available at **http://
www.netscape.com/comprod/smartmarks_install.html** and **ftp://
ftp1.netscape.com/pub/smart/**. And a version named Smart Bookmarks
was available from First Floor Software—the people who actually created
SmartMarks—at **http://www.firstfloor.com/**.

Download the program file from the Netscape site (go to the Netscape home page for information). Open Windows Explorer, place the file in an empty directory you've created for it, and double-click on it. This is a compressed archive file, so when it runs, it will extract several files from within. Double-click on the SETUP.EXE file, and follow the instructions to install SmartMarks.

Adding SmartMark bookmarks

You'll find, once you've installed SmartMarks and started the program, that the Netscape Bookmarks menu has changed. The original Add Bookmark menu option has changed to Add SmartMark, and there's another option, File SmartMark.

Adding a bookmark (or SmartMark) can be the same as before. Display the Web page for which you want to create a bookmark, then choose Bookmarks, Add SmartMark. A bookmark is placed in Netscape's Bookmarks menu, as before. But you can also add a bookmark to the actual SmartMarks system. Choose Bookmarks, File SmartMarks. You'll see the dialog box in figure 6.4.

Fig. 6.4
Choose Bookmarks, File SmartMarks to open this box and place the bookmark in a particular folder.

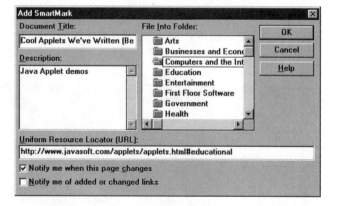

You have a lot more options now. First, you can change the document title, if you wish, by typing over, or editing, the text in the Document Title text box. You can also add a Description. Then you can decide which folder you want to place the bookmark into; click on it and you'll see the folder icon "open."

Now, notice the Notify Me When This Page Changes check box near the bottom. Check this if you want SmartMarks to tell you when the document changes; that's right, this is an interactive bookmark system that goes out onto the Web to see if anything's changed! There's also the Notify Me Of Added Or Changed Links. Check this if you want to be informed when the links in the document are modified. Then click on the OK button, and your bookmark is added.

The SmartMarks window

Bookmarks you add in the manner I just described won't appear on the Bookmarks menu. You'll have to open the SmartMarks window to see them— choose Bookmarks, View SmartMarks to see the window in figure 6.5. In the left pane, you'll notice three types of folders. First, there's the SmartFolders, a whole range of which have already been added for you (Government, Health, Netscape, News, and so on). Then there's the Bookmark Menu folder. This displays the contents of Netscape's Bookmarks menu, bookmarks added using the Add Bookmarks or Add SmartMarks menu options. Finally, there's the Monitored Items folder, which contains a list of all the monitoring operations you have requested. Remember I said that you could tell SmartMarks to inform you when a document or its links change? Well the Monitored Items area is where SmartMarks stores a list of the jobs it needs to do.

Fig. 6.5
The SmartMarks window dramatically improves your bookmark system.

SmartFolder

Bookmark Menu folder

Monitored Items folder

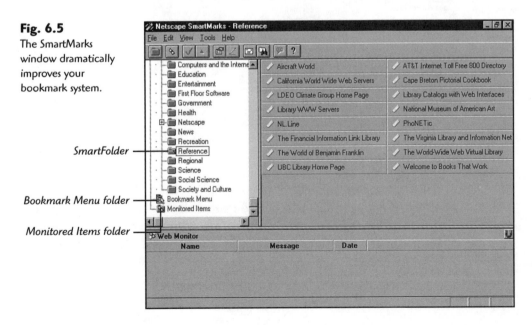

To view the contents of a folder, simply click on it. In the right pane, you'll see a list of the bookmarks in that folder. In figure 6.5, you can see the contents of the Reference folder.

How do I use these?

Now that you've got the window open, what can you do with it? The following table explains your options.

To carry out this operation...	Do this
View a bookmarked document	Double-click on the bookmark, or right-click and choose <u>O</u>pen.
Monitor a page for changes.	Click the bookmark and click on the Monitor Changes button, or choose <u>F</u>ile, Moni<u>t</u>or Changes. Or drag the bookmark onto the Monitored Items folder.
Add a new folder.	Click on the folder in which you want to add a subfolder, then click on the New Folder button or choose <u>F</u>ile, <u>N</u>ew Folder.
View a bookmark's properties.	Click on the bookmark and then on the Properties button, or choose <u>F</u>ile, Proper<u>t</u>ies.
Add notes to a bookmark.	Click on the bookmark and then on the Comments and Bulletins button; or choose <u>F</u>ile, Co<u>m</u>ments and Bulletins. Then type a note into the New Comment text box, and press Enter.
E-mail a bookmark to someone.	Click on the bookmark and then on the Send button; or choose <u>F</u>ile, <u>S</u>end. SmartMarks will automatically include the name, location, description, and Comments and Bulletins.
Search SmartMarks for a particular bookmark.	Click on the Smart Finder button; or choose <u>T</u>ools, <u>F</u>ind. (You can also use this to search the Web itself; we'll look at this in chapter 7.)
Turn on Smart Captions.	Click on the Smart Captions button; or choose <u>V</u>iew, Smart <u>C</u>aptions. Each time you point at a bookmark, a little "balloon" pops up, showing the bookmark's Description, Location, and Modified date.

continues

To carry out this operation...	Do this
Update a monitored bookmark.	Click on the bookmark, then on the Update button; or choose File, Update.
Clear the change flags.	SmartMarks marks bookmarks that reference changed documents with a small flag. Remove all the flags by clicking on the Clear Flags button or choose File, Clear Flags.
Copy an entry to the Netscape Bookmarks menu.	Click on the bookmark; and choose File, Add to Bookmark menu. Or drag the bookmark onto the Bookmark Menu folder.
Delete an entry from SmartMarks.	Click on the bookmark; and choose Edit, Delete. Be careful with the Edit, Remove command. In theory, this simply removes the entry from the current folder, not from throughout the system (if there's a duplicate in another folder, it remains). But if there are no duplicates, it removes the entry anyway, without warning.
Move a bookmark to another folder.	Drag it to the other folder.

TIP   **You can select multiple bookmarks, and then carry out opera-**
tions. Hold Ctrl while you click on the ones you want to select; or click on
one, hold Shift, then click on another at the end of a contiguous block. Or
choose Edit, Select All. Also, notice that there's a right-click pop-up menu
containing many of these commands.

The neat stuff—automatic monitoring

The really unusual and useful feature provided by SmartMarks is the way it
can automatically check documents for you to see whether there have been
any changes. Here's how it all works. First, you have to tell SmartMarks that
you want to monitor a particular bookmark; I showed you how to do that
when you created a SmartMarks bookmark (by choosing Bookmarks, File
SmartMark in Netscape).

 You can also tell SmartMarks to monitor an existing bookmark by clicking on
the bookmark and then choosing File, Monitor changes; or by clicking on the
Monitor Changes button. You can even drag one or more bookmarks into
Monitored Items folder; this places a copy in that folder.

When will SmartMarks check the documents referenced by the bookmarks? That depends. The first thing it does, when you tell it to begin monitoring a bookmark, is to take a look at the existing document, to give it "baseline" information about the document. It will then check the bookmarks later, depending on what you've set up in the Preferences dialog box. Choose Tools, Preferences, and click on the Internet tab to see the dialog box shown in figure 6.6.

Fig. 6.6
You can define exactly when SmartMarks checks your monitored items.

Notice that in the Update Monitored Items area, you can update three ways:

- **Manually.** If this option is selected, SmartMarks only updates your monitored bookmarks when you tell it to do so.

- **At Program Start-up.** SmartMarks updates the bookmarks every time you start the program.

- **Every.** You can define how often SmartMarks should check—the number of minutes, hours, or days.

You can wait and let SmartMarks do its thing—check the bookmarks automatically. To manually check your bookmarks, do one of the following:

- Select the ones you want to check, and click on the Update button; or choose File, Update. (Note that you can use this and the next method to manually check bookmarks that you haven't even defined as Monitored Items.)

- Select a folder in the right pane (not the tree in the left pane), and click on the Update button; or choose File, Update—this updates all bookmarks within the folder.

- Click inside the Web Monitor pane or on the Monitored Items folder; and choose View, Refresh to update all the monitored items.

SmartMark then takes a look at the documents you've told it to monitor, looking for changes. If it finds any, it places an entry in the Web Monitor pane (see fig. 6.7) at the bottom of the window (you can detach this from the window by choosing Tools, Detach Web Monitor). You can now double-click on the entry to go to the document.

Fig. 6.7
When SmartMarks finds changes, it places an entry in the Web Monitor pane.

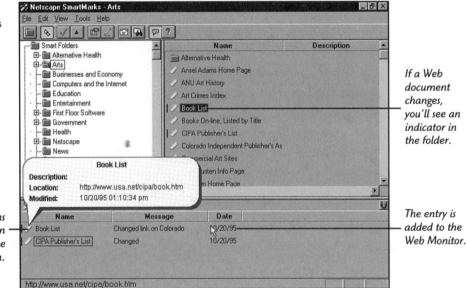

If a Web document changes, you'll see an indicator in the folder.

With Smart Captions turned on, you can point at an entry to see more information.

The entry is added to the Web Monitor.

 A few Web pages—very few right now, but the number's growing—use a feature called **bulletins**. A bulletin is a special little text message associated with the Web document; you don't necessarily see it when you read the document, but when SmartMarks checks the document for changes, it can grab the bulletin. Click on the bookmark, and then click on the Comments and Bulletins toolbar button. The bulletin may inform you of changes to the page, plans for the Web site, or anything else the author wants to tell you.

When you've finished with an updated bookmark, click on it and then click on the Clear Flags button.

Importing and exporting catalogs

You can import and export **catalogs** (the folders). This is an especially handy feature because you can download new catalogs from online. Choose Help, New Catalogs, and Netscape will go to the following page, from which you can obtain new catalogs:

http://www.firstfloor.com/catalogs/

Right now, you'll find the Health and Fitness, Investment Resources, Investment Markets, Windows 95, and U.S. Government catalogs, with more to come.

You can view the catalogs you are interested in (they are Web documents), then save the ones you want as .HTM files (choose File, Save As). Then go to SmartMarks, click on the top-level folder (the Smart Folders folder), choose Tools, Import; and select the file you just saved. SmartMarks will import the information from the .HTM file, creating new folders for each Heading 1 in the document (if you look in the .HTM file using a word processor, or using Netscape's View, By Document Source command, the Heading 1 text is the text between the <H> and </H> tags).

 CAUTION **Unfortunately, the current version of SmartMarks (version 1)** isn't being very smart about this, and is jumbling the folders up a little, creating subfolders incorrectly (and sometimes not displaying the little + icon that shows that the folder has subfolders). I suspect this will be fixed soon; for now, you can't move folders around, although you can create new ones manually and drag and drop bookmarks from one to the other.

 TIP **Before leaving the catalog page in Netscape, place a bookmark on** the page; choose Bookmarks, File SmartMark, and tell SmartMarks that you want to monitor the page for changes. So when new links are added to the catalog, you'll be informed.

You can export catalogs, too, so that you can give them to friends (they don't need SmartMarks to use them, the exported catalog is an HTML file, remember). You can even put them on the Web at the New Catalogs page I just mentioned. You can also export bookmarks or entire folders. Select the bookmark or folder you want to export, then choose Tools, Export. You'll be able to choose Selection (to export the selected folder or bookmarks), Folders (this one isn't working correctly; it seems to export the entire system, but it should export only the selected folder or the folder holding the selected bookmarks), or All Folders (to export your entire SmartMarks system). You can also pick what information should be exported: comments, keywords, and subfolders.

Q&A ***What's all this about SmartFinder and bookmarking searches?***

SmartMarks also lets you search Internet "search engines" and save the search so that SmartMarks can automatically run it again and let you know if it finds anything new. We'll take a look at this in chapter 7.

Creating desktop shortcuts

If you are using Windows 95, Netscape also allows you to create **desktop shortcuts**. A shortcut is a special icon placed on the Windows 95 desktop that, when double-clicked, carries out some kind of operation. In this case, when you double-click on a Netscape shortcut, Netscape will open and display the referenced document. You can create a shortcut to a document you are viewing in Netscape, to a document referenced by a link in the document you are viewing, or to a document referenced by a bookmark. Here's how it works:

- To create a shortcut to the current document, right-click in a blank space and choose Internet Shortcut from the pop-up menu. In the dialog box that appears (see fig. 6.8), modify the Description if you wish, and click on OK.

- To create a shortcut to a document referenced by a link in the document, right-click on the link and choose Internet Shortcut.

- To create a shortcut to a document referenced by a bookmark, choose Bookmarks, Goto Bookmarks, right-click on the bookmark, and choose Internet Shortcut (this currently only works for true bookmarks, not SmartMarks).

bookmark or folder you want to export, then choose <u>T</u>ools, <u>E</u>xport. You'll be able to choose <u>S</u>election (to export the selected folder or bookmarks), <u>F</u>olders (this one isn't working correctly; it seems to export the entire system, but it should export only the selected folder or the folder holding the selected bookmarks), or <u>A</u>ll Folders (to export your entire SmartMarks system). You can also pick what information should be exported: comments, keywords, and subfolders.

Q&A *What's all this about SmartFinder and bookmarking searches?*

SmartMarks also lets you search Internet "search engines" and save the search so that SmartMarks can automatically run it again and let you know if it finds anything new. We'll take a look at this in chapter 7.

Creating desktop shortcuts

If you are using Windows 95, Netscape also allows you to create **desktop shortcuts**. A shortcut is a special icon placed on the Windows 95 desktop that, when double-clicked, carries out some kind of operation. In this case, when you double-click on a Netscape shortcut, Netscape will open and display the referenced document. You can create a shortcut to a document you are viewing in Netscape, to a document referenced by a link in the document you are viewing, or to a document referenced by a bookmark. Here's how it works:

- To create a shortcut to the current document, right-click in a blank space and choose Internet Shortcut from the pop-up menu. In the dialog box that appears (see fig. 6.8), modify the Description if you wish, and click on OK.

- To create a shortcut to a document referenced by a link in the document, right-click on the link and choose Internet Shortcut.

- To create a shortcut to a document referenced by a bookmark, choose <u>B</u>ookmarks, <u>G</u>oto Bookmarks, right-click on the bookmark, and choose Internet Shortcut (this currently only works for true bookmarks, not SmartMarks).

When you've finished with an updated bookmark, click on it and then click on the Clear Flags button.

Importing and exporting catalogs

You can import and export **catalogs** (the folders). This is an especially handy feature because you can download new catalogs from online. Choose <u>H</u>elp, <u>N</u>ew Catalogs, and Netscape will go to the following page, from which you can obtain new catalogs:

http://www.firstfloor.com/catalogs/

Right now, you'll find the Health and Fitness, Investment Resources, Investment Markets, Windows 95, and U.S. Government catalogs, with more to come.

You can view the catalogs you are interested in (they are Web documents), then save the ones you want as .HTM files (choose <u>F</u>ile, <u>S</u>ave As). Then go to SmartMarks, click on the top-level folder (the Smart Folders folder), choose <u>T</u>ools, <u>I</u>mport; and select the file you just saved. SmartMarks will import the information from the .HTM file, creating new folders for each Heading 1 in the document (if you look in the .HTM file using a word processor, or using Netscape's <u>V</u>iew, By Document <u>S</u>ource command, the Heading 1 text is the text between the <H> and </H> tags).

CAUTION **Unfortunately, the current version of SmartMarks (version 1)** isn't being very smart about this, and is jumbling the folders up a little, creating subfolders incorrectly (and sometimes not displaying the little + icon that shows that the folder has subfolders). I suspect this will be fixed soon; for now, you can't move folders around, although you can create new ones manually and drag and drop bookmarks from one to the other.

 TIP **Before leaving the catalog page in Netscape, place a bookmark on** the page; choose <u>B</u>ookmarks, <u>F</u>ile SmartMark, and tell SmartMarks that you want to monitor the page for changes. So when new links are added to the catalog, you'll be informed.

You can export catalogs, too, so that you can give them to friends (they don't need SmartMarks to use them, the exported catalog is an HTML file, remember). You can even put them on the Web at the New Catalogs page I just mentioned. You can also export bookmarks or entire folders. Select the

Fig. 6.8
When you create a
shortcut, you may
want to modify the
description to help
you remember the
document.

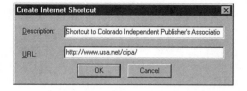

You can also create a shortcut to a document referenced by a link by dragging it onto the desktop. First, position the Netscape window so that you can
see your Windows 95 desktop. (You can also place shortcuts in desktop
folders or in Windows Explorer—open the folder or Explorer, and position
the shortcuts so they are visible.). Now, point at a link in a Web document,
then press and hold the mouse button down. With the button held down, drag
the mouse pointer off Netscape and onto the Windows 95 desktop (or over a
desktop folder or Windows Explorer folder), then release the mouse button.
The shortcut is created.

How do you use these shortcuts? Simple. Double-click on a shortcut at any
time to open Netscape and display the referenced document. You can open
these shortcuts and take a look, by the way. Right-click on the bookmark,
and choose Properties to see the Properties dialog box. Click on the Internet
Shortcut tab to see the URL of the referenced document.

 TIP **If you drag a link and drop it into an OLE application, such as**
Word for Windows, the URL will be pasted into the program.

7

Searching for Information on the Web

● **In this chapter:**

● **Searching the Internet with search engines**

● **Using Internet directories**

● **A few dozen search sites**

● **How can I search with Smart Finder?**

● **Using Smart Finder to automatically search**

The Web is huge...so where's the road map?. . . . . ➤

The Web is enormous, and thousands of new pages are being added every week. How can you possibly know what's out there, and how can you find the information you need? For instance, I recently wanted to find information about a particular printer I was considering buying. I was sure that the company that made the printer must have a Web site—most companies in the computer business seem to these days. But what was the URL I needed to get to the site? I also wanted to find the public-television Web site, so I could search for a particular show I was interested in. How was I going to find this site?

Of course, I could spend several years wandering through hyperlinks on the Web, and maybe eventually I'd wander into the pages I needed. Or I could go to a search or directory site, and search a vast index of Web sites, or view lists of sites broken down by category.

Netscape's search tools

Netscape provides you with several search tools; well, they're not really Netscape's tools, but Netscape puts them within a button's click distance, making them quickly available. You can use the following buttons and commands to find sites:

| Net Search |

- **Net Search (Directory, Internet Search).** Takes you to a document that enables you to search the InfoSeek search engine, and get to several other search sites.

| Net Directory |

- **Net Directory (Directory, Internet Directory).** Takes you to a page with links to a variety of Internet directories.

| What's New! |

- **What's New! (Directory, What's New).** Displays the Netscape Communications What's New page; you won't use this to search for a particular site, but it provides links to interesting new sites on the Web.

| What's Cool! |

- **What's Cool! (Directory, What's Cool).** Displays the Netscape Communications What's Cool page with a variety of links to interesting sites. Again, you won't search, but it's interesting just to peruse.

- **Directory, Internet White Pages command.** Takes you to a list of links to directories of Internet e-mail addresses, so you can track down other users.

TIP **You may want to remove the button bar (choose <u>O</u>ptions, Show <u>D</u>irectory Buttons)** to make more room for the Web documents. You can still get to the documents linked by these buttons by selecting from the <u>D</u>irectory menu.

66 *Plain English, please!*

Directories and search engines—what's the difference between an Internet directory and an Internet search site? A **directory** provides categorized lists of Web pages; select a category, then a subcategory, then another subcategory, and so on, until you find the site you want. A search site lets you use a **search engine**, a program with which you'll search a database of Web pages. Type a keyword, then click on a Search button or press Enter, and the search engine searches the database for you. Some sites—such as Yahoo—contain both directories and search engines. 99

How do I use the search engines?

Internet **search engines** allow you to search a database. Click on the Net Search directory button, or choose <u>D</u>irectory, Internet <u>S</u>earch. Scroll down the page that appears, and you'll see something like figure 7.1.

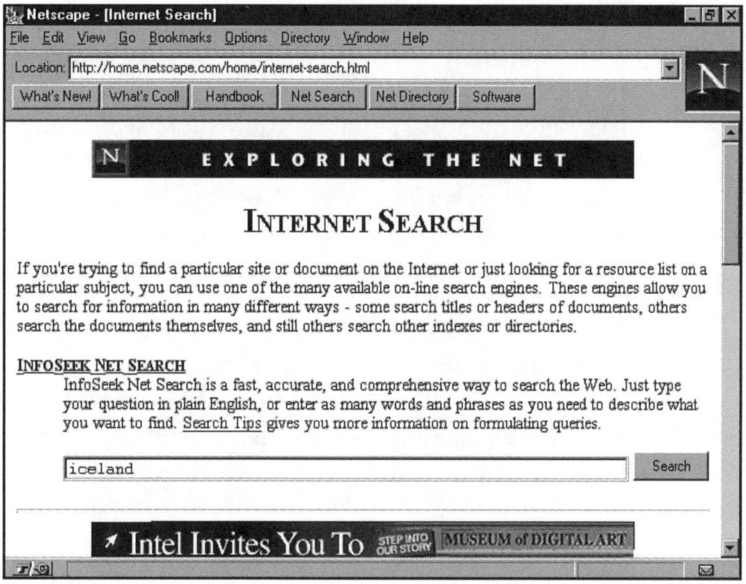

Fig. 7.1
The Internet Search page, which lets you search InfoSeek and go to other various Search sites.

![Screenshot of Netscape Internet Search page showing the EXPLORING THE NET banner, INTERNET SEARCH heading, introductory text about on-line search engines, the INFOSEEK NET SEARCH section with a search box containing "iceland" and a Search button, and an Intel advertisement at the bottom.]

You now need to type a search term into the list box. What are you going to type, though? You could just type a single word, but you may want to get fancy—in which case you should read the instructions. Notice the *special query operators* link above the text box. Click on that to go to a document that describes exactly what you can type. Read this because it gives you a lot of suggestions and hints. For instance, here are a few things you can enter:

- **Words between quotation marks.** Tells InfoSeek to find the words in that exact order, next to each other. For instance, "**the here and now**."

- **Proper names.** Should be capitalized correctly: **Colorado, England, Gore**.

- **Words separated by hyphens.** Tells InfoSeek to find the words, as long as they are close together in the document: **diving-scuba**.

- **Words in brackets.** Should appear together, but not necessarily in the order you've entered them: **[diving scuba]**.

Each search engine is a little different, allowing different sorts of search terms. You can always search by simply entering a single word, but the more you know about each search engine, the more efficiently you will be able to search. When you first go to a search engine, look around for some kind of link to a help document.

Now, back to InfoSeek. When you've finished reading the help information, click on the Back button to return to the page with the text box (refer to fig. 7.1). Enter the word or phrase you want to search for and press Enter, or click on the Search button. Netscape sends the information to InfoSeek, and, with a little luck, you may see a result page soon, as shown in figure 7.2. On the other hand, you may see a message telling you that the search engine is busy; try again in a few moments and you may well get through.

What, then, has InfoSeek found? Well, when I searched for `iceland`, it found 100 links to Web sites that contain information about Iceland. (InfoSeek may have more than 100 such links, but I've just used the free search. If I signed up for the commercial service, there would be no limit; that is, it would show me everything it can find related to Iceland.)

Fig. 7.2
InfoSeek found a few links to Icelandic subjects for me.

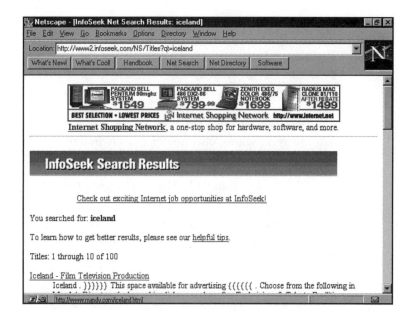

The document I'm viewing doesn't show me all 100 links. It shows me the first 10, but there's a link at the bottom of the page to show me the next 10. It found links to things such as the *Iceland Export Directory*, *Icelandic Horses*, *Heimasida Mals og Menningar* (it's a bookstore in Iceland), *Alphabetical Index of Books*, *The Complete Fly-Fishing School of Iceland*, and plenty more. If any of these links interest me, all I need to do is click on the link, and away I go, over the North Atlantic and into Iceland.

Loads more search engines

InfoSeek is but one of many search engines on the Web. If you click on the Net Search button again and scroll down the page, you'll find links to Lycos, WebCrawler, Deja News (which searches newsgroups—you'll learn more about them in chapter 13), and Excite (which lets you search Web sites, newsgroups, classified ads, and NetReviews—reviews of Web sites).

One good search engine that isn't currently listed in the Internet Search document is Yahoo; but that's also a directory site, and we're going to take a look at those in a moment.

Search multiple engines quickly!

There are many more search engines, and you can quickly search dozens of
them using a couple of special forms. At the bottom of the Internet Search
document, you find a couple of links to lists of search engines:

- **W3 Search Engines**. This is neat; not only will you find a list of many
  search engines, but you can search directly from the W3 Search Engines
  form: **http://cuiwww.unige.ch/meta-index.html**

- **CUSI (Configurable Unified Search Interface)**. Another great site
  for searching, this one also allows you to search a variety of engines
  from one form. It's perhaps a little easier to use than the previous one:
  http://Web.nexor.co.uk/susi/cusi.html

- You might also check out the **Search Engine Room**, which contains
  links to a number of search engines, though you can't search without
  going to the engine sites first: **http://www.nosc.mil/planet_earth/
  Library/sei_room.html**

Q&A *Which is the best search or directory site?*

There is no "best." I really like Yahoo and Jump City (**http://
www.jumpcity.com/**), but there may be other sites that you prefer. Each
is different; each works in a different way, and each will give you a different
result. Try a few and see which you like.

Browse the Internet directories

Now let's see the Internet directories. Click on the Net Directory button;
or choose <u>D</u>irectory, Internet <u>D</u>irectory. You see the document like the one
shown in figure 7.3. Right at the top of this document is the Yahoo directory.
As I mentioned a moment ago, Yahoo has a search engine; if you'd like to use
this, click on the *Yahoo Directory* link; you'll go directly to the Yahoo site.

Fig. 7.3

Yahoo provides lists of Web sites, broken down by category.

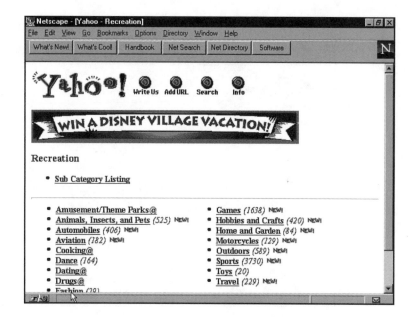

But notice the category links: Art, Education, Health, Social Science, and so on. Each of these links points deeper into the Yahoo system, a level lower down in the hierarchical system of document categories. For instance, click on *Recreation,* and you see a document from Yahoo with a list of more categories: *Amusement/Theme Parks@, Aviation, Drugs@, Motorcycles,* and so on.

What does the @ sign at the end of some of these mean? It means that this entry is a sort of cross-reference, that you will be crossing over to another category if you select this link. For instance, click on *Drugs@,* and you see the page in figure 7.4, which is in the Health:Pharmacology:Drugs category, and contains links to other drug-related categories, along with links to Web pages that are related to recreational drugs (from alcohol to XTC), political and legal issues, pharmacology, and many other subjects.

Fig. 7.4

Finally, you arrive at a page with links out across the Web.

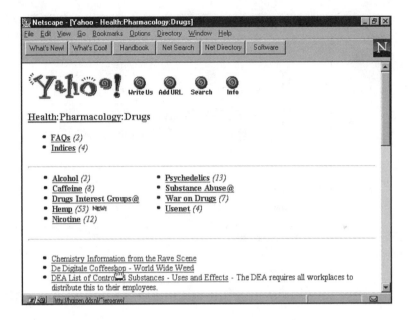

Now, notice that figure 7.4 contains links shown with bold text and numbers in parentheses after them (such as ***Alcohol (2)***), and links that are not bolded (such as *DEA List of Controlled Substances—Uses and Effects*). The bold links take you further down the hierarchy; you see another document that contains more links. The number in parentheses after the link shows the number of links you'll find in that document.

The regular-text links are links across the Internet to Web documents containing the information you're looking for. Select *A short introduction to smart drugs*, for instance, and you'll find yourself viewing a document in Finland.

Need more directories?

Go back to the Internet Directory page, and scroll down a little to find links to more directories:

- **The Mckinley Internet Directory.** This is a directory of Web pages, Telnet, Gopher, FTP, newsgroups, and mailing lists. The entries are also rated by reviewers.

- **Point.** Another directory that rates sites.

- **World Wide Arts Resources.** A directory of Web sites related to artists and the arts.

- **Excite.** Select from a list of a few dozen categories, or search the database. Each link has a short description, which is very handy.

- **World-Wide Web Servers.** A list of Web servers. It doesn't help you find a particular subject, but allows you to select Web servers by country or state.

- **Virtual Tourist.** This site provides a map of the world; click on a region on a large-scale map to see a smaller scale map, then click on a country to see a map showing where the servers are, or perhaps a list of servers. Click on a button to see a list of Web servers, color-coded according to the city (see fig. 7.5).

Fig. 7.5
The Virtual Tourist provides a wonderful way to see where the world's Web servers are.

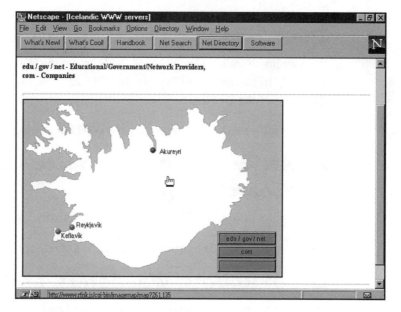

Other search sites

There are loads of other Web sites set up specifically to help people search for a subject of interest. I'm going to describe a few of them now; you may want to go to **http://www.mcp.com/authors/pkent/**, which I set up some time ago when I wrote *The Complete Idiot's Guide to the World Wide Web*.

You'll find links to *Chapter 25*, which contains links to all the sites I'm about to mention, and to *Chapter 26*, which contains links to a potpourri of interesting sites.

Let's take a look at a few other directories you may want to visit.

Directories of directories

We'll start with a general category, a list of Web documents that will help you find more specific directories.

 TIP Remember that URLs sometimes end with **.html**, and sometimes with **.htm**. Make sure you use the correct one. And if one doesn't work, try the other.

The World Wide Web Initiative

"Everything there is to know about the World Wide Web is linked directly or indirectly to this document" (from the W3 Organization, the people planning the future of the Web).

http://www.w3.org/hypertext/WWW/TheProject

ANANSE: Internet Resource Locators and Search Engines

This directory contains links to lots of other directories.

http://ananse.irv.uit.no/law/nav/find.html

List of Robots, Wanderers, and Spiders

This is a directory of programs that dig around on the Web, creating indexes, and measuring its size.

http://info.webcrawler.com/mak/projects/robots/active.html

Plain English, please!

A **robot** is a program that wanders around on the Internet doing things. In this case, a program that wanders around collecting information about Web sites. (You'll often see the suffix **bot**, too, as in **mailbot**, a mail-related robot.) **Wanderer** and **spider** are simply alternative names for World Wide Web robots.

General search engines and directories

The following lists are directories of Web documents. You can search or browse for just about any subject.

Jump City

I really like this one. You can search Web sites and newsgroups, or view category lists (à la Yahoo). The items that are found have short reviews, so you know what you are getting.

http://www.jumpcity.com/

The World Wide Web Worm (WWWW)

The World Wide Web Worm is a system that digs around on the Web looking for documents. It follows links through the Web, and builds an index of Titles and URLs. You can enter keywords to search for any subject, and you find detailed instructions on how to search.

http://www.cs.colorado.edu/home/mcbryan/WWWW.html

Web Crawler

This system crawls around on the Web, creating an index. You can search that index.

http://www.webcrawler.com/

The WebCrawler Top 25

The Web Crawler also publishes a document that lists the 25 most-referenced documents on the Web. That is, the documents that are referenced by other document links more than any others.

> **http://www.webcrawler.com/WebCrawler/Top25.html**

The JumpStation

Another simple index that you can search.

> **http://www.stir.ac.uk/jsbin/js**

Wandex

Wandex (World Wide Web Wanderer Index) lets you search an index of thousands of documents.

> **http://www.netgen.com/cgi/wandex**

The Spider's Web

Over 1000 links to "cool places." (See fig. 7.6.)

> **http://gagme.wwa.com/~boba/spider1.html**

Fig. 7.6
The Spider's Web; loads
of interesting links.

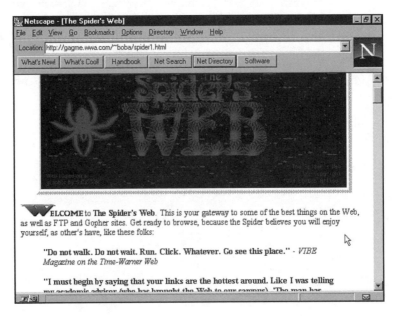

Nikos

This is an index created by Rockwell Network Systems and Cal Poly, San Luis Obispo. Type the keyword you are looking for.

http://www.rns.com/cgi-bin/nomad

RBSE's URL Database

The RBSE (Repository Based Software Engineering) spider "walks the web" grabbing URLs. You can search the resulting database.

http://rbse.jsc.nasa.gov/eichmann/urlsearch.html

Best of the Web '94

A list of the "best" Web documents, chosen in an online contest and announced at the International W3 Conference in Geneva. From the NCSA (Best Overall Site) to the Sports Information Service (Best Entertainment Service), and Travels With Samantha (Best Document Design) to the Xerox Map Server (Best Use of Interaction).

http://wings.buffalo.edu/contest/

ALIWEB

ALIWEB, which stands for Archie-Like Indexing for the Web, lets you search for Web sites in the same way you can use Archie to search for FTP files (we'll get to that in chapter 11). There are several different interfaces—a form-based search, a multiple-keyword form-based search, and a simple index search.

http://web.nexor.co.uk/aliweb/doc/search.html

The Mother-of-all BBSs

Search this giant database of Web sites or select a category first; from Agriculture to Writing on the Net, and find subjects as diverse as Underwear and the Sheffield Ski Village.

http://www.cs.colorado.edu/homes/mcbryan/public_html/bb/ summary.html

NCSA's What's New on the Web

A list of new Web pages. You can view the current month's crop of new stuff, or go back and view previous months. This is a great way to get a feel for just how much new information is being added to the Web.

> **http://www.ncsa.uiuc.edu/SDG/Software/Mosaic/Docs/whats-new.html**

NCSA's Starting Points

This site is handy for newcomers wanting to get an overview of what's on the Web. You'll find links to useful services and other directories.

> **http://www.ncsa.uiuc.edu/SDG/Software/Mosaic/StartingPoints/NetworkStartingPoints.html**

The WWW Virtual Library

This is at CERN, the home of the Web. Select a category and you'll be shown a list of related Web sites.

> **http://www.w3.org/hypertext/DataSources/bySubject/Overview.html**

The CUI W3 Catalog

This directory (the Centre Universitaire d'Informatique W3 Catalog in Geneva) lists thousands of Web pages. You type the word you are looking for, and the catalog looks for matches. It's actually an index of the WWW Virtual Library.

> **http://cuiwww.unige.ch/w3catalog**

Virtual Libraries

This site points you to Web reference documents, such as Scott Yanoff's Internet Services List and Big Dummy's Guide to the Internet. You'll find pointers to useful directories, as well as individual documents.

> **http://www.w3.org/hypertext/DataSources/bySubject/Virtual_libraries/Overview.html**

EINet Galaxy

This site is another directory that can be searched by entering a keyword or by browsing through links to different subjects. There's also a What's New page.

http://galaxy.einet.net/

The Harvest WWW Home Pages Broker

Another searchable index of Web sites. This system also displays information about a Web document that it finds, even showing part of the document's text.

http://www.town.hall.org/brokers/www-home-pages/

GNN NetNews

This one isn't really a directory, but it's worth mentioning because it's a great way to discover lots of interesting things. It's an online magazine about the Internet. It's a great place to find out about new programs and services, Internet news stories and controversies, and other neat stuff.

http://nearnet.gnn.com/news/index.html

Internet Services List

Scott Yanoff's Internet Services List has been around in text files for about three years, but it's now available on the Web—in interactive form, of course. When you find something of interest—a Web site, an FTP site, a chat service, or whatever—you can go right there.

http://slacvx.slac.stanford.edu:80/misc/internet-services.html

Commercial and business lists

These are lists of Web documents maintained by businesses.

Open Market's Commercial Sites Index

A large alphabetical listing of commercial Web documents. You can also search for a keyword or look at the What's New section.

http://www.directory.net/

Interesting Business Sites on the Web

A small list of interesting business Web pages. There's no searching, just select a category—Pick of the Month, Financial Services, Virtual Malls, and so on.

http://www.rpi.edu/~okeefe/business.html

Sell-it On the WWW

This is a Directory of Advertisers' Web sites. You find links to companies selling CD recordings, business supplies, computer equipment, books, and general services.

http://www.xmission.com/~wwwads/index.html

CommerceNet

A Silicon Valley-based directory. You can find out about products and services, associations, news, information and events related to the participants in CommerceNet. Companies like American Express, Amdahl, Apple, FedEx, and many more. (Cool graphics in this directory.)

http://www.commerce.net/

MecklerWeb

Select the category you are interested in—Business and Finance, Travel, Seniors, Arts & Entertainment, Computing, Education, and so on—and you'll see information about companies related to that subject. Or view a list of companies with information at this site. Mecklermedia, the owner of MecklerWeb, publishes Internet World magazine.

http://www.mecklerweb.com/

More Specific Stuff

The following are directories that are designed to help you find more specific information.

Commercial Newspapers on the Web

This lists magazines and newspapers on the Web. It also contains links to other lists of publications. (See fig. 7.7.)

http://www.jou.ufl.edu/commres/webjou.htm

Fig. 7.7
WWW Daily: a great
way to find newspapers
on the Web.

Campus Newsletters on the Net

This list has links to dozens of college newspapers.

http://ednews2.asa.utk.edu/papers.html

Journalism and Communications Schools

Links to journalism and communications colleges.

http://www.jou.ufl.edu/commres/jouwww.htm

The Journalism List

In theory, this provides information about Internet and Web resources that might be of use to journalists. But it's a great list for *anyone* who wants to find their way around. Not only does it have Web resources, but newsgroups, finger, FTP, Gopher, WAIS, and more.

http://www.jou.ufl.edu/commres/jlist.htm

 Plain English, please!

WAIS means Wide Area Information Server. It's a system—that predates the World Wide Web—which allows you to search hundreds of databases. (We'll look at WAIS in chapter 14.) **"**

Internet Law Sites

These are good places on the Web to find information about the law. The General Lists of Various Law Sites (**http://ananse.irv.uit.no/law/nav/law_ref.html**) and law-related sites on the Internet (**http://www2.waikato.ac.nz/law/law-related.html**).

Multimedia Information Sources

This is an index to Web sites related to multimedia. You'll find links to documents with information about current events in multimedia, various company sites, software archives, and more.

http://viswiz.gmd.de/MultimediaInfo/

Web Exhibits

This list links to dozens on Web exhibits, from art to the Dead Sea Scrolls.

http://155.187.10.12/fun/exhibits.html

US Government Web

This is a Web site that lets you search for U.S. Government Web documents. White House press releases, the National Trade Data Bank, the President's speeches (audio files), and more.

http://sunsite.unc.edu/govdocs.html

Irena, Australia's Beauty

Irena is, apparently, named after "one of the most attractive women in Australia."

It lets you search the Web server at the Australian National University for information on the social sciences, humanities, and Asian Studies.

http://coombs.anu.edu.au/bin/irena.cgi/WWWVL-Aboriginal

SmartMarks, your personal agent

Have you heard the term **personal agent**? It's a bit of jargon that's turning up frequently in the press these days; it refers to a program that automatically carries out tasks for you (particularly searching for information that you need).

Well, you have an honest-to-goodness personal agent available to you, in the guise of SmartMarks. Chapter 6 shows the way SmartMarks can be used to improve Netscape's bookmark system, but it can also be used to improve your Internet searches. You can use SmartMarks to set up searches that you want to carry out more than once. The next time you want to do a particular search, you can simply select the search from SmartMarks, and it will carry it out for you. But it does more; it even carries out searches automatically at preset intervals and tells you if it's found anything new.

For instance, let's say you want to search for information about Iceland. You could set up a Yahoo search for the word **iceland**, and run the search. You can then come back next week and select the search from SmartMarks. Or you can tell SmartMarks to run it automatically once a day or once a week, and tell you if it finds anything new.

Searching with SmartMarks

Here's how to set up a search with SmartMarks. First, go to the SmartMarks window; choose <u>B</u>ookmarks, <u>V</u>iew SmartMarks, or simply swap to the window using the taskbar or Alt+Tab.

Next, click on the Smart Finder toolbar button, or choose <u>T</u>ools, <u>F</u>ind. You'll see the dialog box in figure 7.8. If you open the <u>S</u>earch drop-down list box, you see that Smart Finder allows you to search a number of items; you can search Yahoo, Lycos, InfoSeek, and WebCrawler, four well-known search engines. You can also search All Folders and Folders, but these are related to searching the bookmark folders—we're only interested in using the search engines right now.

Fig. 7.8
Smart Finder will help
search the Internet and
automatically re-search
it later.

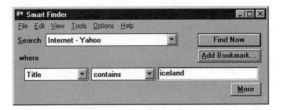

Here's how to set up your search:

1 Select the search engine you want to use from the <u>S</u>earch drop-down
list box.

2 Select the item that you want to search from the drop-down list box
below the Where label; if you are searching Yahoo, you can search
through the database of Web-page Contents, Title, URL, and Comments.
The other search engines only allow you to search the comments.

3 Select an option from the next drop-down list box. Depending on the
search engine you have selected, you may be able to select Contains or
Matches. In other words, if you select Contains, the search engine looks
for any word containing the text you are going to enter; if you search
for **ice**, it finds *ice, iceland,* and *icecream.* However, if you select
Matches, the search engine only finds words that exactly match what
you've entered—you find *ice,* but not *iceland* or *icecream.*

4 Type the word or phrase you want to search for in the text box on the
right.

TIP **You must know how each search engine works—the type of search**
words you can enter. You may be able to enter phrases or multiple words,
for instance. Go to these sites for more information about how to search:
Yahoo: **http://www.yahoo.com/**
Lycos**: http://lycos.cs.cmu.edu/**
InfoSeek: **http://ww2.infoseek.com/**
WebCrawler: **http://webcrawler.com/**

5 If you plan to use this search again, either automatically or manually,
you need to create a bookmark. Click on the <u>A</u>dd Bookmark button to
see the dialog box in figure 7.9.

Fig. 7.9
Place a bookmark on your searches, so that you can run them again manually or automatically.

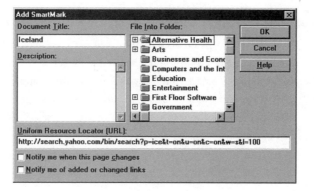

6 Replace the Document Title text with a more appropriate title; the word you are searching for, for instance.

7 Select a folder into which you want Smart Find to place the bookmark. You may want to create a special Search folder for these search book-marks (see chapter 6).

8 Enter a Description, if you wish.

9 If you plan to have Smart Finder automatically rerun the search for you—once a week, for instance—click on the two check boxes at the bottom of this dialog box.

10 Click on the OK button to return to the Smart Finder dialog box.

11 Click on the Find Now button to begin the search. Smart Finder opens a Netscape window, and sends the search word or words to the search engine you selected. In a few moments, you should see the results.

Well, setting all that up was easy enough. But how about this automatic searching stuff? You've just created a bookmark to the search, and SmartMarks will treat that bookmark like any other (and I've discussed that in some detail in chapter 6). You can tell it to check the document referenced by the bookmark every time SmartMarks opens, only when you select a bookmark and tell SmartMarks to check, or after a specific interval—every few days, every couple of weeks, or whatever you prefer. When SmartMarks checks the bookmark, it reruns the search, then tells you if anything's changed. If it hasn't, there's no need for you to look at the search results. If it has, though, you'll be informed that there are changes. See chapter 6 for more details.

Q&A *How about other search engines or directories?*

You can also place bookmarks on other searches you carry out using other search engines or lists you view in directories; you're not limited to the four listed in the Smart Finder drop-down list box. Simply run the search through Netscape in the normal way. Then, once you've got the results, place a bookmark on the results page using the <u>B</u>ookmarks, <u>A</u>dd SmartMark command.

8

Saving Stuff from the Web

● **In this chapter:**

- **Saving documents as text and HTML files**

- **How can I grab images out of Web documents?**

- **How can I save the document background?**

- **Printing documents and saving URLs**

- **Transferring files across the Web**

- **Embedding documents in your word processor**

You can see something in the Netscape window—how do you save it for later?. . . . . ●

Netscape provides a number of ways for you to get information from a Web document into your other Windows applications or saved on the hard disk. You can perform the following operations:

- Save the document text

- Save the HTML **source** document

- Save the text or HTML source for documents you haven't even viewed

- Save inline images in graphics files

- Save the document background

- Print the document

- Save URLs to the Clipboard so you can copy them into another program

- Grab files directly from the cache

- Save computer files referenced by links

- Drag-and-drop

 CAUTION **Remember, much of what you come across on the Web is** copyrighted material. In fact, unless you are sure that what you are viewing is not copyrighted, you should assume it *is*. You can take this material for private use, but not for publication. For information about what you can and can't do with copyrighted material, refer to a book on copyright law. (Many writers' references contain copyright law information.)

How can I grab document text?

Let's begin by looking at how to get text out of a Web document. Use any of the following methods:

- Choose File, Save As. In the Save As dialog box, select *Plain Text (*.txt)* from the Save As Type drop-down list box, select the directory you want to place it in, enter a file name, and click on Save. Netscape will save all the text in the document (not the underlying HTML codes, though).

TIP **When you enter a file name, include the file extension .TXT. Even** though you select *Plain Text (*.txt)*, Netscape currently doesn't automatically change the extension. If you don't change it, the file will be saved with the .HTML extension.

- Highlight the text; choose <u>E</u>dit, <u>C</u>opy or press Ctrl+C. The text is copied to the Clipboard, so you can now go to another application and paste it.

TIP **To highlight text, choose <u>E</u>dit, Select <u>A</u>ll; right-click inside the** document and choose Select <u>A</u>ll; or point at the beginning of the text you want to highlight, click on the mouse button, hold the button down, and drag the pointer across the text. (Make sure you are not clicking inside a link, of course, or you won't highlight the text; you'll see another document.)

Saving the HTML source document

Why would you care about the **source** document? Most people won't want the source document, but if you are interested in creating your own Web pages, you *will*. If you view a source document, you can learn the techniques that other Web authors have used to create documents.

The source document is the ASCII text document that is the basis of the Web page you are viewing. As you saw back in chapter 1, each Web document is an ASCII text document with special codes, or **tags**, that tell Web browsers what to do. When you transfer a document to the browser, the browser renders the document; that is, it takes a look at all the codes, then figures out what it has to do to turn the document into something you can read.

To save the source document, choose <u>F</u>ile, <u>S</u>ave As. Enter a file name, choose a directory, and make sure that *Source (*.htm;*.html)* is displayed in the Save As <u>T</u>ype drop-down list box. Then click on <u>S</u>ave. (If you are using Windows 95 or Windows NT, you'll have the .HTML option: Netscape will automatically save the document with the .HTML extension, not .HTM. Windows 95 and NT accept file extensions over three digits. If you are working with Windows 3.1, you have to use the .HTM extension.)

TIP   **To see the HTML codes before you decide whether to save the** file, choose View, By Document Source, and the View Source window will open. You can then either highlight the text in the window and press Ctrl+C to copy it, or close the window and use the File, Save As command.

By the way, you can tell Netscape to use a different program to display the source; choose Options, General Preferences, click on the Apps tab, and enter a program name into the View Source text box. You may want to use the Windows 95 word processor, WordPad.

Saving documents you haven't even seen

You don't have to view a document before you save it. As long as you have a link to the document, you can save it without viewing it first. Simply right-click on the link, and choose Save This Link As. You'll see the Save As dialog box, and can choose *Source (*.htm;*.html)* or *Plain Text (*.txt)*, as described earlier (see "How can I grab document text?"). After you enter the document title you want to use, select the directory, and click on Save. Netscape will transfer the document. It won't display it, though; it will simply save it as instructed.

How can I save inline images?

You can save pictures that you find inside Web documents. Right-click on the picture and choose Save This Image As. You'll see the Save As window. Enter a file name, and click on Save to save it to your hard disk. It will be saved using the original format: if the picture is a .GIF file, Netscape will save it as a .GIF; if it's a .JPG or .XBM, it will be saved as such.

Note, by the way, that there's a way to remove all the text from around the picture, displaying the picture in Netscape as if it were in a document by itself. Right-click on the picture and choose View This Image *(image name)*. Netscape will request a copy of the picture from the Web server that has the picture and display the picture in a document by itself. In other words, even though the picture is in the cache, Netscape will get a fresh copy. You won't see the original text or document background; all you'll see is the image you selected.

TIP **You can quickly copy a picture of this image into another** application. Press Alt+Print Screen to place a copy of the Netscape window in the Clipboard. Then go to the application in which you want to paste the image, place the cursor where you want it, and press Ctrl+V to paste it. You may, depending on the capabilities of the program into which you pasted it, be able to cut the area around the image away, leaving just the inline picture.

What about document backgrounds?

A new feature that's becoming popular on Web pages these days is the **background** pattern. A Web author can add a special background to his documents; the background may be a plain color or some sort of pattern. Many Web sites use the company name or logo as a sort of watermark in the background. Others use some kind of marble or rock effect. (Some authors aren't doing a good job here. I've noticed that a lot of Web pages are almost illegible, thanks to a poorly chosen background color.)

Right now, Netscape provides no *direct* way to save the background image. (It may soon, though; remember the Netscape vs. Explorer "war" I mentioned in chapter 5. Well, Explorer *can* save the background, so Netscape may add that feature.) The following is a fairly simple technique by which you *can* save the background:

1 Choose View, By Document Source. You'll see the View Source window.

2 Near the top of the window, look for something like this: <BODY BACKGROUND="/netstore/images/background.gif". This is the command that places the background image into the document.

3 Use the mouse to highlight the file name and the path to the file (the text that appears inside quotation marks immediately after the = sign). In this case, it's /netstore/images/background.gif. (You can highlight text by pressing the mouse button and dragging the pointer across the text; or by placing the cursor at the beginning or end of the text, pressing Shift, and using an arrow key to move across the text.)

4 Press Ctrl+C to copy this text to the Windows Clipboard.

5 Open a word processor or text editor, and paste the text (Ctrl+V). Look closely at what you've got. If it's something like the example (`/netstore/images/background.gif`), you don't have the full URL. This is what's known as a **relative URL**. It shows where the image is in relation to the document. (If the image starts with `http://`, then you have the full URL; skip to Step 8.)

6 Switch to the Netscape window, click in the Location bar, and press Ctrl+C. Go back to the word processor and paste the text. Again, look closely at what you've got. In this case, you have the following:

`/netstore/images/background.gif`

`http://merchant.netscape.com/netstore/index.html`

7 You need to take the beginning of the URL, all the way to the end of the host name, and add it to the beginning of the path to the image file, like this:

`http://merchant.netscape.com/netstore/images/background.gif`

In some cases, you may only have a file name (`background.gif`, for instance). This would mean that the image file is in the same directory as the .HTML file. In such a case, remove the .HTML file name from the full URL, and replace it with the image file name.

8 Copy the new URL, and paste it into the Location text box.

9 Press Enter, and Netscape will transfer the image and place it in the Netscape window.

10 Right-click on the image and choose Save This Image As.

That's it! You've got the background image.

CAUTION   **Remember that you don't *own* this image! You can use it for your** own private purposes, but you probably can't publish Web pages using it without the permission of the artist who created it or the author of the Web site from which you took it.

Also, you'll probably see that the image you transferred is just a small square; it doesn't fill a document. A browser knows how to take these small squares and **tile** them all across a document's background.

Web to paper—printing the document

If you want a paper copy of something you've found in a Web document, you can print the document directly from Netscape. First, define your default page setup (you only have to set this up once, not every time you print). Choose File, Page Setup to see the dialog box in figure 8.1.

Fig. 8.1
You can define margins, headers, and footers; and tell Netscape how to print text.

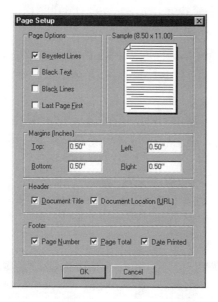

This box lets you select a variety of options, as follows:

- **Beveled Lines.** Many Web documents contain dividing lines across the page (these are created by the Web authors using the <HR> tags). Select this option if you want to print these lines as beveled lines the way they appear on-screen—a sort of 3-D effect. (Well, okay, it just looks like two lines close together on my printouts.) If you don't use this option, the lines will appear as single black lines.

- **Black Text.** Select this to print all the text, even colored text, in black. This is only needed if you are using a color printer, of course.

- **Black Lines.** Select this to print all lines, including colored lines, in black.

- **Last Page First.** If you select this, Netscape will print the document back-to-front, the last page first.

- **Margins.** Set up the margins (the distance from the edge of the paper to the edge of the text). If you enter a number and then Tab out of the field, you'll see that the Sample in the top right of the box changes to show you the new margin.

- **Header.** You can print two items in the header (the line at the very top of the page): **Document Title** and **Document Location (URL)**. These are handy because they help someone reading the document identify and find the original Web document.

- **Footer.** You have three choices for the footer: You can print the **Page Number**, the **Page Total**, and the **Date Printed**.

Before you print—the preview

Before you print a document, you may want to look at the preview to see how it will turn out. Choose File, Print Preview to see something like the window in figure 8.2. You can see more or less how the document will turn out on the printed page. You'll see the header and footer, the images, and the text. (You *won't* see any background graphics because Netscape strips it out before printing.)

Fig. 8.2
The preview shows you how the printed document will look.

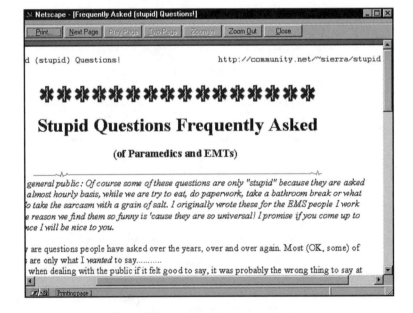

Notice the following buttons at the top of the window:

Print. If you like what you see, go ahead and print the document.

Next Page. If there's more information than will fit on one sheet of paper, click on this button to see the next page.

Prev Page. This button takes you back to the previous page.

Two Page. This displays two pages on your screen.

Zoom In. Click here to zoom in on the document. You can zoom in twice, which gets you pretty close. You can also click inside the document to zoom in (you'll notice that the mouse pointer is a small magnifying glass).

Zoom Out. Click here to zoom back out.

Close. Click here to return to the main document.

Printing the document

When you are ready to print the document, choose File, Print to see a typical Windows Print dialog box. You can pick the printer you want to use, select which pages you want to print (you'll have to guess here a little because a Web document is a single, perhaps very long, page while it's on-screen), and decide how many copies you want to print.

I want that URL!—Saving URLs to the Clipboard

Once you're a regular Web user, you'll find that you want to save URLs, the Web "addresses." Perhaps you want to share them with a friend or colleague. Maybe you want to include a URL in a memo or article you are writing or want to save the URL in a database with other research materials. Netscape provides the following ways to save URLs:

- Click in the Location text box, and the URL of the current document will be highlighted. Then press Ctrl+C; the text is copied to the Clipboard.

- Right-click on a link (a text or graphic link), and choose Copy This Link Location from the pop-up menu. This is a very handy method for copying a URL without even going to the referenced document.

- To copy the URL that identifies a picture, right-click on the picture and choose Copy This Image Location.

Stealing directly from the cache

Long after you've been to a Web document—days or weeks later, depending on how big your hard-disk cache is (see chapter 4)—you can grab information from that document by digging around in the cache. However, the cache is not always very easy to work in.

First, to see where your cache directory is, choose Options, Network Preferences, then click on the Cache tab. The Disk Cache Directory text box shows where your cache has been placed. (It's generally in the CACHE subdirectory of the Navigator directory.)

Now, use Windows Explorer (or File Manager if you are using Windows 3.1) to view that directory. You'll find all the inline images—.GIF, .XBM, and .JPG files—from your cached documents, along with the .HTML documents themselves. You can simply open them in another application or copy them to another directory.

Unfortunately, though, these files have all been renamed, and it's quite difficult to figure out what they are. They've all been given a special *M* number: M007J0PL.HTML, for instance. Double-click on the .HTML files, and they'll open in Netscape—though the links to the inline graphics won't work. If you have some kind of file viewer, you can use that to quickly view entries. For instance, if you are using Windows 3.1 and have PC Tools, you know that the PC Tools File Manager has a good file viewer; once you've opened the file viewer, each time you click on a file the image or text within, the file is displayed in the viewer.

There are a variety of file viewers available for Windows 3.1 and Windows 95. In Windows 95, you can sometimes also use the Quick View window (it should really be called "Slow View" because it's not particularly quick). If the file is "quick-viewable" (.HTM, .GIF, and .JPG are not; .TXT and .DOC are), right-click on the entry, and choose Quick View.

You can also get a file viewer especially created for Netscape: CacheMan. Actually, it's much more than a file viewer; it's really a cache manager. Yes, it helps you view files in the cache—it has a built-in viewer for .GIF, .JPG, .BMP, .TIF, .RLE, .LBM, .PCX files, and more. And you can set up external viewers for other file types. But it also allows you to selectively remove items from the cache (remember that Netscape allows you to clear the entire thing, but not bits and pieces), to fix (**localize**) the .HTML files so that when you open them the inline graphics are displayed, set up a separate directory to store renamed files, and so on.

 TIP **When Netscape retrieves a file from the cache, it can retrieve** the inline pictures, too. It's only when *you* open an HTML file by double-clicking on it in Windows Explorer or File Manager, for instance, that the problem occurs with the inline images not being found.

At the time of writing, there's a version for Windows 3.1, but not for Windows 95 or Windows NT. You can use CacheMan for free if you wish, though if you register it, you'll get free upgrades e-mailed to you and product support.

 CAUTION **CacheMan is *very* difficult to track down. I couldn't find it** on the Internet; the only place I could find it was on CompuServe (GO PCCONTACT, Library 5). I couldn't get the author to respond to my e-mail, so I don't know if CacheMan is a work in progress or simply dead.

How do I grab files from the Web?

Many links on the Web point not to other Web documents, but to computer files of various kinds. You can group these files into the two following types:

- **Files that you want to transfer to your hard disk.** For instance, a link may point to a program that is in an .EXE or .ZIP file. You want to transfer this program to your computer and then install it.

- **Files that you want to play or view.** These include sound files (music and speech), video, graphics of many kinds, word processing documents, Adobe Acrobat documents, PostScript files, and so on.

Of course, in order to play or view a file, it has to be transferred to your hard disk, and you may choose to save it. So in one sense, there's no difference between these two types of files—in each case, a file is transferred to your computer. But if you want to play or view a file, that's part of the **hypermedia** or **multimedia** experience of the Web, the purpose of the transfer is different.

But it's also different in another way: you may have to configure a special **viewer** so that when Netscape transfers the file, it knows how to play or display it. (For the first of these file types, Netscape doesn't care what happens to the file; it's simply going to save it to your hard disk and let you figure out what to do with it later.) You'll look at viewers in chapters 9 and 10. For now, we're only interested in the first type of file, one that you want to transfer and save on your hard disk.

File transfers

Why transfer files back to your computer? In chapter 11, you'll learn how to use Netscape to run **FTP** (File Transfer Protocol) sessions. FTP is an Internet-wide system that allows you to copy files to your computer from software archives all over the world. You can get shareware programs, clip art, various documents, sound clips, and more. There are literally millions of files waiting for you at these archives.

But Web authors can also distribute computer files directly from their Web documents. They create special links from their documents to the files that they believe their readers may want to transfer. Clicking on the link begins the transfer to your computer. The following are a few reasons for grabbing files from across the Web:

- Many sites are run by companies that want to distribute their shareware, freeware, or demo programs. (You'll look at one of these in a moment.)

- Some authors want to distribute non-Web documents. They may create links to PostScript, Word for Windows, Adobe Acrobat, and Windows Help documents, for example.

- Some authors have placed clip-art archives on the Web. You can transfer the files and then use them in your own Web documents.

As you can see, there is some overlap here between the two types of files mentioned before. This list points out that a Web author may want to distribute an Adobe Acrobat file (**Acrobat** is a hypertext document format). But Acrobat files fall into the second category of files: ones that are part of the multimedia experience that Netscape wants to "play."

Well, they may be files that can be played, depending on the following two factors:

- How is the document formatted? If the file has its original extension and is in its original format, the Web author has set it up so that it can be played. For instance, the Acrobat extension is .PDF, and when the file is transferred, Netscape can automatically send this file to an Adobe Acrobat viewer so that you can view the document immediately. But the Web author may have saved the file in a compressed, or archive, format. The extension may be .ZIP (a PKZIP compressed file), or .EXE (a self-extracting archive file). This means that the Web author expects people to transfer the file, extract the software, and then load the file into another program.

- Have you set up Netscape to play the file? If you haven't set it up to play a particular file (and I'll discuss that in chapter 9), the only thing Netscape can do is transfer it to your hard disk. So even if the file extension is .PDF, for instance, if you haven't configured Netscape to "call" an Adobe Acrobat viewer, it can't do so. Netscape will want to simply transfer the file and drop it onto your hard disk.

Here's how it works

Let's take a quick look at how all this works. As an example, I'm using The Consummate Winsock Apps List site (**http://cwsapps.texas.net/**), which contains a fantastic library of Internet software.

I went into the Windows 95 area and then into the Web Accessories area, where I found a program called WebWatch. It's another program that automatically checks Web pages to see whether anything changed, and is similar in concept to SmartMarks (see chapter 6). There's also a version available for Windows 3.1. I clicked on the link that names the file, and Netscape opened the Unknown File Type dialog box, which you can see in figure 8.3.

Fig. 8.3
The Unknown File Type dialog box appears whenever you begin transferring a file that Netscape doesn't recognize.

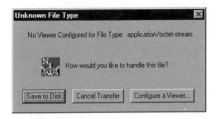

Why did Netscape display this dialog box? Because it doesn't know what to do with it. Netscape can't do anything with the file itself because it's not one of the file types that has been designed to work with Netscape. It doesn't have a viewer installed for this file type (an .EXE executable self-extracting compressed file), so it can't send the file to another program. It needs your help. You have the following three choices:

- **Save to Disk.** Click here to see the Save As dialog box, in which you can tell Netscape where to put the file once it has transferred it.

- **Cancel Transfer.** Click here to remove the dialog box and return to the document.

- **Configure a Viewer.** Click here to tell Netscape which program to send the file to (I'll cover that in chapter 9).

 TIP **As you'll see in chapter 9, you can configure a viewer for another** common compressed file format: .ZIP files. This program opens the file, shows you what is inside, and even extracts the files for you.

If you clicked on Save to Disk, Netscape begins transferring the file. You'll see the window in figure 8.4, which has all sorts of handy information: the name of the file being transferred, the directory into which it's being placed, the file size and the percentage already transferred, and an estimate of how much longer it will take to transfer the file.

Fig. 8.4
Netscape provides plenty of useful information while transferring a file.

Note that you don't have to wait for this transfer. You can simply click on the window's minimize button (the third from the right on the title bar), and continue working in the Netscape window—selecting another file to transfer or moving to another document.

CAUTION It's a good idea to check software you transfer with a computer-virus program before using them. Many sites on the Internet don't check for viruses, so you don't always know for sure what you are getting. There are a number of commercial and shareware programs available.

Embedding Web pages into other documents

Now we'll get really fancy. We're going to use **OLE** (Object Linking and Embedding) to embed Web pages in other programs. Netscape is an OLE **server**, a program that can provide information to an OLE **client**. We're going to use Word for Windows (only because that's the word processor I use—you can use any OLE client program).

Follow these steps:

1 Choose Insert, Object. (That's the command in Word for Windows; in other programs, the menu option may be different, so check your documentation.) The Object dialog box opens.

2 In the Object Type list box, find *Netscape Hypertext Document*.

3 If you wish, click on the Display as Icon check box (see fig. 8.5). With this selected, Netscape will insert an icon to represent the document; if it *isn't* selected, Netscape will insert an actual document that you can view. If you select this check box, you can also click on the Change Icon button to select a different icon to represent the document. (Not much choice last time I looked. You can pull an icon from a different application if you wish.) Right now, you're going to look at what happens when you *don't* use the icon.

Fig. 8.5
Select Netscape
Hypertext Document,
and click on OK.

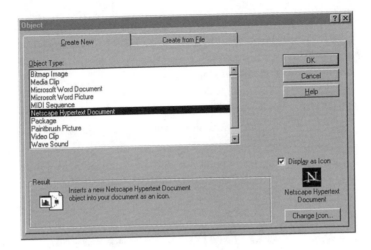

4 Click on the OK button and the Netscape window opens. You can now navigate to the Web page you want to embed into your document. Type the URL of the document you want to embed into the Location bar, and press Enter. (You can also select the URL from the drop-down list box or use a bookmark.)

5 Choose File, Close to close the Netscape window and embed the Web page into the document.

6 You'll see the Web page in your word processing document. You can double-click on it to open it. The normal word processor menu and toolbars are removed, and you'll see Netscape's menu bar and Location bar in their place (see fig. 8.6).

That, then, is the theory. At the time of writing, it wasn't working too well, though. By the time you read this, it should be fixed, although it might work in a slightly different manner.

What good is this embedded document? Well, you can read and view the visible contents. But you can also double-click on the document to bring the Netscape components back again. You can now navigate the Web using your word processor as the browser! When you are finished, click outside the document to remove the Netscape components.

Fig. 8.6

Now you've got a Web
document embedded
inside your word
processor.

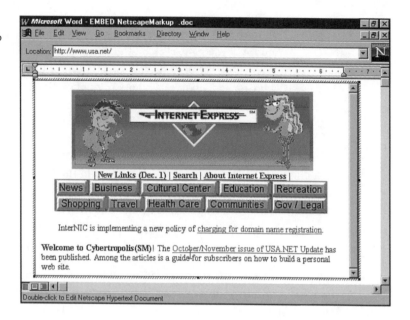

Note that you can resize this window. There are little black **handles** on the
corners and in the middle of each side; drag a handle in or out to modify the
size of the image in your word processing document. Or point at an edge,
wait until the mouse pointer changes to a four-headed arrow, and drag the
edge to move the entire window.

You'll also find several menu options that let you do things to the document.
Click in the document and then, in Word for Windows, choose one of the
following (the options may vary between applications):

Edit, Hypertext Object, Edit. Choose this to edit the document
within the word processor; this is the same as double-clicking on the
object.

Edit, Hypertext Object, Open. Choose this to open Netscape and
place the document within the Netscape window, where you can begin
navigating from the document.

Edit, Hypertext Object, Convert. You *may* be able to convert the
document into another format. Then again, you may not.

TIP **You may also have some right-click menu options. In Word for Windows,** if you right-click on the document, you can select Edit Hypertext and Open Hypertext. You can also Cut or Copy the document to the Clipboard, add a border or caption, or place the item in a frame.

If you use an icon

What happens if you choose to represent the document as an icon? (That is, you click on the Display as Icon check box in the Options dialog box.) When you click on the OK button, a Netscape icon appears in your document, and the Netscape window opens (although not with its normal complement of menus). Find the Web document you want, then close the window by choosing File, Close.

The document is now represented by an icon. You won't be able to view the document within your word processor, but if you double-click on the icon (or choose Edit, Hypertext Object, Edit or Edit, Hypertext Object, Open), the Netscape window opens and displays the document.

**9**

Music, Video, and Other Neat Things— Installing Viewers

● **In this chapter:**

- **What file formats will I run into?**

- **What happens when Netscape transfers a file?**

- **External viewers and inline plug-ins**

- **External files and embedded ("live") objects**

- **Installing a "viewer" for .WAV sound files**

- **Working with plug-ins**

- **How do I install a viewer through the Preferences dialog box?**

The World Wide Web is a multimedia system. It's a lot more than text and inline pictures. Here's how to use the neat stuff . . . .

What happens when you click on a link in a Web document? Well, it might take you to another Web document. It might also transfer a .ZIP or .EXE file, an archive, a program, or a self-extracting archive file that you want to transfer to your hard disk. (I covered that in chapter 8.) But it might be something different. Table 9.1 describes the way Netscape works with a variety of file formats.

Table 9.1 File formats that Netscape can handle

File format	What it does
.AU, .AIF, .AIFF, .AIFC, .SND	Sound files often used on Macintosh systems—Netscape can open a special sound utility and play these.
.EXE	A program file or a self-extracting archive file. You saw these in chapter 8. Netscape will let you save the file to your disk.
.GIF, .JPG, .JPEG, .JPE, .XBM	These are graphics files. They share one thing in common: they are the formats that are used for inline graphics images. But a Web author may also place one of these files at a Web site with a link pointing to it. The file will be transferred, but it won't be **inline**. That is, it won't be part of a Web document—as a graphic separate from a document, it's often known as an **external** image. They will appear in the Netscape window.
.HTM, .HTML	You know all about these; the basic Web-document format.
.TXT, .TEXT	A text file. These are displayed in the Netscape window.

Netscape needs a viewer for the following files—Windows has built-in programs that can handle these (the suite of available programs varies between Windows 3.1, Windows 95, and Windows NT):

.AVI	Video for Windows. This will play in Media Player.
.BMP, .PCX,	Common bitmap graphics formats. These can be displayed in Paintbrush.
.DOC	If you have Word for Windows, .DOC files will open in that program. However, Windows 95 comes with a word processor called WordPad, which can also open Word for Windows .DOC files.
.FLC, .FLI, .AAS	Autodesk Animator files. These can play in Media Player.
.HLP	Windows Help files. The Windows Help-system program opens them.

File format	What it does
.MID, .RMI	MIDI (Musical Instrument Digital Interface) sounds. These will play in Media Player.
.MMM	Microsoft Multimedia Movie Player files. Again, these run in Media Player.
.RTF	Rich Text Format, word-processing files that work in a variety of Windows word processors. If you haven't installed a program such as Word for Windows, the .RTF files are opened in WordPad.
.WAV	The standard Windows wave file sound format. These can play in Sound Recorder.
.WRI	Windows Write word processing files. These can be opened in WordPad.

There are no available built-in Windows viewers for the following file types, so you'll have to find something else if you want to use them:

File format	What it does
.EPS	A PostScript image.
.MOV. QT	The QuickTime video format.
.MPEG, .MPG, .MPE, .M1V	The MPEG (Motion Pictures Expert Group) video formats. (Windows 95 currently doesn't support MPEG, but an upgrade pack may be issued late in 1995 or early in 1996 to add support.)
.MP2	An MPEG audio format.
.PDF	The Portable Document Format, an Adobe Acrobat hypertext file. This format is becoming a very popular way to distribute electronic documents.
.PS	A PostScript document.
.RAM, .RA	RealAudio. This is a sound format that plays while it's being transmitted. Click on a link to a RealAudio file and it begins playing within a few seconds, rather than making you wait for the entire file to be transferred before starting.
.SGML	A document format.
.TSP	TrueSpeech, a sound format similar to RealAudio, though of a higher quality.
.TIF	A common graphics format.
.WRL	A VRML (Virtual Reality Modeling Language) 3-D object.
.XDM	The StreamWorks webTV and webRadio format. Similar to RealAudio, although it allows the real-time playing of video in addition to sound.
.ZIP	A PKZIP archive file. These files contain other compressed files within them.

TIP **You'll find compressed files in a variety of formats. If you find a** .ZIP, .LZH, or .ARC file, it's probably for a DOS or Windows computer. (The .ZIP format is currently the most-used archive format by far; you'll rarely find the other formats these days.) The .EXE self-extracting archive is very common in the DOS and Windows world, too, as you saw in chapter 8. If the file is a .HQX, .SEA, or .SIT file, it's for the Macintosh. The .Z, .TAR, and .GZ files are generally for UNIX computers. (Although the .GZ format can work on all three of these computer types, you'll rarely find a .GZ file for the PC or Mac.)

Have I missed some? There are as many possible file formats on the Web as there are file formats in existence. But the ones I've mentioned here are the ones you'll most likely find. (In fact, even some of the ones I've mentioned are not used very often on the Web—I think I've covered the ground pretty well with this list.)

TIP **Here's a quick way to see which file types Netscape can handle** (there are new types each time Netscape is updated) and which viewers are installed. Choose Options, General Preferences. In the Preferences dialog box, click on the Helpers tab. In this list box, you see file types marked as *Ask User* (Netscape can't display them and doesn't know which program can), *Naplayer* (Netscape's built-in sound player will play this type of file), and *Browser* (Netscape can display the file).

Let's take a look at the way Netscape figures out what it's supposed to do when it transfers a file.

What happens when Netscape transfers a file?

When you click on a link, the Web server sends information about the file that is about to be transferred. Netscape looks at this information to see what type of file is being sent. The Web server may send the MIME information (see "What's this about MIME?"), which tells Netscape exactly what the file is. If the server doesn't send the MIME information, Netscape takes a look at the file extension and uses that to figure out what sort of file it is. The procedure is as follows:

1 If the file is a Web document (MIME type *text/html*, extension .HTM or .HTML), it knows just what to do: display the file in the Netscape window because it's a Web document.

2 If the file is a text file (MIME type *text/plain*, extension .TXT), it's not a true Web document, but it can be displayed easily (it's a text document), so Netscape displays it in the window. You'll often find .TXT files when working in Gopher sites—see chapter 14.

3 If the file is an inline image file (MIME types *image/jpeg*, *image/gif*, *image/x-xbitmap*, extension .JPG, .JPEG, .JPE, .GIF, or .XBM), Netscape displays the file in the Netscape window; all of these are graphics types.

4 If the extension is one of the sound types that the Netscape sound program, NAPLAYER, can handle (MIME types *audio/x-aiff* or *audio/basic*, extension .AIF, .AIFF, .AIFC, .AU, or .SND), Netscape opens NAPLAYER and plays the sound.

5 If the file is none of these, Netscape looks at its list of **viewers** (also known as **helpers**) to see if any have been configured. For instance, you may have configured a viewer for .WAV files—you can use Windows Sound Recorder to play these. Netscape looks in its viewer or helper list, finds that the .WAV format is associated with Sound Recorder, so it "sends" the file to Sound Recorder.

6 If the file is not in the file-association list, Netscape is stuck; there's nothing more it can do, so it has to ask you, as you saw in chapter 8, and as you can see in fig. 9.1.

Fig. 9.1
If Netscape doesn't know what to do with a file, it will ask you.

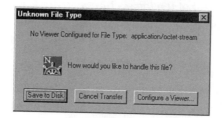

You have three choices. You can choose Save to Disk to save the file to your hard disk—absolving Netscape from any further responsibility. You can choose Configure a Viewer to tell Netscape which application it should use to open this file type (we'll look at this in a moment). Or you can choose Cancel Transfer to remove the dialog box and return to the Netscape window.

Two types of viewers

In a moment, we'll look at ways to configure a viewer. But first, I want to describe the two different types of programs that you can use to display file types that Netscape can't handle:

- **External viewers (or helpers).** Viewers are more properly called **external viewers**. They're sometimes known as **helpers** (the tab in the Preferences dialog box says Helpers). An external viewer is one that Netscape opens when it needs it. Netscape sends the file it's just received to the viewer, and the viewer displays or plays it. For instance, you might configure the Windows Sound Recorder to play .WAV files.

- **Inline Plug-Ins.** These are viewers that are built into Netscape. Instead of opening another program and sending the file to that program, Netscape will use a special program code that you've added to display or play the file *within* the Netscape window.

The concept of **inline plug-ins** is similar to that of Windows OLE (Object Linking and Embedding), in which one Windows program can use program code from another Windows program to display a file within itself. For instance, using OLE, Word for Windows can display Excel spreadsheet data, or Excel can display Word for Windows word processing data. Inline plug-ins are not OLE programs, but the idea is the same: they allow Netscape to display data that it normally would be unable to handle. We'll look closer at plug-ins under "More about plug-ins and live objects," later in this chapter.

For now, be aware that if there's a plug-in available for a particular file type, it's probably better than using an external viewer program. Rather than waiting for another program to launch and display a file, the file will be displayed within Netscape (though there may be cases in which you prefer to have the file type played or displayed *outside* Netscape). For instance, if you want to view .PDF files and can get the Adobe Acrobat plug-in, use that rather than installing the Adobe Acrobat reader program.

Two types of objects

There are also two different types of objects: external objects and live objects. An **external object** is a file that is not embedded into a document. You click on a link, and the Web server sends the file referenced by the link. For instance, the link may "point to" an Adobe Acrobat .PDF file (an Acrobat hypertext file, which you'll learn more about in chapter 10). Click on the link, and the Web server sends the .PDF file, which is then sent to the external viewer, or displayed in the inline plug-in.

Live objects, though, are embedded into a document; the Web author uses the `<EMBED SRC="file">` tag, so that when you open the document containing the tag, the embedded object is displayed. Netscape will run the appropriate inline plug-in, which will display the document. For instance, an .MPEG file can be embedded in a Web document. When you click on a link that takes you to the Web document, Netscape automatically opens some kind of .MPEG player plug-in, and the video begins playing in a rectangle within the Netscape window.

I'll come back to inline plug-ins and live objects later in this chapter. For now, though, I'll stick with external viewers.

Installing a viewer

We're going to quickly install a viewer; we'll set up Netscape so that whenever it transfers a .WAV file (a Windows audio file), it opens Sound Recorder.

When you first install Netscape, it doesn't know how to handle .WAV files. Choose Options, General Preferences, click on the Helpers tab, then look for *audio/x-wav*. You'll see that in the Action column it says Ask User (see fig. 9.2). In other words, when you click on a link to a .WAV file, Netscape will ask you what it should do with the file.

Fig. 9.2
The Helpers area of the General Preferences dialog box shows you that if Netscape finds a .WAV file it will ask you what to do.

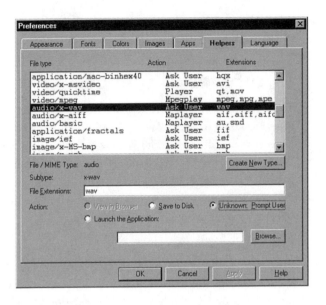

What's this about MIME?

What's this *audio/x-wav* thing shown in the Preferences dialog box? That's the file's **MIME (Multipurpose Internet Mail Extensions)** type. Originally, this system was designed to allow Internet e-mail programs to transfer binary files, and it's still in use today for that purpose. MIME provides a way for a program to identify a file type. Some Web servers, when transferring a file to a browser, send the MIME description.

Netscape can use this MIME information to identify the file type and figure out what to do with it (which viewer to send it to or which plug-in to use). If the server doesn't send the MIME information, Netscape then looks at the file extension and identifies the file that way. (Using the MIME information is the preferred way to handle files; a single file type may be identified using a range of different extensions.)

There are two parts to the MIME description: the **type** and the **subtype**. For instance, here's a MIME file description: *video/mpeg*. The type is *video* (the file is a video file), while the subtype is *mpeg* (just one of several different types of video files). If you look in the Helpers list, you'll see more *video/* subtypes: *video/quicktime* (an Apple video format) and *video/x-msvideo* (a Microsoft video format).

What if Netscape can't recognize the MIME type?

There are dozens of different MIME types, and Netscape has only been configured for a few of them. Notice also that some of the MIME types have the letter "x" in the name—x-msvideo, x-gzip, and so on. The x means that the MIME type is non-standard. Someone has created this MIME type, and it may be in common use, but it hasn't been approved by IANA (the Internet Assigned Numbers Authority).

You may encounter MIME types that Netscape hasn't been configured for. That's okay, though. You're about to see how to set up Netscape to send .WAV files to SoundRecorder. The procedure for setting up a viewer for a MIME type that Netscape can't recognize is the same—Netscape will simply grab the MIME information that it needs from the message sent by the Web server.

Q&A *Where can I find more info about MIME types?*

Try these URLs: **http://sd-www.jsc.nasa.gov/mime-types/** (where you'll find a large list of types) and **http://home.netscape.com/assist/ helper_apps/mime.html**.

Adding the .WAV viewer

Okay, it's time to configure the .WAV viewer. Let's begin by going to the Rolling Stones Web site: **http://www.stones.com**. When you get there, use the RealAudio link to go to the Live Audio Clips page (or simply jump directly there: **http://www.stones.com/audio/index.html**).

Now, scroll down the page, and you'll find various Rolling Stones songs in a variety of formats. You'll see *AU, WAV, AIFF,* and *RealAudio* (which are .RA or .RAM). Netscape can play the .AU and .AIFF files itself, and I'll discuss a little about RealAudio in chapter 10. But it can't handle .WAV files yet. So click on a *WAV* link.

1 In the Unknown File Type dialog box, click on the Configure a Viewer button.

2 The Configure External Viewer dialog box opens. All you need to do is tell Netscape which program you want to use to play .WAV files: Sound Recorder.

3 Click on the Browse button, and the Select An Appropriate Viewer dialog box opens—a typical File Open box, which you can see in figure 9.3.

Fig. 9.3
Click on a link, on Configure a Viewer, on Browse, and then find the program.

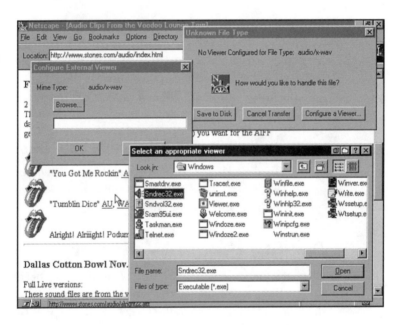

4 Remember the Files of Type bug we saw in chapter 8? Make sure that the Files of Type drop-down list box shows *Executable (*.exe)*.

5 Find SNDREC32.EXE or SOUNDREC.EXE (it's in your WINDOWS directory), click on it, then click on the Open button to place the program name into the Configure External Viewer dialog box.

6 Click on OK, and Netscape begins transferring the .WAV file. When it's finished, Sound Recorder opens. Click on the play button to hear the music.

By the way, Netscape saves the viewer information you've just added to the NETSCAPE.INI file (in Windows 3.1) or the System Registry (in Windows NT or Windows 95) when you close Netscape. If Netscape crashes the next time you open the program, the viewer will *not* be configured; you'll have to go through this process again or add the viewer manually.

Installing Sound Recorder

Sound Recorder is optional. If you didn't load it when you installed Windows, you can do so now. In Windows 95, double-click on the Add/Remove Programs icon in the Control Panel, click on the Windows Setup tab, click on the Multimedia item in the list, click on Details, click on Sound Recorder in the list, and click on OK a couple of times.

In Windows 3.1, double-click on the Windows Setup icon (in the Main program group); choose Options, Add/Remove Windows Components; click on the Accessories Files button; double-click on Sound Recorder in the left list box; and click on OK.

Adding viewers manually

There's another way to add viewers. You don't have to wait until you click on a link to a file type that Netscape doesn't recognize. Instead, you can go into the Preferences dialog box and add viewers beforehand.

Choose Options, General. When the Preferences dialog box opens, click on the Helper Apps tab. You'll see the dialog box in figure 9.4. The large list box in the middle shows you many of the MIME types. As you already know, some of these are handled by Netscape itself (look in the Action column for *Browser*), and some are handled by NAPLAYER, the Netscape sound program.

Fig. 9.4
The Preferences dialog box shows all the viewers configured and many file types for which you haven't configured a viewer.

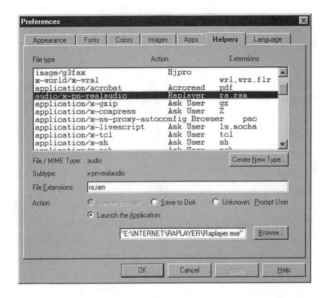

Click on an item in the list, then look below the table. You'll see the File/MIME Type, the Subtype, and the File Extensions. Below, you'll see four Action option buttons with the following attributes:

View in Browser. This button is disabled in most cases; it's only enabled if you have selected one of the file types that Netscape can handle directly. You'll only use it if you have previously told Netscape to do something else with one of these file types, which is unlikely.

Save to Disk. Click on this button if you want to save this file type to disk. As soon as you click on a link that points to this file type, Netscape opens the Save As dialog box.

Unknown: Prompt User. This is the default. If this is selected, Netscape displays the Unknown File Type dialog box.

Launch the Application. Select this option if you plan to configure a viewer. This tells Netscape to open the application specified in the text box immediately below the option button.

These options allow you to tell Netscape what to do with a particular file type. Click on the file type in the list box, then click on an option button.

 CAUTION **Don't think you can come into the Helpers area, fool around** with various changes, then click on Cancel to get out without saving your changes. You can't! As soon as you make a change, it's saved and clicking on Cancel will not retrieve the original settings.

Configuring a new viewer is very easy with the following steps:

1 Click on the file type in the list box.

2 Click on the Launch the Application option button.

3 Click on the Browse button.

4 In the Select an Appropriate Viewer dialog box, find the program you want to use, and click on the Open button.

 Q&A *Oh, I picked the wrong viewer. What now?*

Simply click on the file type in the list, then click on the Unknown: Prompt User option button. Or click on the Browse button, and pick another application to act as the viewer.

Can't find the correct file type?

Now and again, you may want to install a viewer for a file type that doesn't appear in the list. For example, you may want to use the Adobe Acrobat player. This uses the *application/acrobat* or *application/pdf* MIME type, which, at the time of writing, doesn't appear in the list box. (There are files identified as *application/acrobat*, and some as *application/pdf*; you may want to add both MIME types.) You add it as follows:

1 Click on the Create Ṇew Type button to open the dialog box shown in figure 9.5.

2 Type the MIME Type (the bit before the /, *application*), and the MIME SubType (the bit after the /, *acrobat*).

3 Click on OK to close the dialog box.

Fig. 9.5
You can add new MIME types, if necessary.

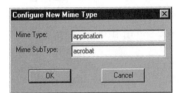

4 Now, with the new MIME type selected, enter the file extension in the File Ḛxtensions dialog box (don't include the period—enter **pdf**, not **.pdf**). Many file types actually use several different extensions, as you can see by clicking on different file types in the list. With Adobe Acrobat, there's only one common format: .PDF. (If you were adding two extensions, you would separate them with a comma and no space, for instance: **ra,ram**.)

5 Next, select the appropriate option button. If you plan to use the Adobe Acrobat player (see chapter 10), click on the Launch the Ḁpplication option button.

6 If you selected the Launch the Ḁpplication option button, click on the Ḇrowse button to find the application.

TIP **When you enter a file extension for a MIME type, the file** extension is not added to the table right away; it won't be added until you leave the dialog box, though the information is saved as soon as you enter it.

More about plug-ins and live objects

How about installing plug-ins so that you can use live objects? Well, you may already have plug-ins installed without realizing it. A Web author can embed a live object that will use a program that you have installed on your system. For instance, the Web page may automatically use Microsoft Paint in order to display a .BMP file inside a Web document.

Aside from these "automatic" plug-ins, there were few plug-ins available at the time of writing. In fact, there are currently only three available: the WebFX VRML (Virtual Reality Modeling Language) 3-D viewer plug-in, the NCompass OLE Control plug-in, and the Macromedia Director Shockwave plug-in.

 TIP By the time you read this, of course, there will be a few more around. You can find a list of plug-in developers, with links to their sites, at **http://home.mcom.com/comprod/products/navigator/ version_2.0/plugins/plugin_developers.html**.

Installing a plug-in—WebFX

How are plug-ins installed? Let's take a look at the WebFX one as an example. You can get hold of the program at the **http://www.paperinc.com** Web site. Run the program file, and a setup program will begin. Follow the instructions, and the plug-in is installed. Is that easy enough for you? No messing around with entering configuration data; the setup program will do it for you. Other plug-ins will probably be the same: run a setup program and the plug-in is installed.

Once you've got your plug-in installed, how do you use it? Simply click on a link to the appropriate object type, and the plug-in takes over. For instance, in figure 9.6, you can see WebFX in action. I went to the **http:// www.paperinc.com/** site, then clicked on the *New, What's Cool* link, which took me to a variety of sample VRML sites. I clicked on a link that pointed to a 3-D object (a .WRL file) and, after a few moments, saw the image in figure 9.6

Fig. 9.6
WebFX adds a 3-D viewer to Netscape; you can move around in VRML objects within Netscape. Go to **http:// www.paperinc.com/ vrml/models/ urlhouse.wrl.**

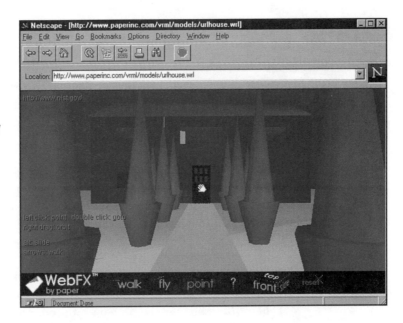

This is a 3-D image. You can move around the object using the control bar at the bottom, the mouse, or the keyboard. The **control bar** is the bar immediately above the status bar; the bar with the big WebFX sign on the left side. Each word on the bar is a sort of button; click on the word to carry out some kind of command, or select a mode.

I'd suggest that you start by clicking on the ? button. This will turn on the help mode, which places command instructions in the lower left corner of the window; you can see them in the figure.

Then try the different motion modes: Walk, Fly, and Point. Each mode has a different set of commands. For instance, holding the left mouse button down and dragging the pointer across the screen in the Walk mode will move you in the direction that you drag. The same procedure in the Fly mode is the "pitch, roll, yaw" command, which allows you to fly around the object (difficult to control, this one). Experiment with these different motions. They're difficult to explain, and the best way to get the feel for how they work is to try them.

There's also a Reset button on the bar; click this to return to the image's original position. And the Top/Front/Side button has three parts; click on Top to look down at the image from above, Front to look at it from the front, and Side to look at it from the right side.

Also, try moving the mouse pointer across the image; now and then it will turn into a hand pointer. You'll also see a URL appear in the top left corner of the content area (see the figure), or perhaps a description of the referenced image (*Robins Castle, 36k,* for instance). Yes, that's right, the image can contain links to other images or to a normal Web page. Click to leave the current image and see what the link points to.

Q&A *How do I know which plug-ins are installed?*

There's no easy way to figure this out. However, try this: type **about:plugins** into the Location text box at the top of the Netscape window, and press Enter (or choose <u>H</u>elp, About <u>P</u>lug-ins). You'll see a document listing the plug-ins, which *may* give you an idea of what you've got. For instance, after installing WebFX the document showed x-world/ x-vrml; this is the MIME type of the file handled by the plug-in. It indicates that I've got a plug-in installed for VRML (Virtual Reality Modeling Language), but doesn't show much else; it doesn't show *which* plug-in I've got.

Different types of plug-ins

Embedded. An embedded plug-in is one that runs an embedded object. It appears as a rectangular area within the Web document, just as an inline image appears as a rectangular area. The difference is that while the inline image is static, the embedded plug-in will "do stuff," such as play a video, and it is interactive—you may be able to use mouse clicks, for instance, to determine what's happening in the plug-in.

Full-screen. The full-screen plug-in takes over the entire Netscape content area. When an external file is transferred to Netscape, the full-screen plug-in opens and displays the file contents (it may be an Adobe Acrobat hypertext file or Apple QuickTime video file, for example). The normal Netscape controls will remain in view, but the plug-in may add controls too (a video-player plug-in would have start, stop, pause, and rewind buttons, for instance).

Hidden. A hidden plug-in is one that runs without any visible sign. A plug-in that plays sounds, for instance, may be hidden.

Plug-ins will be clever little guys, too. They'll be able to grab information from other Netscape windows, grab data from the Internet (using URLs), create information that can be used by Netscape or other plug-ins, and so on. It'll be interesting to see just what sort of plug-ins are on the way.

In the planning stages are plug-ins that will let you run Windows applications across the Internet, index Web documents you view, move through 3-D images, restrict kids' or students' access to the Internet (by time or specific Internet sites), play RealAudio sounds, and play MPEG audio and video. There are also loads of multimedia plug-ins on the way.

When you use an embedded plug-in

When you open a document with an embedded item, you may see a warning dialog box (such as the one in fig. 9.7), telling you which program Netscape is opening in order to run the embedded object. For instance, it may automatically open MSPAINT to display an embedded .BMP file within the document.

Fig. 9.7
When Netscape transfers an embedded object, you may see a warning.

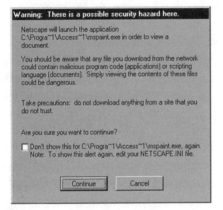

The warning tells you that files downloaded from the network (the Internet, generally speaking, though Netscape can be run on a network that is not connected to the Internet) can contain `malicious program code or scripting language`—in other words, viruses. At the bottom of the dialog box, you see a Don't Show This check box. The label names the program that is being used. If you click on this, the next time Netscape tries to run this particular program to display an embedded object, you won't see the warning message again.

Why turn off the warning message? Some file types are *not* dangerous. If the file type can't do anything, it's not dangerous. What file types *can* do something? **Executable** files (also known as **program** files, such as .EXE and .COM files), **script** files (such as .BAT files), and document files from programs that allow internal **macros.** (Many word processors these days

allow users to create macros—mini programs—that run when the document is opened.) But many file types are not dangerous because they are essentially nothing but dumb data. Bitmap files, such as .BMP or .TIF files, can't do anything. They can be displayed by a program, but they can't do anything themselves.

Q&A   ***What's this about editing the NETSCAPE.INI file?***

The warning box says that if you use this check box, you won't see the message again—for this particular program—unless you edit the NETSCAPE.INI file to add the line back in. If you are using Windows 95, you don't have a NETSCAPE.INI file—all the NETSCAPE information is stored in the System Registry. However, I'd recommend that you leave the registry alone; if you damage the Registry, you can really mess up your Windows 95 system. (If you really feel you *have* to mess with this, you can open the Registry Editor by choosing Start, Run; type **regedit**; and press Enter. The setting is in the HKEY_CURRENT_USER\Software\Netscape\Netscape Navigator\User Trusted External Applications "directory.")

The NCompass plug-in

Here's another useful plug-in you may want to install: the **NCompass OLE Control**. It's a special utility, run by NCompass, which allows Web authors to embed small programs into their Web pages; the program is transferred to Netscape when you open the Web page.

You can get a copy of NCompass from ExCITE at **http:// oberon.educ.sfu.ca/NCompass/**. Download and install the program (simply double-click on the file you download and follow instructions), then return to the NCompass site to check out some of the demos. (NCompass was released just before we went to print, so the only NCompass Web pages are demos at the ExCITE Web site.)

When you enter a page containing one of these little programs, you'll see a dialog box similar to that in figure 9.8. You are about to transfer an actual program, and it may be a vindictive little program that's about to destroy everything on your hard disk! Not very likely, but possible. For that reason, you are given a chance to decide whether or not you want to transfer the program—it's up to you to decide the sort of risks you wish to take on the Web.

CAUTION **How do you know that the program is safe? Will you really lose** your hard disk? Why would you ever want to risk it? Can I reassure you in some way?

Well, you *don't* know for sure that it's safe, though the risk is probably slight. I personally believe that the whole virus scare is exaggerated—few people have their computers infected by viruses. All I can say is that if you find one of these little programs at a well-known site, it's almost certainly okay. If you find it in some strange little Web backwater... you'll have to decide whether the benefits of having this program run in your browser is worth the risk.

Fig. 9.8
Before an NCompass program is transferred, you have the chance to abort the transfer.

WARNING	✕

NCompass Plugin will download the application listed below if you click on the OK prompt. Please note that this will be a fully functional application used by pages on this website. Protect yourself from and do not download anything from a site you do not trust.

Product Name :	WWW MIDI/WAVE OLE Co
Company Name :	NCompass
File Description :	WWW MIDI/WAVE OLE Co
Product Version :	3.0.001
Legal Copyright :	Copyright © 1995, Dr.Gerri Si
Legal Trademarks :	$
HTTP Site :	http://oberon.educ.sfu.ca/N

Do you still want to download ?

[Yes]   [No]

If you decide that this Web site is okay, that the program won't do any harm, click on the Yes button to continue, and the program transfers. You can see an example of a demo program in figure 9.9. This is an example of a "billboard" that changes every few seconds, using a variety of different transitions between screens. (Notice the three different panes inside the Netscape window? We'll look at that in more detail in chapter 17.)

NCompass can be used to transfer background sounds, too. In figure 9.10, you see the Mozart demo page. When you enter this page, the music begins playing automatically (assuming you have a sound card installed and correctly configured). Because this is a sound file and not an executable file, you won't see the warning box first.

Fig. 9.9
The billboard's
currently changing
from the Radisson
Hotel ad to the Advil
ad, using a block
transition.

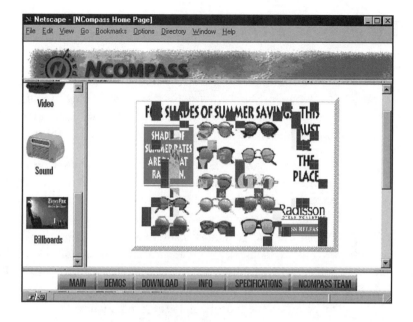

Fig. 9.10
ExCITE's Mozart demo
page.

Shockwave for Director

The third plug-in available at the time of writing was the Shockwave for Director plug-in. Director is an animation program sold by a company called Macromedia; Shockwave is the name of the plug-in that plays these animation files. There's currently very little Director animation on the Web, but the folks at Macromedia hope that the availability of this plug-in will change that.

You can find the Shockwave plug-in at **http://www.macromedia. com/Tools/Shockwave/**. Download and install it, then go to **http:// www.macromedia.com/Tools/Shockwave/Vanguard/index.html** to find links to sites using Macromedia Director. You'll find some sites that use Director to play animations and others that simply use it to play sounds. At the Yahoo Shockwave site, for instance (**http://shock.yahoo.com/shock/**), you'll find the familiar Yahoo search page (see chapter 7). But you'll also hear a jingly little tune playing in the background, and you'll see the Yahoo banner "dancing" to the tune, each letter jumping around in turn.

In figure 9.11, you can see the MTV site; the Tubescan picture has a TV that flickers intermittently (you can hear the hissing sound, too), and bars that keep changing in size (the bars with the ball at each end). Also, the picture has links in it (though the mouse pointer won't change to a small hand when you point at one). Click on Real World or Weekly Schedule, for instance, to move to a different page.

 TIP These animations can be quite large. The small ones may be as small as 20K, but the really neat stuff is much larger—the MTV picture, for instance, is 355K, which will take a few moments to transfer if you are using a modem.

Fig. 9.11
The MTV Tubescan
animation, created
in Macromedia
Director **(http://
www.mtv.com/
shock/tube/)**

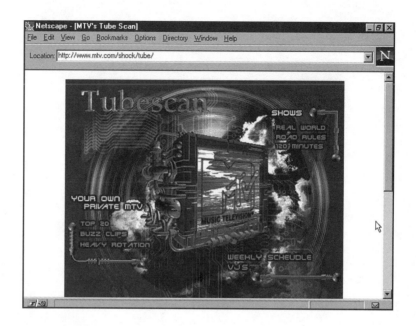

10

More on Viewers

You'll need a number of viewers to make the most of the multimedia World Wide Web. I'll show you where to find them. . . . . >

I n chapter 9, you learned the basics of adding viewers to Netscape. This chapter covers a bit more information that you'll find useful: how to save the multimedia files that you find on the Web, where you can find more viewers (mostly freeware or shareware), and details about specific viewers.

Saving what you played

Once you played a file, you can save it for future use. Most viewers have a command to help you save the file. For example, you may be using Sound Recorder to play a .WAV file. This program has a File, Save command that lets you save the sound to whatever directory you wish.

But some viewers *don't* provide a way to save files. For example, NAPLAYER, the built-in sound player, is not even visible; you might see a speaker icon, but you can't get to the program. And once the sound has finished playing, the program closes anyway. How can you save a file that's been played by a program that doesn't let you save it? Grab it from the hard disk.

When Netscape transfers a file, it has to place it on your hard disk. In some cases, it places the file in the cache directory (see chapter 4 for information about the cache). For example, when it transfers files that are played by NAPLAYER, it puts them in the cache directory. Go to Windows Explorer, look in your cache directory, and sort the files by date (View, Arrange Icons, by Date). Near the top, you'll find the file that was just transferred and played.

Netscape doesn't place all the files in the cache, though. If the file is being played by an external viewer, it's placed in your TEMP directory—look in \TEMP or \WINDOWS\TEMP. It should have the correct name.

TIP **Netscape doesn't rename files it places in the TEMP directory.** If you are using Windows 3.1, however, it may have to shorten the name to restrict it to the DOS eight-character file name rule.

What viewers do I have?

You have plenty of viewers. As you've already seen, Netscape can deal with .TXT, .GIF, .JPG, .JPEG, .JPE, .XBM. .AU, .AIF, .AIFF, .AIFC, and .SND files by itself. But what about other types of files? Windows already has a variety of built-in viewers—Sound Recorder, Media Player, and WordPad. You may have installed more without knowing it, too. For example, I installed Hijaak Pro, a graphics program. That program can work with *loads* of file formats, including .TIF and .EPS, two common graphics formats.

I need more viewers!

You can find more general-purpose viewers on the Internet. These are often freeware or shareware. You may want to take a look at the following Web sites to see what else you can pick up:

http://home.netscape.com/assist/helper_apps/index.html (The Netscape helper applications page)

http://cwsapps.texas.net/ (The Consummate Winsock App page)

http://www.ncsa.uiuc.edu/SDG/Software/WinMosaic/ viewers.htm (The Mosaic and External Viewers page)

http://vsl.cnet.com/ (The Virtual Software Library)

http://www.tucows.com (The Ultimate Collection of Winsock Software page)

http://www-dsed.llnl.gov/documents/WWWtest.html (The WWW Viewer Test page)

http://www.iuma.com/IUMA-2.0/help/help-windows.html (The IUMA Microsoft Windows Utilities page)

http://www.law.cornell.edu/cello/cellocfg.html (The Cello FAQ—Frequently Asked Questions—page)

 CAUTION **Be careful when entering URLs; some names end in .htm, while** others end in **.html**. If you add an **l** when it's not needed or miss it when it is, you won't get to the document. Also, make sure you type them with the correct case; uppercase where shown.

You can also try the following FTP sites (see chapter 11 for instructions on getting into FTP sites):

ftp://ftp.law.cornell.edu (In the /pub/LII/Cello/ directory.)

ftp://ftp.winsite.com (You'll have to dig around a bit to find anything, but there's a *lot* of software in here.)

If you can't find what you need through these sites, try searching the Web (see chapter 7) or use Archie (see chapter 11). I suspect, though, if you can't find what you need in the sites I've just listed and in the sites that I've provided for specific file types later in this chapter, it's just not available.

RealAudio (.RA and .RAM) files

The **RealAudio** links at the Rolling Stones site (see chapter 9) are to .RA and .RAM files. RealAudio is a new format that greatly improves the way sound is played over the Web. With other sound formats you've looked at, you click on a link and then wait. Twiddle your thumbs for a while, or go get some coffee, because it can take a long time to transfer a sound file. Once the transfer is finished, Netscape plays the file or sends it to Sound Recorder.

RealAudio, on the other hand, begins playing almost immediately. Netscape begins the transfer and then starts the RealAudio player within a few seconds. (You don't have the RealAudio player yet—I'll explain how to find it in a moment.) The music begins playing right away, and it continues playing while the file is being transferred. (It doesn't have to be music; National Public Radio uses RealAudio files for its news broadcasts—go to **http://www.npr.org/**). In fact, this is the way that a radio works. The radio receives a signal over the airwaves and plays the signal immediately (it doesn't wait until it has received the entire song and then play it).

If you want to try RealAudio, go get the player. You can find it at the RealAudio Web site (**http://www.realaudio.com/**). Read this page; you'll find lots of background information and links to sites that use RealAudio sounds.

On the RealAudio main page, click on the *Download* link to go to the download page, and click on the *Windows download* link to transfer the file.

Once you've downloaded the file, close Netscape. Then open Windows Explorer, find the file you just downloaded, and double-click on it. The RealAudio Setup program begins. Follow the instructions to install the program. I suggest you select the Custom installation, which lets you choose the directory into which you want to place the program.

The Setup program looks for various Web browsers on your hard disk, and asks if you want to install the RealAudio player for those browsers, too. If you don't have these browsers, you can simply click on the Cancel button. Make sure you select Netscape, though, so RealAudio can configure itself for that program. Finally, the RealAudio player opens and informs you—vocally—that the setup is complete.

That's it; RealAudio is ready to play—if all went well, it even entered the correct information into the Netscape list of viewers (Helper Apps). Let's go back to the Rolling Stones site (**http://www.stones.com/audio/index.html**) and find a RealAudio file. Or go to NPR (**http://www.npr.org/**), or back to the RealAudio page (or directly to **http://www.realaudio.com/ othersites.html**), where you'll find links to RealAudio sites all over the world.

Playing RealAudio

At one of the sites I've just mentioned, find a RealAudio link and click on it. The RealAudio program opens (it may take a few moments), Netscape starts transferring the file, and the music (or newscast, or whatever) begins (see fig. 10.1).

Fig. 10.1
Listening to National Public Radio news over the Internet using RealAudio.

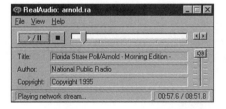

You can click on the Stop button in the RealAudio player to cancel a file transfer. You can use the other controls to determine which parts of the sound file you play, as shown in the following table:

Button	What it does
▶/ ‖	Pauses the transmission and restarts.
■	Stops the transmission and moves to the beginning.
◀ ▶	Rewinds or forwards the sound.
◁⟩)	Adjusts the volume.

Q&A ***I increased the volume, but it's still too quiet. What can I do?***

Your sound system may have another sound control somewhere. For example, in Windows 95, look in the taskbar's **tray**, the small panel where you'll find the clock and various small icons. Click on the speaker icon to open a small volume control.

You can also drag the vertical bar along the horizontal scroll bar—immediately to the right of the Stop button—to move to a different part of the sound.

Q&A ***Why is the sound so bad?***

Well, for a start, RealAudio doesn't sound as good as the .WAV, .AU, and .AIF formats. It's a compromise between instant gratification and sound quality. Also, if you have a low-quality sound card and cheap speakers, you'll get low-quality sound. Finally, sound files can vary in quality, depending on how they were recorded.

TrueSpeech (.TSP) files

RealAudio is not the only program that plays a sound at the same time it transfers, though it is currently the most popular. You may want to also take a look at the TrueSpeech program, which plays .TSP files. These files are of higher quality than RealAudio files—TrueSpeech sounds are much clearer.

Go to **http://www.dspg.com** to find more information and to download the free TrueSpeech player. TrueSpeech is likely to become very popular on the

Web, not only because of the high quality, but because a variety of companies, such as Microsoft, Cirrus Logic, and Sierra Semiconductor, like the product.

 TIP **Another product, called StreamWorks, allows you to play a sound** at the same time it transfers...and can do the same thing for video, too. (These are .XDM files.) Go to **http://www.xingtech.com**.

Adobe Acrobat (.PDF) files

You're going to see a lot of .PDF files on the Web very soon, for several reasons. You might think of .PDF as a sort of extension of the Web's hypertext or hypermedia. Adobe Acrobat files are self-contained hypertext documents with links between pages. Unlike HTML, though, Acrobat files allow the author to determine exactly what the document will look like.

When a browser **renders** an HTML file into the document you see on your screen, the browser decides how to display the different document components—the headers, body text, pull quotes, and so on. But with Acrobat, this control is left in the hands of the author; the Acrobat viewer displays the document just as the author intended. Also, Acrobat files are independent of the Web. You can take an Acrobat file and send it to everyone with an Acrobat reader; they don't need a Web browser. In fact, Acrobat began its life far from the Web; it was intended to help companies distribute online documentation to a variety of different computer systems. The same document can be read by viewers on Windows, DOS, Macintosh, SunOS, and Solaris computers, with more viewers to be added soon. It also allows companies to produce online documents that look the same as their paper documents.

Two of the most important companies on the Web—Netscape Communications and Spyglass (the people who make Microsoft's Internet Explorer, among other browsers)—have decided that Adobe Acrobat will be merged into the Web. Both companies plan to make their browsers work with .PDF. Netscape will soon work with Acrobat through the use of an inline plug-in. Also, Adobe is working on a system called Weblink (go to **http:// www.adobe.com/Acrobat/Plug-Ins/** for information) that will allow Acrobat authors to add links from their Acrobat files to Web sites. Users will be able to click on a link in Acrobat, causing their Web browser to retrieve the specified Web document. Once the Acrobat plug-in is available, Acrobat files will appear to work within Netscape seamlessly; a link at a Web page will display the Acrobat document within Netscape, and links in the Acrobat document will take you out, back to various Web documents. In the meantime, you'll have to add a .PDF browser if you want to view Acrobat files.

You'll find the Adobe Acrobat reader in a variety of places, but you might want to try the source first, Adobe itself, at **http://www.adobe.com/Software.html** (the viewer is free; Adobe wants to sell the authoring tool, so they've made the viewer easy to get). Once you've installed the program (just run the file you download and follow the instructions), you can try it out at a variety of sites:

Web Sites with Cool PDF: **http://www.adobe.com/Acrobat/PDFsites.html**

U.S. Patent Office: **http://www.uspto.gov/hearings.html**

Centers for Disease Control Morbidity and Mortality Weekly Report: **http://www.cdc.gov/epo/mmwr/mmwr.html**

Time-Life Virtual Garden: **http://www.timeinc.com/vg/TimeLife/Project/**

TimesFax: **http://nytimesfax.com/**

Axcess Magazine: **http://www.internex.net/axcess**

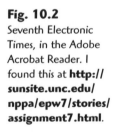

Fig. 10.2
Seventh Electronic Times, in the Adobe Acrobat Reader. I found this at **http://sunsite.unc.edu/nppa/epw7/stories/assignment7.html**.

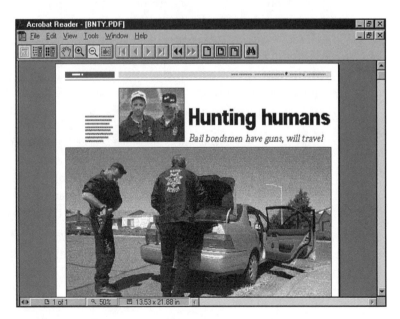

.ZIP, .ARC, .ARJ, & .LZH files

You may want to associate these file types with an application. These are all archive, or compressed, file formats. If a Web author wants you to be able to transfer a very large file, or a collection of files, he can compress it in one of these formats so that it transfers more quickly. You'll often find .ZIP files (PKZIP files); less commonly, you *may* run across .ARC, .ARJ, and .LZH files.

If you have a Windows Explorer utility that lets you view these files as if they are directories, you probably won't want to associate these files with anything. For example, I have Norton Navigator, which has a Windows Explorer replacement. This program treats .ZIP files as if they are directories; click on one and you can see the contents, drag files to other directories, and so on.

If you don't have a utility like this, you can associate these files with an archive-specific program, such as WinZip. (You can find WinZip from the **http://www.winzip.com/winzip** Web page.) Once associated, Netscape automatically places the archive file in your TEMP directory (\TEMP or \WINDOWS\TEMP) directory, and then opens WinZip. WinZip displays the contents of the file (see fig. 10.3), and lets you extract the compressed files to another directory.

Fig. 10.3
I just transferred a new FTP program (see chapter 11) from **http:// cwsapps.texas.net/ top20.html**, and Netscape sent the .ZIP file to WinZip, which is displaying the contents.

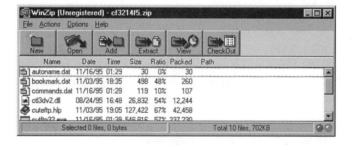

Motion on the Web—video viewers

You'll find a variety of video images on the Web. Perhaps the most popular are the MPEG (.MPEG, .MPG, .MPE) and QuickTime (.MOV) formats, neither of which can be played by Media Player. (However, Microsoft plans to add MPEG support to Windows 95 at some point, probably by late 1995 or early 1996. It's not entirely clear how the program will be distributed, but it might be part of the "Tune-Up" packs that Microsoft says they'll be selling.) Also, there *may* be another way to play MPEG movies—using Apple's QuickTime for Windows. (Most of you *won't* be able to use this method, though, as I'll explain in a moment.)

I've installed the MPEGPLAY program. (I found it at the **http://www-dsed.llnl.gov/documents/WWWtest.html** Web page. You can also get it at **http://cwsapps.texas.net/**.) It plays MPEGs well, but it has a size limit. I'm not exactly sure what the limit is, but it won't play 5M movies, for instance. (When you register the program, you get a version that has no limit.) You can also try VMPEGLite, a demo version of VMPEG (which hasn't been released yet). You can find this at the Consummate Winsock Apps list (**http://cwsapps.texas.net/**) and the Virtual Software Library (**http://vsl.cnet.com/**), among other places. However, I had trouble getting it to run correctly in Windows 95 (the file-selection dialog box doesn't like long names).

TIP As neat as video on the Web might be, it can get old fast. The problem is that transferring video across the Internet is very slow, even if you're using a 28,800 bps modem. If you have an ISDN (Integrated Services Digital Network) connection or a LAN connection, you're okay, but many people are still working with 14,400 or 28,800 bps modems, which take a *long* time to transfer the 5M or 6M that many videos on the Web take up. A small video can easily take an hour, or several hours, to transmit when using a 14,400 bps modem! When the transfer begins, wait a few moments for the transfer speed to settle down, and then look at the Saving Location dialog box to see what the estimated transfer time is.

You can see an example of a movie running in MPEGPLAY for Windows in figure 10.4. This is from the Enternet Skateboarding Videos, at **http://www.enternet.com/skate/birdhouse.html**.

Fig. 10.4
A rather murky MPEG movie, from the Enternet Skateboarding Video site, playing in MPEGPLAY.

Q&A *Where can I find MPEG videos on the Web?*

A good place to start is **http://www.cs.tu-berlin.de/~phade/ mpegwww.html**. You'll find links to dozens of MPEG-related sites. Try **http://www.netvideo.com/technology/videosites.html**, too. Or search for MPEG at a Web search site.

QuickTime is another very popular movie format (.MOV). I ended up using QuickTime for Windows, which, in theory, plays both MPEG and QuickTime movies. I couldn't find a shareware QuickTime program for Windows 95—there's QuickTime Extensions for Windows mplayer, which is a system that runs in Windows 3.1 by somehow making the Windows Media Player program compatible with QuickTime, but it doesn't seem to work in Windows 95. But Apple sells QuickTime for Windows for only $9.95, so I downloaded that program.

Unfortunately, while QuickTime for Windows plays .MOV files well, it only plays MPEG movies if you have a special MPEG video board installed in your computer, which, of course, few people have.

See **http://quicktime.apple.com/ordering-qt.html** to download the file from the Web (or call 800-637-0029). Right now, you can only get an external viewer version, although a plug-in should be available soon. There are a couple of things you should know about downloading this program. First, you can only download from the Web if you have a First Virtual account. This is a special account that allows you to use your credit card online, without using your actual credit card number (you'll use a special account number that you choose when you open an account). It costs $2 to open an account. You can learn more about this in chapter 15 (or go to First Virtual and follow instructions: **http://www.fv.com/newacct/**).

Once you've downloaded and installed the program, you can go in search for QuickTime movies. The best places to start are **http://quicktime.apple.com/ content.html** and **http://w3.one.net/~flypba/QT/index.html**, where you'll find lists of QuickTime sites. You can see an example in figure 10.5.

Fig. 10.5
I found this sample at the Apple QuickTime Movie archive site: **http:// quicktime.apple.com/ archive.html**.

 TIP **While it's not very common yet, we may be seeing the** StreamWorks video format (.XDM) become popular. Go to **http:// www.xingtech.com**.

More sounds on the Web—MPEG audio

MPEG audio is another MPEG format (these files have the .MP2 extension). **MPEG** stands for the **Motion Picture Experts Group**, after the people who came up with the file format. They are a great way to play sound; the files are compressed, so really high-quality sounds can be squeezed down into quite a small space. You won't find a lot of these on the Web, though—most sounds are in the .AU, .AIF, .WAV, or .RAM formats.

I installed XingSound, which I found at the **http://www.iuma.com/ IUMA-2.0/help/help-windows.html** Web document (this is at IUMA, the Internet Underground Music Archive). You can also get it at **http:// www.xingtech.com,** which is the "home site." It was very easy to install, and works well. There should be an inline plug-in version of XingSound soon, too.

It's slow, but...viewers for VRML 3-D images

The new fad on the Web is 3-D images. Click on a link in a Web page, and up pops your 3-D viewer, with a 3-D image inside. Move around in this image, or "walk around" the image. Some images are of landscapes and buildings you can "move through," others are of objects that you can rotate. The only problem is that working in 3-D images is often painfully slow, especially over phone lines.

 Plain English, please!

VRML stands for Virtual Reality Modeling Language.

Check these sites for viewers:

To find this viewer...	Go to this site
A variety of viewers	**http://cwsapps.texas.net/**
WorldView	**http://www.webmaster.com/vrml/**
WebSpace	**http://webspace.sgi.com/WebSpace/index.html** **http://webspace.sgi.com/WebSpace/index.html**
AmberGL	**http://www.divelabs.com/vrml.htm**
NAVFlyer	**ftp://yoda.fdt.net/pub/users/m/micgreen**
Pueblo	**http://www.chaco.com/pueblo/**
VRWeb	**http://hyperg.iicm.tu–graz.ac.at/Cvrweb**
WebFX	**http://www.paperinc.com/**

Note that not all of these programs are available for all versions of Windows.

 TIP WebFX is now available as a plug-in; see chapter 9.

You can also check this page to see an up-to-date list of VRML viewers: **http://www.sdsc.edu/SDSC/Partners/vrml/software/browsers.html**. There will be a number of inline plug-in VRML viewers soon, too.

66 *Plain English, please!*

Just to confuse you a little...programs that display VRML images are often known as VRML **browsers**, rather than **viewers**. 99

Note also that, at the time of this writing, the Windows VRML viewers were a little buggy and didn't work too well. That may change quickly, though. Also, working in 3-D often requires relatively powerful computers. To run WorldView, for instance, you'll need a 486/50 or better and 8M of RAM, and you must be running in 256-color video mode. And it still may not be enough! When you are talking about 3-D images, the more power, the better.

Download a viewer and install it. Read the installation instructions carefully. Then, go to one of the following Web pages, where you can find links to VRML objects you can test:

- **http://www.nist.gov/itl/div878/ovrt/projects/vrml/vrmlfiles.html** (VRML samples from the Open Virtual Reality Testbed.)

- **http://vrml.arc.org/gallery95/index2.html.** (The Arc Gallery—à la VRML.)

- **http://www.well.com/user/spidaman/vrml.html** (Look under the *Actual VRML sites* heading for links to VRML sites.)

- **http://www.nist.gov/itl/div878/ovrt/hotvr.html** (Hot Virtual Reality Sites.)

- **http://www.lightside.com/3dsite/cgi/VRML-index.html** (Loads of links, some of which are to actual VRML sites, though most are to sites with information *about* VRML.)

When you've found a link to a VRML object (it will have the .WRL extension; look in the status bar), click on it, and Netscape will transfer the file and load your viewer. You'll then be able to move around in (or about) the 3-D picture (see fig. 10.6).

Fig. 10.6

Entering a house in a 3-D image displayed by VRweb, an Austrian VRML viewer.

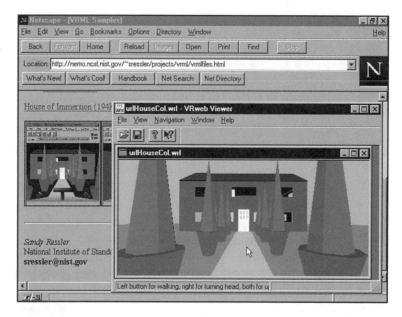

This Web page is a good place to try out all sorts of viewers (including VRML viewers): **http://www-dsed.llnl.gov/documents/ WWWtest.html**. You can also find unusual viewers here—viewers for .PDB "chemical objects," .MA Mathematica files, .V5D dataset objects, and so on.

Note that VRML is very new; there will probably be many changes over the next year. Right now, the viewers are likely to be rather "buggy." You'll soon find lots of new and improved viewers, and perhaps new file formats (there are lots of different 3-D file formats, though most of the files you'll find on the Web are currently .WRL files). You'll also find that some images have Web links inside them. For example, you can walk through a museum, click on a door, and go into another room. For information about VRML, go to the **http://vrml.wired.com/** and **http://www.lightside.com/3dsite/ cgi/VRML-index.html** Web pages.

There's another Virtual Reality/3-D system on the horizon, QuickTime VR. This system, from Apple Computers, has been around for a little while, but the Windows viewer wasn't released until shortly before we went to print. You can find it at the **http://qtvr.quicktime.apple.com/** Web page.

Voyager CDLinks

Here's a brand new format that's an interesting combination of CD-ROM and Web site. Voyager CDLink provides a way for Web authors to link their Web sites to a music CD in your computer's CD-ROM drive. These CDs don't have to be created to work with a Web site. A Web site can be created to work with an existing CD. For example, two of the first CDLink sites were designed to work with Frank Zappa's *Hot Rats* CD (**http://www.rykodisc.com/fzcdlink.html**) and Elvis Costello's *Imperial Bedroom* CD (**http://www.rykodisc.com/eccdlink.html**). You can read reviews of these CDs, and click on links in the reviews to play specific portions of the music (see fig. 10.7). You can download Voyager CDLink from **http://www.voyagerco.com/cdlink/cdlink.html**.

Fig. 10.7
This Web page (**http://www.inmet.com/~mg/wgw/lyrics.html**) contains links to CDLink. When I click on the control box, CDLink (which is hidden in the background) plays music from the CD in my CD-ROM drive.

TIP

To find a registry of Web sites that use the CDLink program—and the music CDs they work with—go to **http://www.voyagerco.com/cdlink/registry/registry.html**. You'll find sites working with CDs from Selena, Amy Grant, Bob Dylan, The Traveling Wilburys, The Beatles, Bon Jovi, and plenty more.

Part III: Traveling the Internet

Not By Web Alone— FTP and More

● **In this chapter:**

- **Using other Internet resources through Netscape**

- **Using FTP to grab files from the Internet**

- **Finding the files you need at the FTP site**

- **How can I search for computer files on the Internet?**

- **Finding a site and searching with Archie**

- **Advanced Archie**

The Internet is much more than the Web. Netscape can help you use other services, such as Telnet, Gopher, newsgroups, e-mail, and much, much more. . . . . ▸

So far, you've seen the standard http:// URLs. When your Web browser sees a URL that begins with http:, it knows that the destination is a Web document. But some URLs begin with other protocols, such as the following:

- **gopher://**   Takes you to a Gopher menu system (see chapter 14).

- **ftp://**   Takes you to an FTP (File Transfer Protocol) site—a site set up so that you can transfer files back to your computer.

- **mailto:**   Used to send e-mail (see chapter 12).

- **news:**   A special newsgroup protocol that enables you to read newsgroups from Web browsers (see chapter 13).

- **telnet://**   Starts a Telnet session, in which you can log in to another computer on the Internet (see chapter 14).

- **tn3270://**   Starts a 3270-mode session, which is very similar to Telnet. (You're connecting to a different type of computer: an IBM 3270) (see chapter 14).

- **wais://**   A relatively little-used URL. It stands for Wide Area Information Servers, systems that are used to search databases. Netscape can use the **wais://** URL if you have a special proxy set up; if not, you can still use WAIS through special **gateways** (see chapter 14).

- **file:///**   Used to "point" to a file on your hard disk. When you choose File, Open File, Netscape uses this URL (you'll see it in the Location bar).

- **mailbox:/**   A special Netscape URL used by the program's e-mail system (which you'll learn about in chapter 12). It simply tells the mail system which mailbox file to use. (It's not a URL that is used by other Web browsers to point to Web resources).

In other words, you can access systems that are not true Web systems. You can use Gopher, FTP, and Telnet; you can send e-mail from Web links; and you can read newsgroup messages. There are even special "gateways" through the Web to systems for which your Web browser isn't prepared. For instance, your Web browser cannot communicate directly with Archie, a system used to search FTP sites for computer files. (You type a file name, and Archie tells you where to find it.) But there are Web documents that do the work for you by using forms. You type the name of the file into a form, and a special program at the Web server communicates with Archie for you (see "How Can I Find Files? Working with Archie," later in this chapter, for information about Archie).

Finding Internet resources

If you'd like to find the sort of non-Web resources that you can get to through the Web, take a look at some of the following documents:

Inter-Links

Select a category to see lists of related documents and tools.

> **http://www.nova.edu/Inter-Links/**

Directory of Service Types

If you want to see where you can use WAIS, newsgroups, Gopher, Telnet, FTP, Whois, and other Internet services through your Web browsers, take a look at this Web document.

 *Plain English, please!*

> **Whois** is a special service that you can use to search for other Internet users. 🟋🟋

> **http://www.w3.org/hypertext/DataSources/ByAccess.html**

ArchiePlex

This is a directory of ArchiePlex servers throughout the world—servers that let you search Archie directly from the Web. You'll find sites for browsers both with and without forms support.

> **http://web.nexor.co.uk/archie.html**

Internet resources—Meta-Index

This is a list of directories containing references to various Internet resources: the Web, Gopher, Telnet, FTP, and more.

> **http://pubweb.nexor.co.uk/public/archie/servers.html**

FTP: the Internet's file library

We've already seen how to transfer files from the Web back to your computer (see chapter 8). The Web contains many files that you might find useful—shareware and demo programs, clip art, press releases, music, video, and plenty more.

But before the Web was born, there was already a system for grabbing files from the Internet: **FTP** (File Transfer Protocol). Using this system, you can log in to a computer somewhere on the Internet, then transfer files back to your computer.

There are many publicly accessible software archives on the Internet, which are known as **anonymous FTP** sites. You can log in to a public FTP site by using the account name *anonymous* and then typing your e-mail address as the password. (Those unfortunate souls still using the Internet through a UNIX command line actually type these entries when they log in to an FTP site. You have Netscape to do it automatically for you—you won't even see Netscape log in for you.)

For example, here are a couple of FTP sites that contain a lot of Windows shareware utilities: **ftp.winsite.com/pub/pc/win95/** and **ftp.wustl.edu/systems/ibmpc/win3**. Or go to **http://hoohoo.ncsa.uiuc.edu/ftp/**, the monster FTP sites list, to find thousands of FTP sites.

What does all this information mean? First, there's the FTP site name (or host name): **ftp.winsite.com**, for instance. This identifies the computer that contains the files you are after. Then there's the directory name: **/pub/pc/win95/**. This tells you which directory you must change to in order to find the files.

There are two ways to use the Web browser for an FTP session. You'll either click on a link to an FTP site that some kind Web author has provided, or enter an FTP URL into the Location text box and press Enter. The FTP URL begins with **ftp://**.

Let's say, for example, that you want to go to the **ftp.winsite.com/pub/pc/win95/** FTP site to see what shareware is available. You would type **ftp://ftp.winsite.com/pub/pc/win95/** into the Location text box near the top of the Netscape window, and press Enter. Watch the status bar, and you'll see a progress message *(Connect: Contacting Host)*. When you connect, you'll see something like figure 11.1. (This site actually has a text message at the top of the directory listing; I scrolled down so you could see more of the files and directories.)

TIP **As with the http:// URL, you don't always need to include ftp://.** If the FTP site name begins with **ftp**, you can omit the **ftp://** bit. For instance, you can type **ftp.winsite.com/pub/pc/win95/** instead of **ftp://ftp.winsite.com/pub/pc/win95/**.

Fig. 11.1
You can use Netscape as an FTP program.

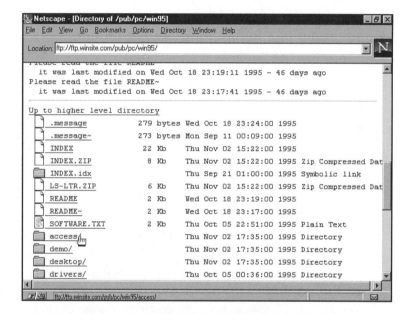

FTP path names use forward slashes

If you're used to working in DOS and Windows, FTP site directory names may appear pretty strange for two reasons. First, I've used a forward slash (/) rather than a backslash (\) to separate each directory in the path. In the DOS world, you use a backslash (\), but in the UNIX world—and most of the Internet still runs on UNIX computers—the forward slash character (/) is used instead.

Also, the directory names are often long. In DOS, you can't have directories with more than 12 characters in the name (if you include a period and an extension). Of course, in Windows 95 and Windows NT you can because this new operating system allows long file and directory names, and UNIX computers allow long names, too.

Each file and directory is shown as a link. On the left side of the window, you'll see a column of icons: plain white sheets represent files of most kinds, white sheets with "writing" on them represent text files, white sheets with ones and zeros represent program files, and yellow folders represent directories.

On the right side of the window, you'll also see a column with descriptions of each item, such as the following:

Zip compressed data. A .ZIP file containing compressed data (see chapters 9 and 10).

Symbolic link. These are special files, allowed by UNIX, that act as links to another directory and provide shortcuts through the directory system. Selecting a symbolic link is the same thing as selecting a directory.

Directory. The location of files and subdirectories.

Plain text. A text file; select this to read the file in the Netscape window.

Binary executable. A program file.

Macintosh BinHex archive. An .HQX file, which is an ASCII text file that contains some form of binary file—a program file, graphics file, whatever—that has been converted to ASCII so it can be transferred across the Internet's e-mail system. BinHex is commonly used on Macintosh systems. In the UNIX and PC world, the equivalent is UUENCODE (see chapter 13).

Macintosh archive. A .SIT file, which is an archive file used on Macintosh systems.

GNU zip compressed data. A .GZ file, which is an archive file used on UNIX systems.

UNIX tape archive. A .TAR file, which is another form of UNIX archive file.

If there's no description shown for an item, then the item is a file of some other kind. Netscape looks at the list of viewers to see if you've set up one for this file type when you begin transferring it. For example, if this is a .WAV file, the description will be blank; but if you configured Sound Recorder as the viewer, Netscape will transfer it and open Sound Recorder when you click on the link to this file.

You'll find more information about an entry, too. You can see that the file or directory's date and time of creation is shown (the date is very handy, providing an indication of how old the file is). The size of each file, in bytes or kilobytes, is also shown.

Click on a directory link to see the contents of that directory. Netscape will display another Web document showing the contents of that directory. There's also a link back to the previous directory—the *Up to a higher level directory* link, at the top of listing. (This is not the same as the browser's Back command, of course. It takes you to the parent directory, the one of which the current directory is a subdirectory.)

 TIP **Don't forget Archie! Archie is a system that lets you search an** index of FTP sites throughout the world for just the file you need. For more information, see "How can I find files? Working with Archie," later in this chapter.

What happens when you click on a link to a file? The same thing that would happen if you did so from a true Web document. If Netscape can display or play the file type, it will; if it can't, it will try to send it to the associated application. If there is no associated application, it will ask you what to do with it, allowing you to save it on your hard disk. For instance, if you've set up WinZip as the viewer for .ZIP files, then when you click on a link to a .ZIP file, Netscape transfers the file and opens WinZip (see chapter 10 for more information).

How can I find my way around?

Finding your way around at an FTP site is often a little difficult. There are no conventions for how such sites should be set up, so you often have to dig through directories that look as if they might contain what you want until you find what you're looking for.

Remember that Netscape can display text files. When you first get to an FTP site, look for files that say INDEX, README, DIRECTORY, and so on. These often contain information that help you find what you need. The more organized sites even contain full indexes of their contents or at least a list of the directories and the types of files you'll find.

TIP   **Many FTP sites are now accessible directly through Web** documents. For example, instead of going to **ftp:// ftp.winsite.com/ pub/pc/win95/**, you could go to **http://www.winsite.com/**.

How can I use my private FTP site?

Many Internet users have private accounts at FTP sites. For instance, Que has given me a username password so that I can access a private area of their FTP site. How can I use Netscape to get into that FTP site?

There are two ways. I can enter both my username and password in the URL, or just enter my username and let Netscape prompt me for the password. Here's how to do each one.

To create a URL in which you enter both your username and password, format it like this: **ftp://*username:password*@*ftp.site***. For instance, **ftp:// pkent:23&*^12@ftp.mcp.com**. Press Enter; Netscape will connect to the site, passing the username and password information to the FTP host when prompted (you won't see it pass the information, it all happens in the background).

You can also enter the information like this: **ftp://*username*@*ftp.site*** (for instance, **ftp://pkent@ftp.mcp.com**). This time, when you press Enter, Netscape will display a small dialog box prompting you for your password; type it and press Enter again to continue.

TIP   **If you want a program designed specifically for FTP—one that will** let you transfer files *to* FTP sites, not just from them—try WS_FTP. You can find this program at **http://cwsapps.texas.net/** or **ftp://ftp.usma.edu/ pub/msdos/winsock.files**. There are both 16-bit (for Windows 3.1) and 32-bit (for Windows 95 and NT) versions of the program. There's also a new Windows FTP program called CuteFTP, which is getting good reviews. You can find this at **ftp://papa.indstate.edu/winsock-l/ftp** or **http:// papa.indstate.edu:8888/CuteFTP/**.

How can I find files? Working with Archie

With millions of files to choose from and thousands of FTP sites spread around the Internet, it's difficult to know where to go to find the file you need. That's why Archie was developed.

Designed at McGill University in Canada, *Archie* is a system that indexes FTP sites, listing the files that are available at each site. Archie lists several million files at thousands of FTP sites and provides a surprisingly quick way to find out where to go to grab a file. Well, sometimes. As you'll find out, Archie is extremely busy and sometimes too busy to help you!

More client/server stuff

As with many other Internet systems, Archie is set up using a **client/server** system. An Archie **server** is a computer that periodically takes a look at all the Internet FTP sites around the world and builds a list of all their available files. Each server builds a database of those files. An Archie **client** program can then come along and search the server's database, using it as an index. Your Web browser is *not* an Archie client. That is, there is no **archie://** URL! Rather, you'll have to use an Archie interface on the Web. There are dozens of these. Go to **http://pubweb.nexor.co.uk/public/archie/servers.html** to find a list. Just in case that's busy, the following are several Archie sites you can try:

> **http://www.lerc.nasa.gov/archieplex/**

> **http://hoohoo.ncsa.uiuc.edu/archie.html**

> **http://src.doc.ic.ac.uk/archieplexform.html**

When you arrive at an Archie site, what sort of search are you going to do? Most of these sites offer both forms and non-forms versions. Netscape is a forms-capable browser; that is, it can display the forms components we've seen earlier: text boxes, command buttons, option buttons, and so on. So select the forms search.

 TIP **It's generally believed in Internet-land that it doesn't matter** much which Archie server you use because they all do much the same thing; some are simply a few days more recent than others. This isn't always true. Sometimes you may get very different results from two different servers. If, for example, one server finds two **hits,** another might find seven.

How do I search?

In figure 11.2, you can see an example of an Archie form, this one at the NASA Lewis Research Center located at **http://www.lerc.nasa.gov/archieplex/doc/form.html**. The simplest way to search is to type a file name or part of a file name into the Search For? text box and click on the Submit button. For instance, if you are trying to find the WS_FTP program that I told you about earlier in this chapter, you can type **WS_FTP** and press Enter.

TIP   **To cancel a search, click on the Stop toolbar button or press Esc.**

Fig. 11.2

The dozens of Archie Web sites provide a way for you to search Archie from your browser.

Netscape - [ArchiePlexForm]

File   Edit   View   Go   Bookmarks   Options   Directory   Window   Help

ArchiePlexForm

This ArchiePlex form can locate files on Anonymous FTP sites in the Internet. Other servers can be found on the List of WWW Archie Services.

Search for: ws_ftp   Submit   Reset

There are several types of search: Case Insensitive Substring Match

The results can be sorted ⦿ By Host or ○ By Date

Several Archie Servers can be used: Israel   You can restrict the results to a domain (e.g. "uk"):

You can restrict the number of results to a number < 100: 95

The impact on other users can be: Nice

Archie searches are often very slow. In fact, they often simply don't work because the Archie server you are working with is busy (I'll show you how to choose another server in a moment). If you are lucky, you'll eventually see something like figure 11.3. This shows what the Archie server found: links to the WS_FTP files. You can see that there are links to the host (the computer that contains the file you are looking for), the directory on the host that contains the file you want, or the directory of the file you want. For example, if you clicked on one of the *ws_ftp.zip* links, Netscape would begin transferring the file.

Fig. 11.3
If you're lucky, when
Archie responds, you'll
get a list of sites and
files.

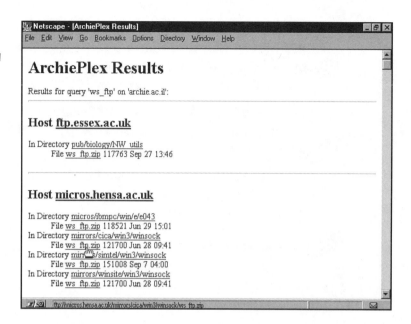

TIP   **Remember, you can choose Edit, Find, to search the list of files.**
For instance, if you are searching for WS_FTP, you don't really want the
WS_FTP.ZIP files; those are probably the 16-bit versions for Windows 3.1.
Rather, search for WS_FTP32 to find the 32-bit versions for Windows 95.

Archie's options

The Archie form (refer to fig. 11.2) has other components that provide more
options for your search. You'll find the following:

> **There Are Several Types Of Search.** There are four types of
> searches, which I'll explain in a moment.

> **The Results Can Be Sorted.** The list of files that is returned to you
> may be sorted by file date or by the host containing the file. The file
> date search is a good idea, as it will help you pick the latest version of
> the file.

> **Several Archie Servers Can Be Used.** There are Archie servers all
> over the world, and you can select the one you want to use from a list.
> If one Archie server is busy or it can't find what you want, try another.
> You might want to try servers in countries that are currently "asleep,"
> and, therefore, less busy than during the day.

Restrict the Results To A Domain. You can tell the Archie server that you only want to see files in a particular domain (a particular type of host computer): UK (FTP sites in the United Kingdom), COM (commercial FTP sites), EDU (educational FTP sites), and so on.

You Can Restrict The Number Of Results. You can tell the Archie server how many results you want to see, though this setting is not always accurate.

The Impact On Other Users Can Be Set. You can tell Archie to be Nice (Extremely Nice, Nicest, and so on) to other people or Not Nice At All.

Q&A *Why are the options I'm seeing different?*

Each Archie form is a little different; the labels may differ, for instance. Still, they're usually close to the example I've shown here, so you'll be able to figure them out quite easily.

What are the search types?

Before you begin searching for a file name, you should figure out the *type* of search that you want to use. You have the following choices:

Exact or **exact match.** You must type the exact name of the file for which you are looking.

Regex or **regular expression match.** You will type a UNIX regular expression. That means that Archie will regard some of the characters in the word you type as wild cards. (If you don't understand regular expressions, you're better off avoiding this type of search.)

Sub or **case insensitive substring match.** This tells Archie to search within file names for whatever you type. That is, it will look for all names that match, as well as all names that include the characters you typed. If you are searching for *ws_ftp*, for example, Archie will find *ws_ftp* and *ws_ftp32*. Also, when you use a sub search, you don't need to worry about the case of the characters; Archie will find *ws_ftp* and *WS_FTP*.

Subcase or **case sensitive substring match.** This is like the sub search, except you need to enter the case of the word correctly. For example, if you enter *ws_ftp*, Archie will find *ws_ftp* but not *WS_FTP*.

You'll want to use the sub search (case insensitive substring match), which is frequently set up as the default. It takes a little longer than the other types, but it's more likely to find what you are looking for.

You should know, however, that file names are not always set in stone. With thousands of different people posting millions of different files on thousands of different computers, sometimes file names get changed a little. If you have trouble finding something, try a variety of different possible combinations.

 TIP **If you are looking for shareware, go to http://vsl.cnet.com/. This** site lets you search for programs by description rather than by file name.

Remember the find limit!

The substring matches *won't* always find file names that contain what you typed. That is, if you type **ws_ftp**, it may not find *ws_ftp32*, or it may only find one or two when there are many files named *ws_ftp32* at many FTP sites. Why? Because it will show you the *ws_ftp* matches before it shows you the *ws_ftp32* matches, so if there are a lot of *ws_ftp* matches, it may exceed the find limit (see "You Can Restrict The Number Of Results" in the list under "Archie's Options"). You can increase the number of results and search again, to see if there are any *ws_ftp32* files. Or search for *ws_ftp32*.

12

Throw Away Your E-Mail Programs!

● **In this chapter:**

● Preparing the e-mail program

● Sending messages

● How can I send files, Web documents, and URLs?

● The address book

● How can I retrieve e-mail messages?

● Reading and managing messages

Netscape can help you with all of your major Internet chores, including e-mail. . . . . ●

Many browsers enable you to send e-mail. It's almost an essential browser function, these days, because so many documents use the **mailto:** URL; click on a link using this URL and the browser's e-mail program opens. The To field is already filled in for you with the address in the mailto: link. All you need to do is write the message and click on Send.

Until recently, though, most browsers would let you *send* e-mail, but not receive it. Netscape 2.0, however, comes with a "full featured" e-mail program. Not only can you send e-mail, but you can receive it, too. You can work with attached files, create folders, view your messages in a "threaded" view, and more.

 TIP If you are a dedicated Microsoft Exchange user (Exchange is the messaging system that comes with Windows 95), you can use that program instead of Netscape Mail. In the Preferences dialog box, click on the Appearance tab, and choose the Use Exchange Client for Mail option button.

Setting up e-mail

Before you can use the e-mail system, you need to enter information into the Preferences dialog box. Choose Options, Mail and News Preferences, and then click on the Servers tab to see the dialog box in figure 12.1.

Right now, we're only using the top area, the Mail area; the News area is related to newsgroups, which we'll look at in chapter 13. Enter the following information:

Outgoing Mail (SMTP) Server. Enter the address of your SMTP (Simple Mail Transfer Protocol) server, the system to which Netscape will send e-mail messages. Ask your service provider what to enter.

Incoming Mail (POP) Server. Enter the address of your POP (Post Office Protocol) server, the system that holds your incoming e-mail until you log on to retrieve it. Again, ask your service provider what to enter here.

Pop User Name. This is your e-mail account or username, usually the same as the account name you use to log onto the Internet.

Fig. 12.1
Here's where you tell
Netscape how to
handle your e-mail.

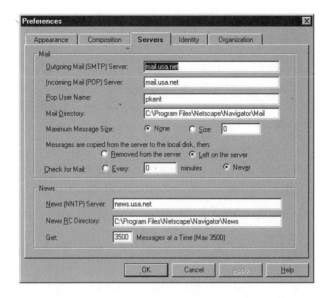

Mail Directory. This is the directory on your hard disk where
Netscape will store the mail-related files (the files containing the
messages, for instance). There's no need to change this.

Maximum Message Size. If you click on the Size option button and
enter a number into the text box, you can provide Netscape with a
message size limit; messages larger than the number of characters you
enter won't be transferred.

Messages are Copied From the Server to the Local Disk, Then.
These two option buttons define what Netscape tells the POP server to
do with your messages. If you select Removed From the Server, once
Netscape has retrieved your e-mail, it tells the POP server to delete the
messages—if you try to retrieve them later using a different e-mail
program, they won't be there. If you select Left on the Server Netscape
doesn't tell the POP server to delete the messages—you can retrieve
them with another e-mail program later.

Now click on the Identity tab to see the information shown in figure 12.2. In
this area, you tell Netscape how you want to be identified in your messages.
Enter the following information:

Your Name. Type your name here. This will be included on the From
line of your outgoing messages, along with your e-mail address.

Your Email. Type your e-mail address. Again, this goes on the From line.

Reply-to Address. You can enter a different Reply-to Address, if you wish, so that replies to your e-mail are sent to a different address. Most users will ignore this option; it's useful if you have more than one e-mail address.

Your Organization. When posting messages to newsgroups (see chapter 13), you can include an Organization line that identifies you in some way, such as by company name.

Signature File. A signature file is a text file containing some kind of "blurb" that's inserted into the end of an e-mail message. You've seen other people use these—they often contain the person's name and address, phone numbers, other e-mail addresses, and so on. If you want to use a signature file, type the text in a word processor or Windows WordPad. Limit it to about 65 characters across, and place a carriage return at the end of each line. Then place the file name in the Signature File text box (see fig. 12.2).

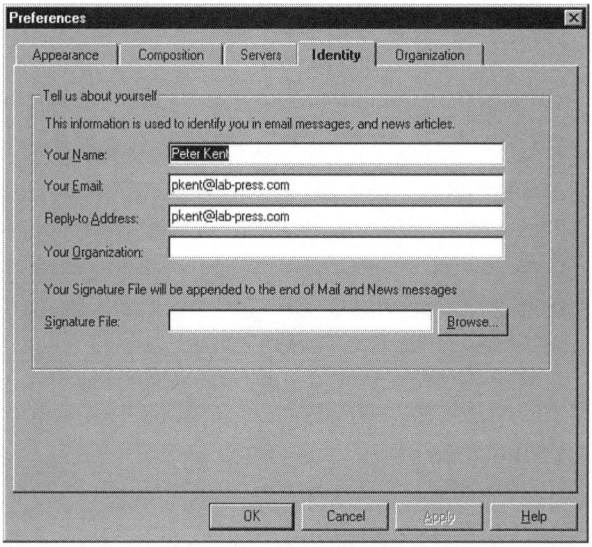

Fig. 12.2
Tell Netscape what identifying information you want to include in your e-mail and newsgroup messages.

Now click on the Composition tab to see the information in figure 12.3.

Fig. 12.3

Tell Netscape what to do when you send e-mail messages.

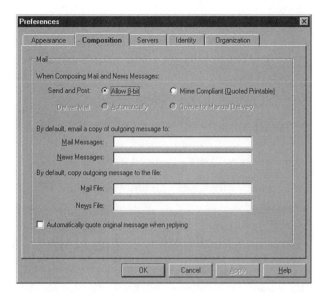

The following list explains what you need to tell Netscape to do when you are composing outgoing e-mail messages:

Send and Post. The following options refer to the manner in which Netscape transfers binary files across the Internet.

> **Allow 8-bit**. Keep this default setting unless you have problems transmitting messages.
>
> **MIME Compliant (Quoted Printable)**. In some cases, messages sent from Netscape may be garbled by the Internet e-mail system. If so, try this setting.

Deliver Mail. These options tell Netscape exactly *when* to send messages.

Automatically. Select this to tell Netscape to send a message when you click on the Send button.

Queue for Manual Delivery. Select this to tell Netscape not to send the e-mail when you click on the Send button. Rather, Netscape stores the message (in the message "queue"), and sends all the messages in the queue when you choose File, Deliver Mail Now.

By Default, Email a Copy of Outgoing Message to. You can have Netscape send a copy of every message you send to another e-mail account. This is handy if you use the Netscape e-mail system only for sending e-mail, and want to keep a record of all the messages you send in your main e-mail program.

By Default, Copy Outgoing Message to the File. Netscape will place a copy of every message you send in the file specified in the Mail File text box. There's no need to change this.

Automatically Quote Original Message When Replying. "Quoting" in Netspeak is placing an original message inside a reply. Select this check box to automatically copy all of the original message's text into the reply. Each line of that text will be preceded by >, to indicate that it's quoted.

You have other mail options, too. Under the Appearance tab, you can define the type of text you want to use for your mail messages. This simply determines what the text will look like when you are reading it, not what the text in messages that you send will look like to the recipient. And under the Organization tab you can tell Netscape to "thread" your messages—that is, replies to your messages are shown next to the original message, making it easier to figure out what's going on. And you can tell Netscape how to sort your messages in the message list: by date, subject, or sender. (By default, messages are threaded and sorted by date.)

Sending e-mail

We'll begin by looking at the basic browser e-mail function: sending e-mail messages. You can open the Compose window, the window in which you will write an e-mail message, several different ways:

- Click on a mailto: link in a Web document. You'll often see Internet e-mail addresses in documents that are colored and underlined just like any other link. Hold the mouse pointer over the link and you'll see the URL in the status bar, something like **mailto:pkent@lab-press.com**.

- Type the mailto: URL into the Location bar (type **mailto:robinhood@sherwoodforest.com**, for instance), and press Enter.

- Choose <u>F</u>ile, <u>N</u>ew Mail Message.

- Choose File, <u>M</u>ail Document to send a copy of the current document to someone.

- In the Netscape Mail window (which we'll look at later in this chapter), click on the New Message toolbar button.

- In the Netscape Mail window, choose <u>M</u>essage, <u>N</u>ew Mail Message.

Whichever method you use, the Message Composition window opens; you can see an example in figure 12.4. With the first two examples—using a link that has the mailto: URL, or entering the mailto: URL directly into the Location text box—you'll notice that the Mail <u>T</u>o address is already filled in for you.

Fig. 12.4
Write your message and click on the Send button.

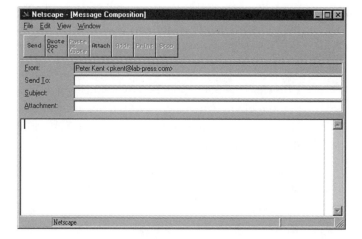

Open the <u>V</u>iew menu. You see a list of text fields that you can display at the top of the Message Composition window: Reply To, Mail To, Mail Cc, and so on. You can select from this list or you can choose <u>V</u>iew, <u>S</u>how All to display all of them at once. By default, the window already has four text boxes, as you can see in figure 12.4. The following list gives a quick description of all the available text boxes:

From. This is your name and e-mail address from the Mail and News Preferences dialog box.

Mail To. The Mail To text box is the address of the person you are sending the message to.

Subject. Type a subject if you wish. If you chose the File, Mail Document from the Netscape window, the current Web document's title will appear here.

Attachment. If you are sending a file (you'll see how in "Sending non-text files," later in this chapter), or using the File, Mail Document command, the file name will appear here.

Reply To. This is from the Mail and News Preferences dialog box, though you can enter a different Reply To address.

Mail Cc/Cc. Choose View, Mail Cc to display the Cc text box. Enter the e-mail address of someone to whom you'd like to send a copy of this message.

Mail Bcc/Blind Cc. Choose View, Mail Bcc to display the Blind Cc text field. You can also enter the e-mail address of someone to whom you wish to send a copy of the message. When you send a **blind copy** (Blind Cc), the original recipient has no indication that a copy of the message has been sent.

File Cc. This field appears only if you choose View, Show All. It shows you the file in which a copy of the outgoing message is saved (from the Mail and News Preferences dialog box). You can delete this text if you don't want to save a copy, or you can enter a different file name.

Post To/Newsgroups. Choose View, Post To to display the Newsgroups text box. You can use this to send a copy of the message to a newsgroup. This text box is really intended for use while working with newsgroups (see chapter 13), but you can send a message to a newsgroup at the same time you send e-mail to someone. Simply enter the newsgroup name.

Followup To. This field is used when you are responding to newsgroup messages (the same window is used for both e-mail and newsgroup messages). It identifies the message to which you are responding.

Once you've entered all the necessary information at the top of the window, place the cursor in the large text area and type your message. Then, when you've finished, click on the Send button or choose File, Send Message. If you chose Deliver Mail Automatically in the Mail and News Preferences dialog box, Netscape now sends the message out across the Internet. Otherwise, it places the message in a queue; it won't send the message until you open the Netscape Mail window (choose <u>W</u>indow, Netscape <u>M</u>ail in the main Netscape window) and choose <u>F</u>ile, <u>D</u>eliver Mail Now.

TIP **You can override this setting by clicking on the Later** button to hold the message; it won't be sent until you choose <u>F</u>ile, <u>D</u>eliver Mail Now in the Mail window, regardless of the setting in the Preferences dialog box.

Sending the Web document

Netscape provides a variety of ways to send Web documents inside e-mail. Experiment with these procedures:

- In the browser window, choose File, Mail Document. The Message Composition window opens, and the current document is attached (you'll learn more about attachments under "Sending non-text files," later in this chapter. Send the message; if the recipient is using Netscape to read his e-mail he'll see the Web document within the e-mail message! (See fig. 12.5.)

Fig. 12.5
This is what the recipient will see if you send a Web document in your message. I attached the Netscape home page to an e-mail message. Notice that the links are active, too!

- Open the Composition window, and click on the Attach button (or choose File, Attach File). You'll see the dialog box displayed in figure 12.6. Click on the Attach File button, and choose a file from your hard disk. Or click on the Attach Location (URL) button, and enter the URL of a Web document. Click on the As Is option button to send the document so that a Netscape recipient will be able to view the Web document. Click on the Convert to Plain Text option button to remove all tags and send plain text.

Fig. 12.6
You can attach a "location" (any page anywhere on the Web—just enter the URL) or a file from your hard disk.

- Open the Message Composition window, and click on the Quote button, or choose File, Include Original Text. Netscape copies the text from the current Web document into your message, replacing the graphics with [Image]. (This is just the text that you can read, not all the HTML tags.) Each line in the text is preceded by >, to indicate that it's "quoted" text.

TIP If you have Netscape Navigator Gold (see chapter 18), you can quickly create messages using bold, italic, centered, and justified text, and then use the File, Mail Document command to send the document to someone else. If the recipient has Netscape, he'll be able to see all the formatting in the document.

Sending non-text files

Netscape's e-mail system is intended to be a full replacement for your current system. And no e-mail program would be complete without the capability to send **binary files** as attachments. A binary file refers to any computer file that is not ASCII text. If you want to send a word processing file, spreadsheet file, or image file with your e-mail message, you can't just place it in the message, you have to use a program that is able to "attach" the file to the message.

UUENCODE and MIME are the two standard systems for doing this. (BinHex, a system used on the Macintosh, is very similar to UUENCODE.) Netscape uses the MIME system, which means that the recipient of the message must be using MIME, too.

We've already seen how to attach a file; when we attached a Web file earlier, by clicking on the Attach button or using the File, Attach File command to open the Attachments dialog box (refer to fig. 12.6). That's right, you'll use the same dialog box to attach any kind of file, not just .HTM or .HTML files. Click on the Attach File button, and find the file you want to send. (Leave the As Is option button selected, of course.)

Q&A *How can I send a file to someone whose e-mail program doesn't use MIME?*

You have a couple of options. You can tell the recipient to get the Munpack program, which will take the MIME message—it will appear like a jumble of text—and convert it back to the original binary file. (You can find Munpack, along with Mpack, at **ftp.andrew.cmu.edu/pub/mpack/**, or by searching for **munpack** and **mpack** at **http://vsl.cnet.com/**.) Or you can use the UUENCODE system. To use that, you'll need a utility such as Wincode, which we'll look at in chapter 13.

What else can I do with Netscape Mail?

The following list describes the variety of other minor procedures that can be carried out in the Message Composition window:

Paste text from the Clipboard. Place the cursor in the Message Composition window and choose Edit, Paste. Or choose Edit, Paste as Quotation to paste the text with each line preceded by a > symbol.

Select all the text. Choose Edit, Select All to select all text in the composition area.

Save the message. Choose File, Save As to save a copy of the message in a text file before you send it.

Print the message. Choose File, Page Setup to define how you want to print your message, and then choose File, Print Message(s) to print the message.

Open the address book. Click on the Address button to open the address book. Huh, the address book? We'll get to that now.

Using the address book

Netscape has a very simple address book. You can open it from the Netscape, Netscape Mail, or Message Composition window by choosing <u>W</u>indow, <u>A</u>ddress Book. You'll see a simple box with a folder icon at the top.

First, here's how you add a name to your address book:

1   Choose <u>I</u>tem, <u>A</u>dd User. You'll see a small dialog box with several fields.

2   Type a Nick Name. This is a name you can use when entering e-mail addresses into the text boxes at the top of the Message Composition window. For instance, if you want to add the **robinhood@sherwoodforest.com** e-mail address to your address book, you might type **robinh** as the Nick Name. Then, when you want to send a message to Robin all you need to do is type **robinh** into the Message Composition window's Send To field.

3   Type the <u>N</u>ame. This is the name by which this entry will be shown in the address book; for instance, type **Robin Hood**.

4   Type the <u>E</u>-mail Address for this person.

5   Type a <u>D</u>escription, if you want. This can be any kind of notes about this person that you wish to keep.

6   Click on the OK button; the new person is added to the address book.

You can view (and modify) an entry's information later by right-clicking on it and choosing Properties (or click once and choose <u>I</u>tem, <u>P</u>roperties).

TIP   **Remember the Mail To and CC buttons in the Message** Composition window? Click on one of these to see the Select Addresses dialog box. Click on a name, then click on the <u>T</u>o, <u>C</u>c, or <u>B</u>cc button to place the nickname into that text field in the Message Composition window. Then click on OK to close the box.

The Netscape Mail window

Well, we've seen how to *send* e-mail. How about dealing with the tons of e-mail that you're going to *receive?* You'll do that in the Netscape Mail window, which you can open by choosing Window, Netscape Mail in the browser window, or by clicking on the little envelope icon on the status bar (see fig. 12.6). When you open this window, you'll see a dialog box asking for your password. This is the password you use to log into your e-mail system and retrieve your e-mail—usually the same password you use to log onto your account with your service provider. If you don't want to get your e-mail yet, press Esc to remove the dialog box.

Fig. 12.6
The Netscape Mail window allows you to organize your incoming mail.

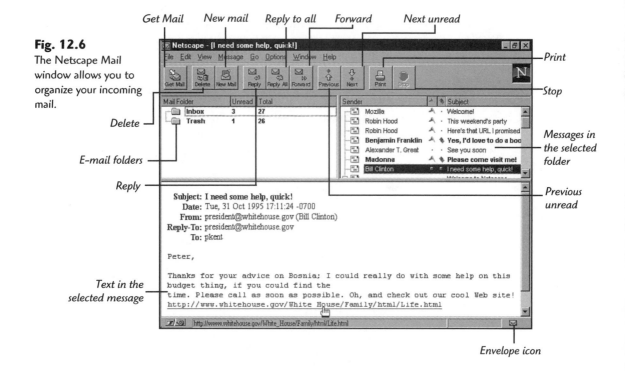

Getting your mail

The procedure for getting your e-mail is simple: click on the Get Mail toolbar button; or choose File, Get New Mail. You may see the password dialog box (if you haven't already entered your password when you opened the Netscape Mail window).

Netscape then goes to your service provider's POP server and grabs the e-mail. In a few moments, you'll see new mail icons appear in the top right pane, and the contents of the first unread message will appear in the bottom pane.

Q&A   *How do I get people to send me e-mail?*

What, no e-mail waiting for you? Well, I can't teach you how to win friends and influence them to send you e-mail. But you can test the e-mail system by sending messages to yourself. Follow the previous instructions for sending e-mail, but enter your own e-mail address in the Mail To text box. Also, you should already have a message from Mozilla, the Netscape mascot. (This message is placed in the Inbox when you install Netscape.)

So, what will you find in your message? You'll see the message header, which contains the Subject, Date, From, Reply To, and To information at the top of the message. Then you'll see the actual message text.

Q&A   *Where's the rest of the message header?*

There's a lot more to a message header than is shown in the message in figure 12.6. All sorts of data (Return-Path:, Received:, Message-Id: X-Sender:, and so on), which most people don't want to see and just clutters up the message pane, is hidden from view. If you *do* want to see this stuff (it's sometimes useful when trying to figure out where a message came from), choose Options, Show All Headers.

Unlike most Internet e-mail programs, Netscape Mail can display Web documents (as shown in fig. 12.5). You may also find pictures inside your messages. If someone sends you a message containing a MIME or UUENCODE picture in .JPG or .GIF format, that picture will be displayed in your message (see chapter 13 for more details).

TIP   You'll only see a Web document if View, Attachments Inline has been selected (it's the default). If View, Attachments as Links is selected, you'll see a link to the Web document; click on the link and Netscape loads the document into the browser window.

Moving between messages

When Netscape first transfers messages, it highlights the first unread message and displays the contents in the bottom pane. You can click on any other message to see that message's text.

You can also use the following menu and toolbar commands:

 Click on the Previous button, or choose <u>G</u>o, Pre<u>v</u>ious Unread to read the previous message that you haven't yet read.

 Click on the Next button or choose <u>G</u>o, Ne<u>x</u>t Unread to read the next message that you haven't yet read.

Choose <u>G</u>o, <u>F</u>irst Unread to read the first unread message in the list.

Choose <u>G</u>o, <u>N</u>ext Message to read the next message in the list, whether you've read it or not.

Choose <u>G</u>o, <u>P</u>revious Message to read the previous message in the list, whether you've read it or not.

Replying to messages

If you'd like to reply to or forward a message, you have a few options:

 To reply to the person who sent the message, click on the Reply button or choose <u>M</u>essage, <u>R</u>eply.

 To reply to the sender *and* to all the people who received copies of the message, click on the Reply All button or choose <u>M</u>essage, <u>R</u>eply to <u>A</u>ll.

 To send a copy of the message to someone else, click on the Forward button or choose <u>R</u>eply, <u>F</u>orward.

About message threads

You saw earlier in this chapter that the Mail and News Preferences dialog box allows you to "thread" your mail messages. That is, when a reply to one of your messages is retrieved, Netscape Mail places the reply indented below the original message in the list. Choose <u>O</u>ptions, <u>M</u>ail and News Preferences, and then click on the Organization tab. If you'd like to use this feature, make sure that the <u>T</u>hread Mail Messages check box has been selected.

You can also turn this feature on and off within the Netscape Mail window by choosing <u>V</u>iew, <u>S</u>ort, <u>T</u>hread Messages.

Working with folders

When you first begin working with Netscape Mail, only one folder, the Inbox, exists. Others will be added automatically; when you delete a message, for instance, Netscape creates a Trash folder and places the deleted message there. If you entered a file name into the Mail Messages text box under the Composition tab in the Preferences dialog box, when you send a message, Netscape creates a Sent folder.

You can create your own folders, too. Choose Eile, New Folder, type a folder name, and press Enter. You might create a variety of folders for different purposes: Business, Family, Friends, one for each mailing list, and so on.

You can sort the messages in your folders. Choose View, Sort, and a cascading menu will open. You can then choose to sort the messages by Date, Subject, or Sender. You can also toggle threading and Ascending search on and off here. (Ascending search controls the order in which the messages appear on your screen. For example, when sorting by date, turn Ascending on to put the newest messages at the top; turn Ascending off to put the newest messages at the bottom.)

 TIP   **Netscape Mail always puts incoming messages at the bottom of** the Inbox list, regardless of the type of sorting you selected. Choose View, Sort, Resort to place the messages in their correct positions.

Moving and copying messages between folders

You can quickly shift messages from one folder to another. Select the message or messages that you want to move, and then choose Message, Move to open a small cascading menu showing all the folders. Select the folder into which you wish to place the message.

You can use the same method to copy messages between folders, too: just choose Message, Copy.

 TIP   **You can carry out operations on several messages at once. To** select multiple messages, hold the Ctrl key while you select each one; or, if the messages are contiguous, select the first in a block, press Shift, and select the last in a block. Or you can choose Edit, Select All Messages or Edit, Select Flagged messages (to select just those messages that have been marked). To select all messages in a thread, select one of the messages and then choose Edit, Select Thread.

Marking messages—the flag and blob columns

In the top right pane, the message-list pane, you'll see two small columns, one with a small flag at the top, and one with what looks like a green diamond or blob of some kind. The flag column shows if a message has been **flagged**. The blob column shows if the message has been read.

You can flag a message by clicking on the little dot in the flag column (or by selecting the message and choosing Message, Flag Message); Netscape replaces the dot with a small flag. Remove the mark by clicking again or by choosing Message, Unflag Message.

Why bother marking messages? Well, it's a way to group them for an operation. For instance, let's say you receive 20 e-mail messages (easy to do if you subscribe to one of the Internet's thousands of mailing-list discussion groups). As you read each one, you can mark the ones you want to shift to another folder. When you've finished reading and marking, choose Edit, Select Flagged Messages. Netscape will highlight all the messages you have marked. Then choose Message, Move, or Message, Copy to move or copy those messages to another folder.

The View, Show Read command displays all the messages in a folder, whether read or unread. It is on by default. If you turn it off, Netscape will show only your unread messages. When Netscape retrieves your messages, each—except the first, which Netscape highlights—is marked with a green blob in the blob column. The green blob indicates that you haven't read that message. Once you open the message, the green blob is removed.

You can mark a read message as *unread*, however. You may want to do this if you open a message and don't have time to read it or if you want to reread it later. This is handy if you've turned the Show Read command off. Click on the dot on the blob column to mark the message as unread. Or select several messages and choose Message, Mark as Unread.

13

All the News Fit to Print (and Much that Isn't)

Netscape provides a link to thousands of discussion groups through its newsgroups window. . . . .

Y ou may already be familiar with Internet newsgroups (discussion groups). Pick a subject, visit the group, read people's messages, respond, and start your own "conversations" or **threads.** There are tens of thousands of Internet newsgroups, spread around the world, on every conceivable subject.

Now, you can't get to all these newsgroups through your service provider. Most Internet newsgroups are of local interest only and are not distributed throughout the world. But thousands are, through a system known as **Usenet.** Each online service has to decide which of these Usenet newsgroups it wants to subscribe to. Service providers typically provide from 3,000 or 4,000 groups to around 10,000 or 12,000, sometimes more. Enough to keep a chronic insomniac *very* busy.

 Plain English, please!

The Internet uses the word **news** ambiguously. Often, when you see a reference to news somewhere on the Internet, it refers to the messages left in newsgroups (not standard journalism). Newsgroups are, in most cases, discussion groups, although there are some newsgroups that contain real news stories.

Netscape's newsgroup system

Netscape provides a great newsgroup program that is integrated into the browser. It's a two-way integration: you can open newsgroups from the Web and open Web pages from newsgroup messages.

Before you can view newsgroup messages, though, you'll have to spend a few moments setting up the newsgroup system. Refer to chapter 12, where I explained how to set up the e-mail system. Setting up the newsgroup system is almost exactly the same. In fact, once you've set up the e-mail system, you've entered most of the information that Netscape News requires.

So return to chapter 12, and follow the instructions for entering information into the Mail and News Preferences dialog box. You'll have to include the following items that I didn't cover in the last chapter:

- **News (NNTP) Server.** Under the Servers tab, enter the host name of your News (NNTP) Server, which is the computer that contains all the newsgroup messages (**NNTP** means **Network News Transfer Protocol**). You can get the host name from your service provider or system administrator.

- **News RC Directory.** This is the name of the directory where Netscape will store information about the newsgroups you've subscribed to.

 Plain English, please!

RC—as in the RC Directory—is a bit of a misnomer here. It's an old UNIX term meaning "run commands." In this context, it refers to the **.newsrc** (news run commands) file that UNIX newsreaders use to determine which newsgroups the user has subscribed to. Netscape has been developed for UNIX, Macs, and Windows, so this reference is left over from the UNIX development process.

- **Get x Messages At a Time.** By default, Netscape will grab up to 3500 messages from a newsgroup at a time, and no more. You can reduce this value if you wish.

- **By Default, Copy Outgoing Message to the File.** Under the Composition tab, remember to enter the name of a file where you want to keep a copy of each newsgroup message you send.

- **By Default, Email a Copy of Outgoing Messages to.** If you want to send a copy of every newsgroup message you post to a particular e-mail address, enter the address under the Composition tab.

The newsgroup hierarchies

Before looking at ways to work in a newsgroup, you need to know about the **newsgroup hierarchies**. Newsgroups use a hierarchical naming system. The first name is the top level. For instance, in *soc.couples.intercultural*, the *soc.* bit is the top level. Below that are sublevels. There are many sublevels within the *soc.* level, just one of which is *couples*. Then, within the *couples* level are newsgroups and perhaps more sublevels—one group below the couples level is called *intercultural*. The top-level Usenet groups are shown in the following table:

Top level	Subject
comp	Computer-related topics.
news	Information about newsgroups themselves, including software used to read newsgroup messages and information about finding and using newsgroups.
rec	Recreational topics: hobbies, sports, the arts, etc.
sci	Science topics; discussions about research in the "hard" sciences—physics, chemistry, etc.—as well as some social sciences.
soc	A wide range of social issues, including types of societies and subcultures, as well as sociopolitical subjects.
talk	Debates about politics, religion, and anything else that's controversial.
misc	Stuff. Looking for jobs, selling things, a forum for paramedics. You know, *stuff.*

Not all newsgroups are true Usenet groups. Many are local groups, although they may be distributed internationally through Usenet just to confuse the issue. Such newsgroups are known as **Alternative Newsgroups Hierarchies**. The top-level groups are:

Top level	Subject
alt	Alternative subjects; often subjects that many people would consider inappropriate, pornographic, or just weird. Can also be simply interesting stuff, but the newsgroup has been created in an "unauthorized" manner to save time and hassle.
bionet	Biological subjects.
bit	A variety of newsgroups from the BITNET network.
biz	Business subjects, including advertisements.
clari	Clarinet's newsgroups from "official" and commercial sources—mainly UPI news stories and various syndicated columns.
courts	Related to law and lawyers.

Top level	Subject
de	Various German language newsgroups.
fj	Various Japanese language newsgroups.
gnu	The Free Software Foundation's newsgroups.
hepnet	Discussions about high-energy and nuclear physics.
ieee	The Institute of Electrical and Electronics Engineers' newsgroups.
info	A collection of mailing lists formed into newsgroups at the University of Illinois.
k12	Discussions about primary and secondary education.
relcom	Russian language newsgroups, mainly distributed in the former Soviet Union.
vmsnet	Subjects of interest to VAX/VMS computer users.

Now and again you'll see other groups, often local newsgroups from particular countries, towns, universities, and so on.

 Plain English, please!
It's sometimes said that **alt.** stands for anarchists, lunatics, and terrorists. (Said by whom? By me, though I freely admit I stole this little quip. I wish I could remember from where.) The alt. groups can be very strange; they're also some of the most popular groups on the Internet. 🙶

Getting the news

How can you view a newsgroup's list of messages? The following are several ways to start:

- Type a **news:** URL into the Location bar (**news:alt.alien.visitors**, for instance), and press Enter. Netscape will open the Netscape News window and connect to your news server. (Note that the **news:** URL does *not* have the two forward slashes after the colon.)

- Click on a link that contains a **news:** URL.

- Choose <u>W</u>indow, Netscape <u>N</u>ews, then click on a news server in the top left pane.

Now and again you'll find Web documents that contain links to newsgroups. Go to Yahoo (**http://www.yahoo.com**; see chapter 7), and follow any hierarchy down a few levels; you'll eventually come to a list of newsgroups. For instance, follow the hierarchy to *Entertainment:Music:Usenet*. (You can go directly here with this URL: **http://www.yahoo.com/Entertainment/ Music/Usenet/.**)

This document provides links to information about dozens of music-related newsgroups: a variety of alt.music newsgroups (**alt.music.prince**, **alt.music.producer**, and so on), **rec.music.info**, **rec.music.marketplace**, **rec.music.misc**, and **rec.music.reviews**. You'll find information about each newsgroup (a short description and the e-mail address of the person running the group) and a link to the group. When you click on the link—a **news:** link—Netscape will open the Netscape News window and load the newsgroup (see fig. 13.1).

Fig. 13.1
The **alt.alien.visitors** newsgroup is a window on another world (well, many worlds).

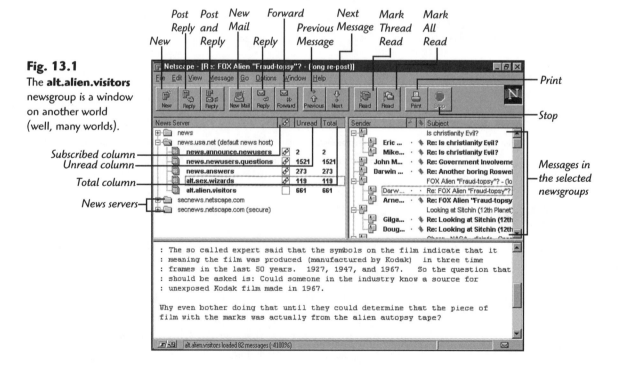

Subscribed column
Unread column
Total column
News servers

Print
Stop

Messages in the selected newsgroups

TIP **Another good search site that references newsgroups is Jump City** (**http://www.jumpcity.com/**). You can select a subject, and you'll find a list of related Web sites and newsgroups. Also, try **http://www.w3.org/ hypertext/DataSources/News/Groups/Overview.html,** which is a large list of newsgroups with links that will open the groups.

Q&A *Netscape opened the News window, but why didn't it display the newsgroup?*

If the news server you've specified in the Mail and News Preferences dialog box doesn't have the newsgroup, Netscape can't display it. Each news server **subscribes** to a different list of newsgroups, so now and again you'll run into a server that doesn't have the newsgroup referenced by the link you clicked on.

If you still want to read the newsgroup's messages, you may be able to choose another news server. See "Give me another news server," later in this chapter.

Working in the newsgroups

What will you see when you open the newsgroup window? Perhaps something like figure 13.1. To display the window like this, I typed **news:alt.alien.visitors** in the browser's Location text box and pressed Enter. The window opened, and after a few seconds (it can take a little while), the list of messages appeared in the top right pane. I then clicked on a message, and the message text appeared in the bottom pane.

TIP **Some newsgroups are huge, and it can take a while to download** the message listing. If it's taking too long, click on the Stop toolbar button or press Esc. Also, consider changing the Get x Messages at a Time value in the Mail and News Preferences dialog box (under the Servers tab).

If you opened the window using the <u>W</u>indow, Netscape <u>N</u>ews command, you saw no list of messages and no message text in the bottom pane because you haven't yet told Netscape which newsgroup you want to read. (This is explained in the next section.)

If you've read chapter 12, you're already familiar with the News window because it's very similar to the Mail window. The major difference is that the top left pane shows a list of news servers (in the Mail window, it shows folders, of course). You'll see one news server at least, the one you defined in the Mail and News Preferences dialog box. You can add more, though, as you'll see in "Give me another news server," later in this chapter.

Displaying the newsgroups—and subscribing to them

If you used the Windows, Netscape News command to open the News window, you haven't yet selected a news server or newsgroup. Here's what you need to do.

First, click in the top left pane on the news server you want to work with. (There's probably only one there, anyway.) Netscape News will display a list of newsgroups below the server icon. These are the newsgroups that you have subscribed to.

Now, notice the column with the glasses at the top, the Subscribed column. Each newsgroup listed will have a check box in this column. If there's a glasses icon in the box, you have subscribed to the group. If you clicked on a link to a newsgroup or typed the **news:** URL, one of the listed newsgroups may show a check box *without* a check mark. This means that the URL took you to a newsgroup to which you haven't yet subscribed.

 TIP   **Because newsgroup names and message subjects are often very** long, you may need to drag the bars between the panes to the left or right to make more room for the text. Also, you can drag the column dividers to the left or right to make more room. (Drag the line immediately before the glasses icon in the left pane or the line immediately before the red flag icon in the right pane.)

Why doesn't Netscape simply show you all the newsgroups that the server has available? That might be thousands and could take a long time. So instead, it allows you to **subscribe** to newsgroups. Then, each time you click on that news server, Netscape gets information about those few newsgroups, which it can do relatively quickly.

Here's how to pick a few newsgroups and subscribe to them. First, choose Options, Show All Newsgroups. You'll see a message box warning that it might take a while; click on OK and Netscape will begin retrieving the information. (How long will this take? Well, as an example, it took Netscape about a minute to retrieve information about my service provider's 6,000 newsgroups; I'm using a 28,800bps modem.)

Take a look at figure 13.2. I've expanded the top left pane a little to the right (by dragging the bar between the two top panes to the right) and removed the bottom pane (by dragging the bar down) to show you what you'll see once Netscape News has retrieved a list of newsgroups:

- **Folder icons with + signs.** Remember the newsgroup hierarchy I told you about? Well, these folders represent groups of newsgroups. Netscape shows how many newsgroups the folder contains in parentheses. Click on one to see a list of the groups (and perhaps more groups of groups) below.

- **Newsgroup names in bold text.** If the newsgroup name is shown in bold, it contains messages.

- **Newsgroup names in regular text**. If a newsgroup name is *not* bold, it's empty; there are no messages in the group.

- **The Subscribed column.** The check box here shows whether you've subscribed to the newsgroup: an empty box means you haven't, a glasses icon mark means you have.

- **The Unread column.** This shows how many messages in the newsgroup you haven't yet read (or which you have marked as unread).

- **The Total column.** The total number of messages held in the group, both read and unread.

- **???** In some cases you may see ??? shown in the Unread column. This means either that Netscape is still grabbing information about the group (the ??? will be replaced with a number after a moment), or that Netscape was unable to get the numbers (perhaps because you're offline).

Fig. 13.2

Adjust the panes and
the columns to make
more room for the
listings; here's a list of
newsgroups.

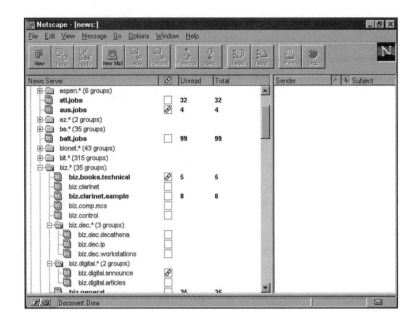

Now that you have a full list of all the newsgroups, you can move down the
list, clicking on the check boxes of the ones you want to subscribe to. You
don't have to subscribe to a group to see its messages, though. You can
always view a group to which you have not subscribed. You can do that by
typing **news:*newsgroup.name*** into Netscape's Location bar and pressing
Enter, or by choosing File, Add Newsgroup (though at the time of writing,
this command wasn't functioning). Or you can choose Options, Show All
Newsgroups again. (Subscribing to a newsgroup is simply a convenience that
allows you to quickly see a list of your favorite newsgroups.)

Once you've finished with the full list of newsgroups, you can choose Options, Show Subscribed Newsgroups to return to your subscribed list. You
can also choose Options, Show Active Newsgroups to show only the
newsgroups that you've subscribed to that contain messages (as you can see
from fig. 13.2, many newsgroups are empty), or Options, Show New
Newsgroups to show the newsgroups that your service provider has recently
begun carrying.

TIP   **If you select another news server, or close and reopen the**
Netscape News window, Netscape News will display only the list of
subscribed newsgroups—it will turn off the Show All Newsgroups option.

Displaying messages

Now that you've got a list of newsgroups, you can display messages from any of them. It doesn't matter whether you've subscribed or not; if the newsgroup name is listed, you can click on it to display its message list in the top right pane—assuming that the newsgroup has messages, of course. Netscape will transfer the list of messages, which may take a moment or two.

Once you've got a list of messages in the top right pane, you can click on one to view the text in the bottom pane. Remember that Netscape may not retrieve a list of *all* the messages, depending on the Get x Messages at a Time setting in the Mail and News Preferences dialog box (under the Server tab). You can get more messages by choosing <u>F</u>ile, <u>G</u>et More Messages.

What's in the text?

What will you find in the message text? This is very similar to what you saw in chapter 12 when you looked at an e-mail message. You'll find the header: the Subject, Date, From, and Organization. (Newsgroup messages typically have an organization identifier; you can enter yours in the Mail and News Preferences dialog box.) You'll often find Newsgroups and References entries too, and you'll see that they are active links (colored and underlined).

The Newsgroups entry shows you to which newsgroups the message has been posted; many are posted to multiple newsgroups. Click on a newsgroup name to open that newsgroup. And the References entries show you related messages, other messages in the thread. Click on a reference to see another message displayed in the main Netscape window. We'll talk more about threading in a moment.

Below the header, you'll find the message text. (If you want to see the *full* header, all the strange routing stuff, choose <u>V</u>iew, Show <u>A</u>ll Headers.)

You may see other stuff, too. If there's a URL in the message, Netscape News converts it into an active link; click on it and the referenced document will appear in the Netscape window. Newsgroup messages often contain lists of newsgroup names at the top of the message in the header; these are newsgroups to which the message has been posted (people often submit a single message to multiple newsgroups). Click on one to open that particular newsgroup.

Pictures from words

Newsgroup messages are simple ASCII text messages. You can't place any character into a message that is not in the standard ASCII character set. So if you want to send a computer file in a newsgroup message—maybe you want to send a picture, sound, or word processing document—you must convert it to ASCII.

There are two ways to do this: you can **"UUENCODE"** a binary file or you can use **MIME**. You saw in chapter 12 how to attach files to messages, and the process is the same when posting to newsgroups—this uses the MIME system. The problem with this is that UUENCODE is a much more common format for this sort of thing; most files you find in newsgroup messages are "UUENCODEd." We'll come back to UUENCODE in a moment (see "If Netscape can't handle it").

How about converting back from UUENCODE or MIME? Let's say you find a newsgroup message that contains a file you want—a picture, for instance. The newsgroup message contains what appears to be garbage text, a huge jumble of mixed-up characters. But Netscape may be able to automatically convert this text for you. When it begins transferring a newsgroup message, it looks for evidence of a MIME or UUENCODE attachment. If it finds one, it tries to convert it, and can do so if the binary file is a .JPG or .GIF image file, as you can see in fig. 13.3.

Fig. 13.3
Netscape converted the UUENCODED message to a picture automatically.

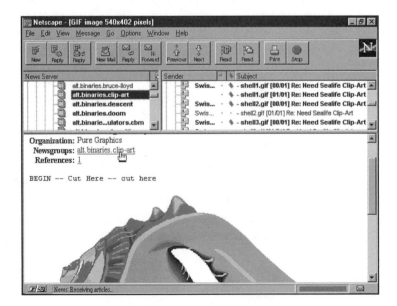

TIP **You can save a picture once it's converted by right-clicking on the** picture and choosing Save This Image As. However, many of the pictures you find in newsgroups have been posted illegally by people who don't own the copyright.

Netscape won't always be able to convert the file, for the following reasons:

- The picture is not one of the image types that Netscape can work with.

- It's the correct image type, but it's split into multiple newsgroup messages. (Many binary files are "UUENCODEd", then divided into several parts because the entire block of text is too big for a single message.) At the time of writing, Netscape could not paste these pieces together, though a later version may be able to because some other newsreaders can do so.

- It's not even a picture; perhaps it's a sound.

- It wasn't encoded properly in the first place. Somewhere between 10 and 20 percent of all the uploaded binary files are damaged in some way and can't be decoded.

If Netscape can't convert the information in the file, you'll see something like that shown in figure 13.4. You'll often see BEGIN -- Cut Here -- cut here near the top of the file, too, meaning that the following text is the encoded binary file.

Fig. 13.4

This sound, from **alt.binaries.sounds.tv,** couldn't be converted by Netscape, so all you get is the "UUENCODEd" text.

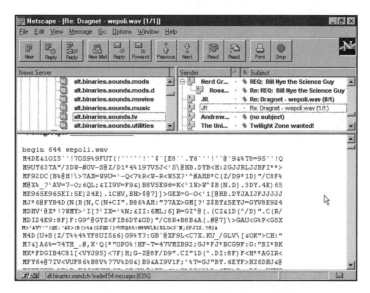

If Netscape can't handle it

What are you going to do if Netscape can't handle the attached binary? Well, you can decode the file using a special UUDECODE program. (The vast majority of files in the newsgroups are attached using UUENCODE, not MIME; however, if you have to convert a file attached using MIME, use Munpack. See chapter 12 for more information.)

If you have Norton Navigator, the Windows 95 add-on utility collection from Symantec, you already have a UUENCODE/DECODE utility in Norton File Manager. Choose <u>F</u>ile, UUEncod<u>e</u>/Decode. You can also use a freeware utility that you can find on the Internet: Wincode. (In theory, Wincode can decode MIME messages, too, although I haven't had much luck.) You can find it at **http://www.winsite.com/** or **ftp://ftp.winsite.com/pub/pc/win3/util/** and at many other shareware sites. Download and unzip Wincode, then read the README.TXT file for information on setting it up.

When you find a file that you want to decode, save it as a text file by choosing <u>F</u>ile, <u>S</u>ave As. Then use Wincode's <u>F</u>ile, <u>D</u>ecode command to select and decode the file. You can also copy the text from the newsgroup message (highlight it and then choose <u>E</u>dit, <u>C</u>opy), then choose Wincode's <u>F</u>ile, <u>D</u>ecode command and click on the <u>C</u>lipboard button to decode the text directly from the Clipboard. (I've found that Wincode's Clipboard system doesn't always work. If you have problems, save the message text and then decode.)

TIP **If the encoded file is split into several messages, you may see** Subject lines that say something like Picture.zip 1/3, Picture.zip 2/3, Picture.zip 3/3. In such a case, save each message in a separate text file. Wincode can pick up each message in sequence while it decodes. See the Wincode instructions for more information.

What's this gibberish message? ROT13

Now and again, especially in the more contentious newsgroups, you'll run into messages that seem to be gibberish. Everything's messed up; each word seems to be a jumbled mix of characters almost as if the message has been encrypted. It has.

What you are seeing is **ROT13**, a very simple substitution cipher (one in which a character is substituted for another). It's actually very easy to read. ROT13 means *rotated 13*. In other words, each character in the alphabet has been replaced by the character 13 places further along. Instead of A you see N, instead of B you see O, instead of C you see P, and so on. Got it? So to read the message, all you need to do is substitute the correct characters. Easy. (Or *Rnfl*, I should say.)

For those of you in a hurry, there is an easier way. Choose <u>V</u>iew, <u>U</u>nscramble (ROT13), and like magic, the message changes into real words.

TIP **So what's the point? Why encode a message with a system that is** so ridiculously easy to break? People don't use ROT13 as a security measure in order to make them unreadable to all but those with the "secret key." After all, anyone with a decent newsgroup reader has the key.

No, encoding using ROT13 is a way of saying, "If you read this message, you may be offended, so if you are easily offended, *don't read it!*" ROT13 messages are often crude, lewd, or just plain rude! Offensive! Nasty! Converting a message into ROT13 forces readers to decide whether or not they want to risk being offended. And if they do, then it's their problem.

Threading and references

Most of the messages you will see in the newsgroups are replies to earlier messages. Someone sends a message with a question or comment, then someone replies, then someone else replies to the reply, and so on.

If all you saw was a chronological list of messages in the newsgroup, you'd find it very difficult to figure out what's going on. For this reason, choose Thread <u>N</u>ews Messages in the Mail and News Preferences dialog box (under the Organization tab). You can also choose <u>V</u>iew, <u>S</u>ort, <u>T</u>hread Messages to turn threading on and off. Figure 13.1 shows threaded messages; you can see that messages are indented one below the other, with the replies below the messages to which they are replying.

Also notice that many messages have a References line in the header. This shows a series of numbers, each of which is a link to a particular message—generally the message to which the one you are reading is a reply. Click on one of these links to display that message in the main Netscape window.

Q&A *I'm using threaded view. Why can't I find the original message in the list of messages?*

Just because you are viewing the messages in a thread doesn't mean you'll see the entire thread. Messages are not held in a newsgroup forever; the newsgroup files your service provider maintains have to be cleaned of old messages to make room for new ones. So if the thread is more than a few days old, you may not be able to find the message that began the thread in the first place.

Moving between messages

You can move between messages by simply double-clicking on each one, or by using one of the following methods:

- Choose Go, Next Message, or click on the Next button to read the next message.

- Choose Go, Previous Message, or click on the Previous button to read the previous message.

- Choose Go, First Unread to move to the first Unread message in the list. (Unread messages are marked with a green circle in the R column.)

- Choose Go, Next Unread to move to the next Unread message in the list.

- Choose Go, Previous Unread to move to the previous Unread message in the list.

Putting in your own two cents: posting and responding

You can just **lurk** in the newsgroups if you wish: just read without taking any part in the discussions. Or you can put in your own two-cents worth by responding to messages or even starting your own discussion. The following are several ways to do this:

- **Reply to a message.** To send a reply to the selected message to the newsgroup, choose Message, Post Reply, or click on the Post Reply button.

- **Reply to the author.** To e-mail a response to the person who origi- nally sent the selected message (not to the newsgroup itself), choose Message, Mail Reply, or click on the Reply button.

- **Reply to the newsgroup *and* the author.** To reply to the newsgroup and e-mail a copy of your reply to the author of the selected message, choose Message, Post and Mail Reply, or click on the Post and Reply button.

- **Forward the message to someone.** To e-mail a copy of the selected message, choose Message, Forward, or click on the Forward button.

- **Send an e-mail message.** You can send an e-mail message to someone (anyone, not just a newsgroup correspondent), by choosing File, New Mail Message, or by clicking on the New Mail button.

- **Send a new message**—To begin a new "conversation" in the newsgroup, choose File, New News Message, or click on the New button.

Read versus unread messages

When you click on a newsgroup and Netscape retrieves the list of newsgroup messages, does it retrieve the entire list? No. It retrieves a list of all the messages that have been marked as Read (up to the Get x Messages at a Time setting from the Preferences dialog box).

How, then, does a message get marked as Read? Well, when Netscape displays the message contents in the bottom pane, it marks the message as Read, removing the green blob from the "Read" column in the top right pane (the column with a green diamond or blob at the top). But there are other ways to mark messages as Read, even if you've *not* read them. You can do this so that you don't see the message the next time you view the contents of this newsgroup. For instance, you might read a message's Subject line and know you're not interested in the message contents. Or maybe you've read the first message in a thread and know you don't care about the rest of the messages in the thread. So they don't appear in the list on your next visit to the newsgroup, mark them as Read by doing the following:

- Click once on the green circle in the Read column, removing the diamond blob thingy.

- Select a message and then choose Message, Mark as Read.

- Select a message and click on the Mark Thread Read button; all the messages in the same thread as the selected message are marked as Read.

- Click on the Mark All Read button; every message in the newsgroup is marked as Read. The next time you view the newsgroup, you'll only see new messages listed.

Of course, you can go the other way, marking messages that you *have* read as Unread. Why bother? So that the next time you view the contents of the newsgroup, that message will still be there. (Maybe you're pondering something in the message, and want to reply to it later.) To mark a message as Unread, do the following:

- Click once on a message and then choose Message, Mark as Unread.

- Click on the little dot in the Read column; Netscape will replace the green blob, marking it as Unread.

 Q&A   ***I read a message in the last session that I want to see again; how do I get it back?***

No problem: choose Options, Show All Messages. Netscape will retrieve a complete list from your service provider's system, marking all the messages as Unread. Of course, this doesn't mean that the message you want is there; it may be too old to remain in the newsgroup. Still, you'll see everything that your service provider has for that newsgroup.

Saving messages

You can save newsgroup messages if you wish. In fact, if you find a useful message, don't simply rely on marking it as Unread so you can come back to it later. If the message is removed from your service provider's computer—as it will be eventually—you won't be able to retrieve it.

To save a message, choose File, Save As. You can also print the message; click on the Print toolbar button, or choose File, Print Message(s).

Give me another news server

If you find a public news server—one that you can connect to, even though it's not provided by your service provider, you can add that server to your Newsgroup window. For instance, you can connect to **secnews.netscape.com**, a secure news server run by Netscape Communications.

Choose File, Open News Host, type the host address of the host you want to use, and press Enter. Netscape will connect to the host and display another host icon in the top left pane. You can now use this in the same way that you use your default host. Click on it and choose Options, Show All Newsgroups to get started.

14

Gopher, Finger, Telnet, and More

● In this chapter:

- **Gophering around in Gopherspace**

- **Searching WAIS through the Web**

- **What's Finger, and how do I use it?**

- **Chatting through the Web?**

- **Starting Telnet sessions**

We haven't finished yet—there are more Internet services available through Netscape. . . . . >

You've looked at three major non-Web services that Netscape can help you with: FTP, e-mail, and newsgroups. But there are other non-Web services out there, many of which Netscape can handle: Gopher, Finger, and WAIS, for example. We'll start with the simplest: Gopher.

Traveling in Gopherspace

Before the World Wide Web became popular (Mosaic wasn't in wide use until the middle of 1994 and Netscape wasn't released until late in 1994), the really easy way to travel around the Internet was through Gopher. Compared to other Internet tools—which were about as easy to use as threading a needle in the dark—Gopher was a revolution.

The Gopher system provided a nice menu system from which users could select options. Instead of remembering a variety of rather obscure and arcane commands, users could use the arrow keys to select options from the menu. Those options took the user to other menus or to documents of some kind. In fact, the Gopher system is, in some ways, similar to the World Wide Web. It's a world-wide network of menu systems. Options in the menus link to menus or other documents all over the world. These Gopher menus made the Internet much easier to use and accessible to people other than long-term "cybergeeks."

The Gopher system is still alive and well for a couple of good reasons. First, there were already many Gopher systems set up before the Web became popular. Second, there are still millions of Internet users who don't have access to graphical Web browsers, so Gophers are the easiest tools available. There's a lot of interesting information on Gopher servers around the world. Fortunately, you can get to it with Netscape. That's right! Netscape may be primarily a Web browser, but you can use the Web to access Gopher.

Digging around with Gopher

You can get to a Gopher server—a computer that maintains a Gopher menu system—in two ways: by clicking on a link that some Web author has provided, or by typing the **gopher://** URL into the Address text box and pressing Enter. For instance, typing **gopher://wiretap.spies.com/** will take you to Internet Wiretap Gopher server, which you can see in figure 14.1.

Fig. 14.1
The Wiretap Gopher
contains a lot of
interesting and strange
documents.

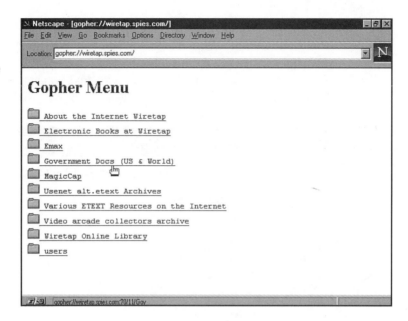

In some cases, you can ignore the **gopher://** bit. You've already learned that you can type a URL into the Address text box without including the **http://** bit. Well, if the Gopher address starts with the word **gopher,** you can type the address and forget the **gopher://** part. For example, you can type **gopher.usa.net** instead of **gopher://gopher.usa.net**. (Of course, the Wiretap address won't work this way.)

TIP   **For a list of links to Gopher servers, go to gopher://gopher.micro.umn.edu/11/ Other%20Gopher%20and%20Information%20Servers**.
If you don't want to type all that, go to **http://www.w3.org/hypertext/ DataSources/ByAccess.html** and click on the *Gopher* link.

How, then, do you use a Gopher server with Netscape? The Gopher menu options are represented by links. Click on the link to select that option. If the option leads to another menu, then it's displayed in the window. If it leads to a file of some kind, the file is transferred in the normal way. And if Netscape can display or play it, it does so. If it can't...well, you'd better go back and see chapters 9 and 10.

You'll find that most of the documents at Gopher sites are text documents; Netscape can display these text documents within its own window. Of course, you won't find any links to other documents within these text documents—they're not true Web documents, after all—so once you've finished, you'll have to use the Back toolbar button (or Alt+left arrow) to return to the Gopher menu. In figure 14.2, you can see a text document that I ran across at the Wiretap site. I chose *Electronic Books at Wiretap*, then *Beowulf*.

Fig. 14.2

If you select a menu option that leads to a text document, you'll see it in the Netscape window.

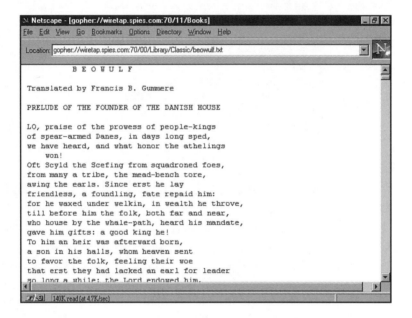

Notice that the icons to the left of the menu options indicate what each option leads to:

 The folder represents a menu (or **directory** in Gopherspeak). Click on this link to see another Gopher menu.

 The page represents a document or computer file of some kind. Click on this link to read the document or view or transfer the file.

 The binoculars represent an index that you can search. Click on this link to see a form for conducting a word search.

Veronica and Jughead

Gopher servers have two types of search tools: **Veronica** (Very Easy Rodent-Oriented Net-Wide Index to Computerized Archives) and **Jughead** (Jonzy's

Universal Gopher Hierarchy Excavation and Display). Do these acronyms mean much? No, but you try to create an acronym from a cartoon character's name!

 Plain English, please!

Why **Veronica** and **Jughead**? They are characters in the famous Archie cartoon strip. **Archie** arrived on the Internet first. Archie is a system that enables you to search the Internet for particular computer files—you can type a file name, and Archie will tell you where the file is (you learned about Archie in chapter 11). Why Archie? The legend is that Archie is derived from the word *archive* with the *v* removed. Some say this is *not* how the name was derived, so who knows? Personally, it makes sense to me. Anyway, the people who created the Gopher search systems figured Archie needed company and named their systems Veronica and Jughead.

Veronica lets you search Gopher servers all over the world. Jughead lets you search the Gopher server you are currently working with (though many Gopher servers don't yet have Jugheads).

If you want to search **Gopherspace**—the giant system of Gopher menus that spreads across the Internet—find an appropriate menu option somewhere. For instance, at the **gopher://gopher.cc.utah.edu/** Gopher site, you'll find menu options that say *Search titles in Gopherspace using Veronica* and *Search menu titles using Jughead.* (The Wiretap site is a bad example because it doesn't seem to have links to either Veronica or Jughead.) At other sites, you may have to dig around a little to find the menu options you need. Most sites have links to Veronica, at least.

Both systems are quite easy to use. Veronica provides two ways to search and also allows you to choose a particular Veronica server. Veronica searches *all* of Gopherspace—Gopher servers all over the world. Something called a **Veronica server** stores an index of menu options at all of these Gopher servers, so you are actually searching one of these indexes, and you get to pick which one.

But at the same time, you have to decide whether you want to limit your search. You can search all menu options or only menu options that lead to other menus. Let's assume, for example, that you went to **gopher://gopher.cc.utah.edu**, then chose the *Search titles in Gopherspace using Veronica* option. You'll see something similar to figure 14.3.

Fig. 14.3
Veronica allows you to choose a server and pick the search type.

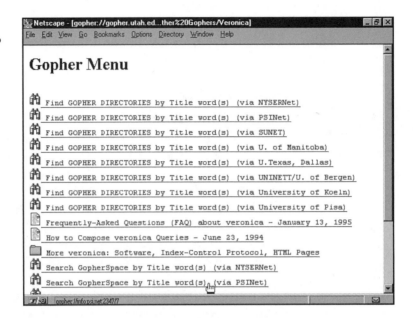

If you now select *Find GOPHER DIRECTORIES by Title Word(s) (via U of Manitoba)*, you will be looking for menu options that lead to other menus (often called **directories** in Gopherspeak) using the University of Manitoba Veronica server. If you select the *Search GopherSpace by Title Word(s) (via PSINet)*, you will search all menu options, both directories and options leading to files and documents, at the PSINet Veronica server.

When you make your selection, a box into which you type the keywords appears. You might type **electronic books**, **publishers**, **sports**, or whatever your interest. Then press Enter and the search begins.

What happens next? Well, there's a good chance you'll get a message saying `*** Too many connections—Try again soon. ***`, or something similar. Try another server. Or perhaps Netscape just seems to wait and wait, and nothing happens. These servers are very busy, so it often takes a long time to get a result. Eventually, with luck, you'll get a list of links you can click on to continue moving through Gopherspace to sites and documents related to your interests.

Using Jughead is similar to using Veronica, but easier: you don't get to pick a server or search type, you simply enter the keywords for your search.

Q&A *Can I use Boolean operators?*

Yes, you certainly can. **Boolean operators** allow you to mix keywords and define how they relate to each other. You can search for **book or publisher** or **book and publisher** or **book not publisher** and so on. For more information on how to search, read the information that most Gopher sites place close to the Veronica and Jughead menu options, such as *How to Compose Veronica Queries* or *About Jughead*. When using Jughead, you can search for **?help** to see a link to the documentation.

WAIS database searches

WAIS means **Wide Area Information Server**. It's a system that's been used for some time to allow Internet users to access information on hundreds of databases around the world.

The WAIS servers are infrequently used, partly because the WAIS interface is rather confusing. You can get to the WAIS servers in several ways. There's a **wais://** URL, but it won't work unless you have a special WAIS proxy installed. (If you installed Netscape on a dial-in line to a service provider, you are out of luck. If you use a copy on your network at work, ask your system administrator if there's a WAIS proxy installed; there almost certainly isn't.)

There are other ways to use WAIS. Many Gopher servers have links to WAIS servers—use Jughead or Veronica to find them. But perhaps the best way to use WAIS is through the WAIS gateway at WAIS, Inc., the company that owns the WAIS software. Use Netscape to go to **http://wais.wais.com/ newhomepages/wais-dbs.html**, where you'll find the WAIS, Inc., Directory of Servers page. (You can also go to **http://wais.wais.com/** to enter the WAIS, Inc. site "at the top," where you can find plenty of information about the WAIS software.)

As you can see in figure 14.4, this page has two elements: a search area and a list of databases.

Fig. 14.4

WAIS, Inc. is the best way to use WAIS through Netscape.

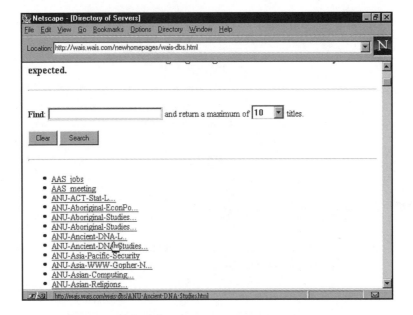

You now have two options. You can search for a useful database by entering a keyword into the Find text box and clicking on Search. The system finds matching databases and then displays a list; you can then search the database that you think will be most useful.

The other option is to scroll down the list of databases (see fig. 14.4) and click on one that looks promising. You'll see information describing the list along with a text box that allows you to search the list.

Using WAIS can be tricky, but it's worth taking a look just to see what's available. You'll find hundreds of databases ranging from *AAS Jobs* (the American Astronomical Society Job Register) to *Zipcodes* (the U.S. ZIP Code directory); from *The Book of Mormon* to *ANU-Buddhist-Electrn-Rsrces* (the Buddhist Electronic Resources Directory). It's a fantastic resource that is well worth learning.

 TIP Try choosing **E**dit, **F**ind to search this and other long lists of links.

Finger

The UNIX **finger** command lets you find information about someone's Internet account. Type **finger username@hostname** at a UNIX prompt and press Enter; you will see information about the user's real name, whether the user is logged on, and so on. And, more importantly, you'll see the contents of the user's *.plan* file. This is often used to distribute information about anything that strikes the user's fancy: sports scores, weather, earthquakes, and so on.

You can't use finger directly from Netscape; there's no **finger://** URL! But there are finger gateways, such as **http://www-bprc.mps.ohio-state.edu/cgi-bin/finger.pl**.

Finger gateways provide a text box into which you can type the address you want. For instance, "fingering" **smith@csn.org** will produce a list of all the Smiths with accounts at that particular host computer. Or "finger" an account that is being used to distribute information. Try **quake@andreas.wr.usgs.gov**, for example. You'll see something like figure 14.5.

Fig. 14.5
This earthquake report was obtained via finger.

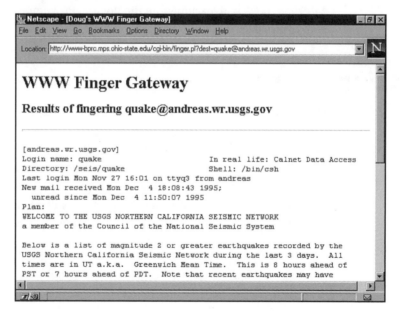

The sort of information you get depends on how the machine you are "fingering" has been set up. Some sites provide a lot of information, some just a little, and some won't give out any finger information at all.

TIP For more finger gateways, search Yahoo (see chapter 7) for the word *finger*, or go to **http://www.yahoo.com/Computers_and_Internet/ Internet/World_Wide_Web/Gateways/Finger_Gateways/**.

By the way, some Web pages have links that automatically use a finger gateway to grab finger information. For instance, search Yahoo for the word *finger*, and you'll find a few of these Finger links. Or go to **http:// www.jou.ufl.edu/commres/jlist/JL_05.htm,** the finger list in the Journalism List Web document. This contains links that will get finger information from a variety of sources on a variety of subjects: auroral activity, NASA's daily news, a hurricane forecast, earthquake information, and all sorts of other, wonderful information.

Some of these finger documents even contain small pictures; although plan files are text files, they can contain links to images just like HTML Web documents. If the document is retrieved through the right sort of finger gateway, those images appear in the document when it's displayed in your Web browser.

Chatting online

Chat is a service that isn't well developed on the Web, but now and again you may run into some kind of chat system. At **http://www.rock.net/webchat/ rwchat.html,** for example, you'll find the RockWeb chat system. You type a message into a form and press Enter. Your "view" of the chat is then updated so you can see your message. RockeWeb has been updated recently to use the Netscape frames feature (see chapter 17), so you can enter your text in one frame and view the conversation in another (see fig. 14.6).

Fig. 14.6
RockWeb is a Web-based chat site; enter your comments in the box at the bottom and watch the conversation in the top frame.

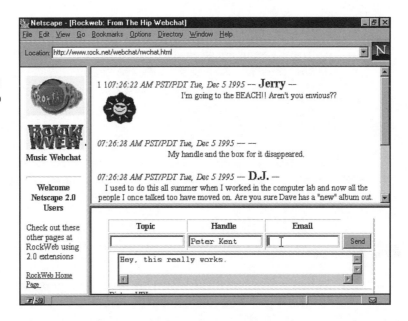

If you know a bit of HTML, you can include HTML tags in your message. You can use bold, italics, underlines, and so on—even include a link to somewhere. In other words, someone reading your message can click on the link in your message to go somewhere else. (If you are going to do this fancy stuff, prepare it beforehand in a word processor, copy it to the Clipboard, and paste it into the chat.)

> **❝ Plain English, please!**
>
> A **chat** system is one that allows people to hold "conversations" in real time. You type a message, and others can read it almost immediately and respond to you. **❞**

If you want to be really geeky, you can tell the system to display a picture next to your name each time you "say" something in the conversation. You'll have to provide the picture, though, and enter a URL pointing to the picture on a system somewhere. (From what I've seen, very few people are using the fancy features that are available in this chat—mostly, it's just plain old text.)

Netscape Chat

Netscape Communications has a product called **Netscape Chat**, which can be integrated into Netscape Navigator. It provides a chat interface through which you can use **Internet Relay Chat** (an Internet-wide chatting system) or set up your own private chat links (similar to what is known as **talk** to UNIX users on the Internet). Those private chats can be between two people or an entire group (either everyone in the group is allowed to take part or one person "presents" to the group). You can find more information about Netscape Chat at the Netscape home page or at **http://home.netscape.com/comprod/chat.html**.

Telnet sessions

Telnet is a system that lets you log in to other computers that are connected to the Internet. You can play games, search library catalogs, dig through databases, and so on. Netscape can't do this for you directly; it doesn't support Telnet sessions. Instead, it can run a Telnet program that you specify.

Choose Options, General Preferences, and then click on the Apps tab (see fig. 14.7). Of the several text boxes that you see, it's the first two that you are interested in: Telnet Application and TN3270 Application. TN3270 is very similar to Telnet; TN3270 sessions run on certain IBM computers. Most Telnet programs don't handle TN3270 sessions very well, so you may need to use an actual TN3270 program to run such sessions.

Use the Browse buttons to select the programs that you want Netscape to launch when you run Telnet or TN3270 sessions. If you are using Windows 95 and have installed the Windows 95 TCP/IP software, you should have Microsoft Telnet available; look in the Windows directory for TELNET.EXE.

Otherwise, you'll have to find a Telnet program elsewhere. Many commercial suites of Internet software contain Telnet programs, and there are a number of shareware programs you can use. Try looking at one of the shareware sites you looked at before, such as the Consummate Winsock Apps list (**http://cwsapps.texas.net/**) or the Virtual Software Library (**http://vsl.cnet.com/**).

Fig. 14.7
You can tell Netscape which Telnet program (and which TN3270 program) you want to use.

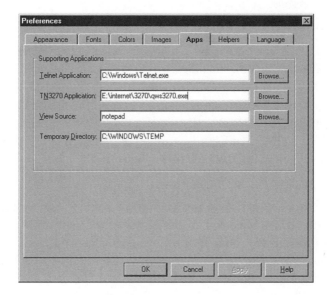

As for TN3270, you can find a commercial program at **http:// www.3270.mcgill.ca/.** There's also a freeware program called Windows Sockets 3270 Telnet Application, which should be available at **ftp.ccs.queensu.ca/pub/msdos/tcpip** or **ftp.sunet.se/pc/windows/ winsock/apps**. Or do an Archie search (see chapter 11) for the qws3270.zip file. Note, however, that TN3270 sites are not terribly common.

Starting a Telnet session

There are several ways to start Telnet sessions from Netscape. You'll occa-sionally find links from Web documents to Telnet sites (using the **telnet://** URL). Clicking on one of these links will launch the Telnet program you have specified. You can also start a Telnet session by typing **telnet://** followed by a Telnet host address into Netscape's Location text box and pressing Enter. For instance, if you type **telnet://pac.carl.org** and press Enter, your Telnet program launches and connects to the Denver Public Library's site. (Type **PAC** and press Enter to log in.)

TN3270 sessions are started in the same way, except that you (or the Web author) use the **tn3270://** URL.

Using HYTELNET

To get a taste for what's available in the world of Telnet, take a look at HYTELNET, the Telnet directory. This used to be available only through Telnet itself, but now you can view the directory at a World Wide Web site. Open your Web browser and go to **http://library.usask.ca/hytelnet/.** (You can also find a HYTELNET site at **http://www.cc.ukans.edu/hytelnet_html/ START.TXT.html**, but it's rather out of date, and at a Gopher site, **gopher:// liberty.uc.wlu.edu/11/internet/hytelnet**).

Each Telnet site is different. You can find Telnet sites where you can play chess, search databases of satellite photographs, or try experimental chat systems. But once you are connected to a Telnet site, that site's rules take over. Each system varies a little and may have different commands or menu options. So if you want to use Telnet, get to know your Telnet program first and then carefully read the instructions that are often shown when you enter a Telnet site.

Part IV: Netscape's Advanced Features

15

Netscape's Security Features

● **In this chapter:**

- The dangers of Web transactions

- Just how real are the dangers?

- What is public-key encryption?

- The two different key sizes

- Working with site certificates

- Personal certificates

The Web is an open system; someone who understands networking can look in on all your transactions. Here's how to make transactions private . . . . ▶

The big question on the Web these days seems to be, "Is it safe?" People are concerned that information they send out across the Internet can somehow be intercepted by someone in-between the Web browser and the Web server.

For instance, let's say that you want to buy something from an online mall; you fill out a form, entering your name and address, the product you want, and your credit card number. You click on the Submit button, and off that information goes, across the Internet, to the Web server that is managing this particular Web store. What happens to that data between here and there? Where is there, even? It might be the other side of the country, the other side of the continent, or even the other side of the world. Could someone take a look at that message as it shoots by and grab your credit card number?

Yes, it can be done. But very few people would know how to do it. Personally, I think the security threat has been exaggerated. There is a threat, and I think companies such as Netscape should be coming up with solutions, but I don't think that at present it's much of a threat. (Do I practice what I preach? Yes, I've sent my credit card number via e-mail to purchase something, and I didn't lose a moment of sleep.)

It's not that dangerous!

I know people who wouldn't dare to send their credit card numbers across the Internet. They seem to have this strange idea that every host computer has some evil soul lurking around, checking every e-mail message for credit card numbers.

Of course, these same people would give their credit card to a waiter in a restaurant, or to the guy in the 7-11, or even read the number over the phone to someone they've never met. They don't know what's happening to that credit card while its out of their sight. They don't know whether the guy at the corner store is copying down the number from the receipt.

In fact, the most dangerous point in a transaction is not while the message is winging its way across the Internet, but what happens once it gets to the other side. Relatively few credit card numbers are stolen online, for a couple of reasons. Very few people know how to do it, yet just about anyone could figure out how to steal a number in the real world. And credit card numbers simply aren't very valuable because they are so easy to steal in the real world.

Public-key encryption—it's magic!

Nonetheless, it does make sense that the companies building software for the Web should do everything they can to reduce the risks, even if those risks are currently minor for most people. The more transactions made over the Web, the more potential for trouble. And once the Web has been made secure, it can be used for transmitting data far more valuable than credit card numbers: corporate financial and management data, research data, even government communications.

Netscape Communications has incorporated something called **public-key encryption** into its browsers and servers to ensure the safety of online transactions.

I don't have a lot of room to explain public-key encryption, unfortunately; it's a concept that few people have heard of and fewer still understand. First, let me describe **private-key encryption**, which most people do understand. A computer file can be **encrypted**—turned into a jumble of garbage characters that make it useless—using a program that works with a **private key** (also known as a **secret key**). The private key is a sort of code word. Tell the program the name of the file you want to encrypt, tell the program the private key, and the program uses a mathematical algorithm to encrypt the file. How can you **decrypt** the file? You do the same thing: give the program the name of the encrypted file, give it the private key, and it uses the algorithm to reverse the process and decrypt the file.

Public-key encryption uses two keys: a private key and a public key. Through the intricacies of mathematics, these keys work together. When you encrypt a file with one key (the public key, for example), the file can only be decrypted with the *other* key! Sounds a little odd, but that's how it works. (Don't ask me how; as far as I'm concerned, it's magic!)

How, then, does this apply to Netscape? Netscape can use public-key encryption to encrypt information from a form before it sends it to the server. Here's how. When you load a secure Web document—a form, for instance—the Web server sends its public key along with the form. (That's why it's called a public key; it's available publicly, and no attempt is made, nor needed, to protect the key.) You fill in the form, click on the Submit button, and your browser takes the public key and encrypts the data in the form. It then sends it back to the server.

The server uses its *private* key to decrypt the message—remember, any file encrypted with the public key can only be decrypted with the private key. Because the people running the server keep that private key secret, your information is safe. If anyone intercepts it, they can't decrypt it.

TIP **Remember, there are two required components in this procedure.** Your browser has built-in security software, but not all servers do. Only special **https** servers (also known as **Secure Sockets Layer** servers) have the security software required for secure transactions. You'll find out how to identify when you are connected to an https server under "How do I actually use this?" later in this chapter.

Different size keys

There are actually two different versions of the Netscape security software: a 40-bit version and a 128-bit version. These numbers refer to the length of the key—the code—that is used to encrypt data. The longer the key, the more secure the transmission. The 128-bit software is built into the Netscape servers and browsers sold to customers within the United States. The 40-bit software is built into Netscape servers and browsers that are sold to customers outside the United States *and* in the browsers that can be downloaded from the Netscape Web and FTP sites and the various mirror sites.

In other words, if you want the very highest security you need to be living within the United States of America, you must (according to law) be a citizen or a resident alien, and you must buy a copy of Netscape—the software will be shipped to you.

Does it really matter? In most cases, no. The 40-bit software is strong enough for all but the most critical of applications. A government department using the Web to transfer information throughout the world would probably want to use 128-bit encryption, ensuring that the message was unbreakable. But for most uses, 40-bit keys are fine.

Why, then, are there two different versions? For one reason only: ITAR, the United States Government's International Traffic in Arms Regulations. Encryption software using keys over 40-bits long is bundled along with armaments—SAM missiles and the like—and cannot be exported. Ridiculous, but true. (How can you stop the export of software, something that can be exported without physically moving anything?)

Q&A   *How safe is Netscape's encryption?*

Very! Data encrypted using the U.S. version, the 128-bit key, is essentially unbreakable. (That's why various U.S. lawmakers have suggested banning this form of encryption; in some countries, it's already illegal.) Messages encrypted with the 40-bit key can be broken, but at a very high price. It takes about 64 MIPS years to break (a million-instructions-per-second for 64 years). A French student recently broke a 40-bit-encrypted message by using spare time on several computers. Netscape estimated that it cost $10,000 of computing time to do so. That's a high price to grab one credit card number! (Note that the 128-bit system is not simply three times as strong as the 40-bit system, it's thousands of times stronger; there's no known way to break it.)

So there are two parts to the security equation: the browser and the server. What happens if you have a 40-bit browser, and you connect to a 128-bit server? The data encryption will be carried out using a 40-bit key. What if you have a 128-bit browser, and you connect to a 40-bit server? The encryption is still carried out using a 40-bit key. You'll get full security only when both browser and server use the 128-bit security software.

How do I actually use this?

Let's see how all this works. Go to the Netscape store; you can get to it from the Netscape home page, or go directly to **http://merchant.netscape.com/ netstore/index.html**. You're going to go through the process of buying something. (Don't worry, you can cancel the operation at the last moment.)

TIP   **If your system administrator has set up your connection to the**

Web behind a **firewall**—a security system that limits the type of communications between your network and the outside world—you may find that Netscape is unable to communicate properly with a secure server. If so, talk with your system administrator about modifying the firewall.

When you get to the store, click on a link to select the type of product you want to buy: *Software* or *Bazaar* (T shirts and so on), for example. Continue following links until you come to a product that is for sale. I went into the Surfer Mozilla Boxer page, for instance; just what I've always wanted, boxer shorts with a surfing lizard on them. Make the appropriate selection—color, size, quantity, and so on—then click on the Add to Basket button. In a few moments, you'll see the dialog box in figure 15.1. This informs you that you are entering a secure form, and that the data you enter into the form will be transmitted back to the server in an encrypted format.

Fig. 15.1
You'll see this message box when you enter a secure document.

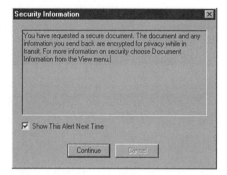

Click on the Continue button. (If you don't want to see these message boxes each time you enter a secure form, clear the Show This Alert Next Time check box.) Now you'll see the secure form, something like the one in figure 15.2.

The URL shows `https://` *rather than* `http://`.

A blue bar appears at the top of secure documents.

Fig. 15.2
Secure forms are identified by the key in the bottom left corner and the blue bar at the top.

The key indicates that this is a secure document.

Notice the blue bar at the top of the content area and the key icon in the left side of the status bar. These both indicate that you are currently working in a secure document—a document at an **https** server (a secure server).

 There are two key icons. The first has just one tooth; it indicates that you will be using the medium security method. You'll see this if either your browser or the server has the 40-bit software.

 The other key icon has two teeth. This indicates that both your browser and the server are using 128-bit software, so the transaction will use high security.

 TIP **You can further confirm the type of security by choosing View, Document Info.** In the lower frame, you'll see something like `This is a secure document that uses a medium-grade encryption key suited for U.S. export.` This refers to the 40-bit key.

What do you have to do to send information from the form using encryption? Nothing. Just leave it up to Netscape. Use the form as you normally would: type the information, click on the Submit or Send button, and so on. Netscape quickly encrypts the data and sends it to the server. It's all transparent to you.

 CAUTION **Just because Netscape provides security features, it doesn't mean** that you are totally safe. There are other things that can go wrong. You have no control over what happens to information you send across the Internet once it's received and decrypted by the server. And if other people have access to your computer, they can subvert your attempts at security.

By the way, Netscape is also selling a secure news server. This would allow you to send messages to a newsgroup and read messages from the group with complete security. The messages would be encrypted between the browser and server. Why bother? After all, newsgroup messages are public anyway, aren't they? Well, a secure news server would let an organization set up private newsgroups. A company might have newsgroups in which employees all over the world could discuss private business securely, for instance. To see a secure news server in action, type **snews://secnews.netscape.com/ netscape.server** into the Location text box and press Enter. (See chapter 13 for more information about newsgroups.)

Keeping you informed—the security messages

By default, Netscape will display message boxes informing you of certain operations; when you enter or leave a secure document, when you enter a document with a secure and insecure mix, and when you submit information insecurely—for instance, if you click on a Send or Submit button in a form that is not on a secure server.

You can turn these message boxes off if you wish; choose Options, Security Preferences, then click on the General tab to see several check boxes that you can use to turn the messages off. Or simply clear the Show This Alert Next Time check box when one of the messages appears.

The most irritating of these messages is the Submitting a Form Insecurely message. Most forms on the Internet are insecure, and in most cases you won't submit anything of importance. For instance, if you go to RockWeb and take part in a conversation (see chapter 14), each time you "say" something by typing your comments and clicking on the Send button, you're submitting data. There's no security risk, though. The Internet is full of such forms, which are systems where you enter data that is not particularly "sensitive." So you may want to turn this message box off.

 TIP **You can save secure documents or view their source, but** Netscape won't save them to the hard-disk cache.

There are a number of other messages that you have no control over:

- Netscape will inform you if a document comes from a secure server, but submits your data to an insecure server.

- Netscape will inform you if a document comes from a secure server, but the script that is used to generate the form (the **CGI**—Common Gateway Interface—script) is not secure. (Perhaps the CGI referenced by the document is on a different server.)

I am who I am—using certificates

A security **certificate** is a special document that is used to **authenticate** a site or person. It's all part of the public-key encryption system. Here's how it works.

A company that's setting up a secure site on the Internet has to get a certificate—otherwise, the server can only operate in an insecure manner. The company applies to a **certificate authority.** Netscape has arranged for RSA Certificate Services (which is owned by the company that created the encryption system used by Netscape) to issue certificates, though other companies will issue certificates eventually.

The company uses special software to electronically create the certificate (this is an electronic certificate), and sends it to the certificate authority, which then checks that the company applying for the certificate is really what it says it is. The authority then digitally signs the certificate.

TIP **This public-key encryption thing can get very involved. You can** sign a document by using a private key to encrypt it. If someone wants to check the authenticity, he can use the associated public key to decrypt it. Because the private key is secret, and because only the associated public key can decrypt documents encrypted with the private key, that person can be sure that the document is authentic.

The company now has a valid https security certificate, and can install that in its server. When you enter a secure document, the certificate is sent to your browser; choose Options, Document Info and you'll see, in the lower frame, that information (see fig. 15.3).

Q&A *Where can I find secure servers that I can experiment with?*

To find a few secure servers to practice on, go to the Netscape Galleria: **http://home.mcom.com/escapes/galleria.html**. You'll find a list of sites using the Netscape server; the ones marked with a key icon are secure servers.

Fig. 15.3
Choose View,
Document Info to see
the site certificate
information.

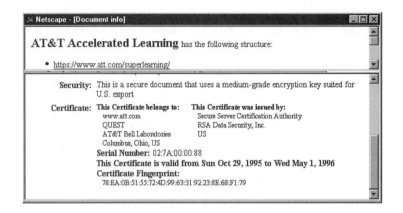

Editing certificates

You can view lists of the certificates that you have accepted and the certifying authorities, by choosing Options, Security Preferences, and clicking on the Site Certificates tab (see fig. 15.4).

Fig. 15.4
The Site Certificates are
in the Security
Preferences dialog box,
where you can view
and edit certificates.

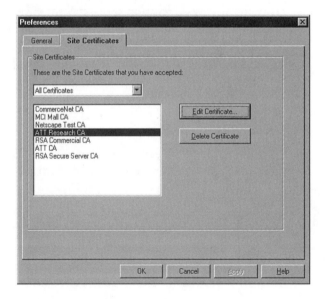

The drop-down list box at the top of this area allows you to modify the contents of the list box; you can view All Certificates, Site Certificates, or Certificate Authorities (the Certificate Authorities list shows the site certificates belonging to the organizations that issue site certificates). Click on an entry, and then click on the <u>E</u>dit Certificate button. You'll see a dialog box like that shown in figure 15.5.

Fig. 15.5
The Edit A Certification Authority dialog box allows you to tell Netscape whether to accept sites authorized by this authority.

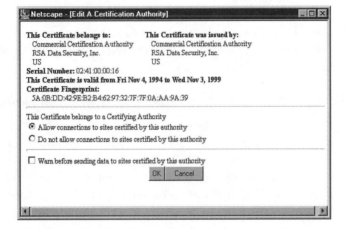

In this case, I clicked on a certification authority in the list. At the top, you can see information about the site certificate; it tells you who owns the certificate and who issued it (in this case, both by the same organization because this is RSA Data Security, Inc., the company that licensed the encryption software to Netscape Communications and also issues certificates).

You'll see the certificate's serial number, its valid dates, and its **fingerprint**. The fingerprint provides a physical way to check the authenticity of a certificate. A company could publish its fingerprint. Anyone who wants to confirm that they really have connected to the correct site—and not one masquerading as the site—could compare the fingerprint in the dialog box with the fingerprint in the company's publications. There's no practical way to forge the fingerprint by adding a forged fingerprint to a forged certificate.

You have two option buttons in this dialog box; the default selection is Allow Connections to Sites Certified By This Authority. In other words, if your browser connects to a secure site, and that site sends a certificate that has been signed by this certifying authority, the browser should assume that it's safe. (How does Netscape know? You won't see any of this and don't need to worry about it; the site sends the certificate to Netscape when you connect to the site, and Netscape can read the digital signature on that certificate.)

The other option is Do Not Allow Connections to Sites Certified by This Authority. Why would you ever use this? If, for some reason you suspect that the certifying authority has certified sites incorrectly. Or perhaps the site accidentally issued certificates to a company that is carrying out fraudulent transactions, or somehow the certification procedure was subverted and certificates were issued incorrectly. Either way, you can block this certifying authority.

Q&A *How will I hear about certification problems?*

I don't know; this is all in its infancy. Perhaps Netscape Communications will issue warnings via e-mail or post such news at its home page.

Finally, there's a check box at the bottom: Warn Before Sending Data to Sites Certified by This Authority tells Netscape to display a warning message if the server you are about to send data to was certified by this authority. Again, there may be a problem with some of the certificates issued by this company.

TIP **There's another way to get to all the security information. Type about:security** into the Location text box and press Enter. You'll see the Certificate Management Web document with links that let you *View Certificates, Delete Certificates, Edit Certificate Trust,* and *List Certificates.*

There's more to come...

At the time of writing, the Netscape security features were not complete. Netscape will eventually allow you to create your own **personal certificate** and to collect certificates from others. You'll soon be able to write encrypted e-mail messages to other Netscape users—you'll retrieve their public keys (perhaps from some form of key server, which is an Internet site that collects public keys), and encrypt messages using those keys. The recipients will decrypt these messages using their private keys.

You'll also be able to digitally sign messages; you'll encrypt a message using your private key. The recipient can then decrypt your message using your public key. Because only your public key can decrypt messages created with your private key, the message is, in effect, signed by you. These features probably won't be completed until Netscape version 2.1. It'll give you something to look forward to.

Other security measures

Although Netscape has introduced some very important advances in Internet security, its current security features are not terribly useful to the average user. Yes, they may come in handy now and again, and maybe soon they'll be essential. But there simply aren't many servers using them yet. I took a look at the list of Netscape secure servers, and there were only about eighty. (You can find the list at the Netscape home page in the Galleria: **http:// home.netscape.com/escapes/galleria.html.**)

But there are other ways to stay safe on the Internet. The following lists a variety of "cybermoney" systems that are in use by a few Web sites here and there:

- **First Virtual.** You can open a First Virtual account, then use your account number to buy things online. The store sends your account number to the First Virtual people who send e-mail to you asking you to confirm. When you confirm, they charge your credit card. For more information, go to **http://firstvirtual.com/.**

- **NetCash.** This is online cash. You apply for an account via e-mail. Then, each time you want money, you ask for a coupon (which is really a serial number representing a sum of money). To buy, you give the merchant the number. It's a little complicated to use, but you can check it out at **http://www.teleport.com/~netcash/ncquick.html.**

- **Ecash.** This is another form of online money, often known as DigiCash—after the company that developed it—or CyberCash. With Ecash, you use a special program to get money from the DigiCash "bank" (which takes it from your checking account) and transfer this Ecash to the store: **http://www.digicash.com/ecash/.**

I saw another interesting security measure the other day. One store splits its order form into two pieces; you enter half of your credit card number into one form and send it, then enter the other half of the number into the other form and send that. Your number crosses the Internet unencrypted, but it's in two parts, reducing the likelihood that it will be stolen.

16

Java and JavaScript: Programs Built into the Web

In this chapter:

- **What is Java?**

- **What can it do for me?**

- **Finding Java sites**

- **Java samples**

- **The trouble with Java**

- **Java made simple—JavaScript**

Web documents are no longer static—Java brings them alive with motion, sound, and interaction . . . . ⊳

One of the most exciting new technologies on the Web is Java. This is a programming language from Sun, a language based on the C++ programming language. It allows a programmer to create a small program that can run "within" a Java viewer. And Netscape 2 has the viewer built into it, so these Java programs—**applets**, as they're commonly known—will run within the Netscape window.

What can Java programs do? They can bring sound and motion to Web documents. The following are a few ways that Java applets can be used:

- **Regular and frequent document updates.** The Web document may contain information that is updated regularly and frequently. As you view the document, the information changes before your eyes: stock quotes, weather reports, news reports, and so on.

- **Expert graphics rendering.** A Java applet may be used to display high-resolution graphics or video.

- **User interaction.** A Java applet may contain a game: a crossword puzzle, chess, a MUD (Multi-User Dimension, a role playing game), tic-tac-toe, word-match games, Hangman, and so on, and can allow a user to search a database or enter information for a survey.

- **Animation.** Web authors can animate their documents, with blinking text, embedded videos and cartoons, and scrolling text and images.

- **Sounds.** Web authors can now use Java to add sounds to their documents: background music, a voice-over, or a welcome-to-the-page statement.

But is it safe?

Java applets are designed to be secure. If the applet provides interaction between you and the server—you might be able to enter information and receive information back from the server—the information is transferred securely. Java also has protection against viruses and tampering. However, that doesn't stop someone writing a Java applet that *intentionally* does harm.

You can disable Java applets. Choose Options, Security Preferences, and click on the Disable Java check box. You'll still be able to view Web pages with embedded Java applets, but a blank space will be left where the applet should go.

Once Java is well integrated into the Web (right now it's in its very early stages), the Web will have a completely different look and feel. It will be more like using a multimedia CD: it will be interactive, in motion, a flow of information rather than static pages transferred one at a time.

Where can I find Java?

Right now, few Web sites have Java applets. You'll rarely run across one by chance. So the following are several places to look for some samples:

- **The Netscape site.** Currently, there are links to various demos from the Netscape site. You can find your way to them from the Netscape home page or go directly to them. (**http://home.netscape.com/ comprod/products/navigator/version_2.0/java_applets/ index.html**)

- **The Gamelan Registry.** Here, you'll find links to a lot of Java sites. (**http://www.gamelan.com/**)

- **Sun's List of Cool Applets**. From the people who brought us Java, here is a list of neat ones. (**http://www.javasoft.com/applets/ applets.html**)

 TIP **There are currently two forms of Java applets: alpha and beta**. Netscape can run **beta** applets, not alpha. Many links, especially at the Gamelan Registry, will indicate whether you are about to view an alpha or beta applet.

Playing an applet

What do you have to do to play one of these applets? Nothing. At least, nothing beyond what you normally do when entering a Web page: click on the link or type the URL and press Enter, or whatever. When the Web page opens, Netscape will load the Java applet at the same time.

Of course once the applet is loaded, you may have work to do, but that's up to the Web author. If the applet is a game, for instance, you have to know how to play the game; a good applet will provide instructions, of course. Each applet is different, so there are no general rules.

TIP **The progress bar doesn't work well with Java applets. It works** while the Java applet is being transferred to your computer, but then the progress bar stops working, even though nothing may be happening. You may see a blank gray box, for instance, and nothing else. However, listen for your hard drive or look for the hard drive light; your drive is probably churning away, preparing the applet.

Here are a few samples that I found. At the time of writing, there simply isn't much that's terribly exciting; Java's very new, very little used, and still a bit "buggy." The majority of sites are simply demo sites with little real utility. So you'll probably want to explore and find your own sites—there'll be many more by the time you read this.

c|net

This is an advertiser-supported Web site that provides a dating service, news, articles, reviews, and contests. It includes a very simple Java applet: a scrolling "ticker tape," displaying news headlines across the top of the main page. (**http://www.cnet.com/**)

Visual music

"Visual music is the notion of expressing musical ideas visually." Yeah, well, it didn't do anything for me, but I'm not very artistic. You see a square with four smaller squares within that flash different colors to represent music. Maybe it'll do more for you. (**http://galt.cs.nyu.edu/andruid/groove.html**)

3-D tennis

A tennis game? Well, it looks more like squash to me. You use the mouse to bounce a ball back along a room; miss the ball and lose "energy." When the energy gauge is down, the game is over. A sort of Web version of the early ping pong video game. (**http://www.sfc.keio.ac.jp/~t93034ei/ja1.html**)

The abacus

An electronic abacus; now there's an interesting concept! See figure 16.1. (**http://www.ee.ryerson.ca:8080/~elf/abacus.html**)

Fig. 16.1
Learn how to use an abacus through the interactivity of Java.

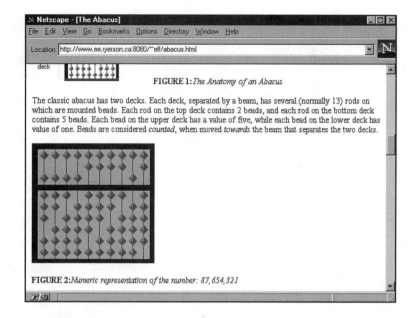

Jumping box

A small box (two-dimensional; nothing snazzy here) jumps around while you try to click on it. You get sound effects when you hit it. (**http://www.javasoft.com/JDK-prebeta1/applets/JumpingBox/example1.html**).

Molecule viewer

You can view a molecule (I don't know what it is, doesn't say) and rotate it if you are lucky. I think you use the mouse, but maybe it's the arrow keys; it's slow, so it's hard to tell what's doing what. See figure 16.2. (**http://java.sun.com/JDK-prebeta1/applets/MoleculeViewer/example1.html**)

Fig. 16.2
The molecule should turn. Well, it *does* turn, but it's kinda slow.

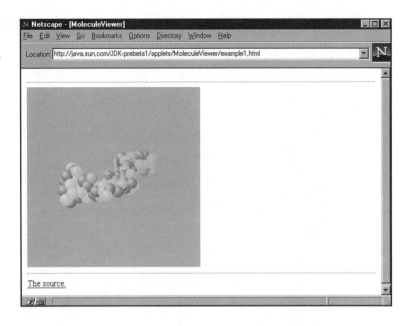

Control the nuclear power plant

Control your own nuclear power plant! Click on valves to adjust the various flows and, if you are lucky, you'll avoid a meltdown (see fig. 16.3). (**http://www.ida.liu.se/~her/npp/demo.html**)

Fig. 16.3
One mistake and the power station blows.

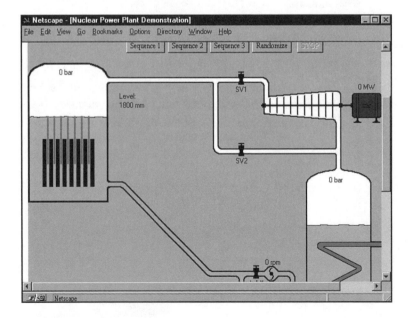

TIP **If a Java applet is a play-once applet—a welcoming message in the** Web author's voice, for instance—you don't have to leave the page to replay it. Simply click on the Reload button.

3-D Netris

Are you a Tetris fan? Want to try a 3-D version (named 3-D Netris)? See figure 16.4. You can move the board around—play it upside down if you want—and then use the control to move the blocks into position. A little slow, though—no match for the experts. (**http://www.earthweb.com/java/Netris/**)

Fig. 16.4
3-D Netris, a three-dimensional version of Tetris.

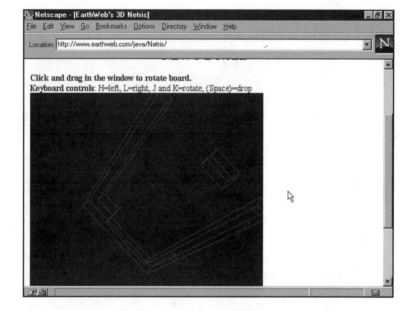

Well, I'm giving up; find your own Java. At the time of writing, most Java sites were hardly worth bothering with; most didn't work in Netscape (they're alpha applets or simply too buggy), and many were *sort* of interesting but not worth coming back to. Java was still a developer's toy, and there wasn't much out there for the user. Still, that will change—perhaps very quickly—as the technology progresses. Check the Java listings I've mentioned to see the current status of the Java world.

The problem with Java

Java applets have the same problem that most of the really neat stuff on the Web has: they can be very slow if you are working through a modem. The introductory voice welcoming you to a Web page, for instance, may not play until you've read most of the page! The animation may be too slow to be fun. Once the Java data has transferred, things work pretty quickly, but having to wait for the stuff to get over the Internet and to your computer spoils the effect to some degree. But hey, what can you do? If you are working on a network, it works well and the rest of us will just have to dream.

Troubleshooting Java

Netscape provides a troubleshooting tool for Java applets: a console that displays the Java program code being run. Click on a link to a Web page containing a Java applet, then quickly choose Options, Show Java Console. A large window opens and displays line after line of gobbledygook, which means little to the average user.

A simpler form of Java—JavaScript

There's another way that a Web developer can create **active** Web documents (documents that do things and allow you to do things to them). Developers can use **JavaScript**, Netscape's new scripting tool. (You may see the term **Livescript**, too; this was the original name given to JavaScript.)

JavaScript is a simplified form of Java. To use Java requires programming skills; it's a true programming language, and developing applets is not to be undertaken lightly. But JavaScript provides a simpler way to jazz up Web pages. If a Web author can understand how to create HTML documents, he can probably understand how to work with JavaScript fairly easily (that's the theory, anyway).

 TIP **It's actually possible to create simple Web pages with very little** HTML knowledge. An author who has created a simple Web page won't necessarily have the skills needed for JavaScript. But anyone who's created complicated Web forms should be able to figure it out.

So what can JavaScript actually do? It allows a Web author to script "events, objects, and actions." The author can tell the document to "watch" for certain actions: when the document is opened by a browser, when the browser moves from the document to another one, when the reader clicks the mouse button, and so on. It also allows the author to link the Web document to inline plug-ins and true Java applets—he can take off-the-shelf Java applets and link them to his documents. It brings the power of Java to developers without the programming skills required to create Java applets.

The developer can use JavaScript to add sounds to a document—a sound may play when the document is opened by the browser or when the reader clicks the mouse button on an icon, or an inline picture may change according to the time of day. Web forms can now quickly check that the correct information has been entered, *before* that information is transmitted back to the server. A Java applet may open or may modify its actions when the reader selects something from a form. For instance, the reader may choose a particular model, type, or color from an order form. The Java applet—on receiving JavaScript instructions generated when the reader makes his selection—then displays the appropriate object.

 TIP **Netscape Navigator Gold provides HTML-authoring tools—these** help you create your own Web documents. At the time of writing, JavaScript hadn't been added to Navigator Gold, but it will be soon. By the time you read this, it may have a special tool to further simplify creating JavaScripts for your documents. See chapters 18 and 19 for information about Navigator Gold.

When do they run?

When can JavaScripts run? Web authors can set up their documents to run JavaScripts when events such as these occur:

- When your browser opens the document.

- When you move from the document to another document—by using the history list or bookmarks, for instance.

- When "input focus" changes; for instance, when you press Tab to move the cursor from one field in a form to another.

- When you select text in a field.

- When you modify text in a field.

- When you click on a button.

- When you click on a command button.

- When your browser sends the contents of the form back to the server.

- When you click on a link.

- When you simply point at a link.

Samples, please

Right now, there are few examples of JavaScript in action. In fact, I've been able to find only a couple. To see a notation calculator, go to **http://home.netscape.com/comprod/products/navigator/version_2.0/script/calc.html.** For an interest calculator, go to the same URL, except use the document name **interest.html**. They don't look much different from a Java applet.

In effect, these calculators are forms, but with much more interactivity than most forms you'll find on the Web. Most allow you to enter information and click on a button to send the information. But these JavaScript examples do more; they respond by returning the results of your actions directly to the form and they work just like a calculator.

17

Netscape Frames— Web Hypertext Grows Up

● In this chapter:

- ● **What are panes and frames?**

- ● **Different uses for frames**

- ● **How do I use frames?**

- ● **Show me some sample frames**

- ● **What is a targeted window?**

Finally... multiple frame (or pane) Web documents. . . . . . ⊙

For all the excitement surrounding the World Wide Web, it's actually a fairly primitive form of hypertext. I'm not talking about all multimedia—sound, video, pictures, and so on. I'm talking about the way that documents are handled. Until recently, Web browsers could only display one document at a time. Click on a link, and the current document would disappear and another would appear.

The best that you could do was to open another window in which to display a new document. For instance, in Netscape, you can right-click on a link and choose New Window With This Link. A new Netscape window opens and displays the document. But what you are really doing is starting a new Web session. You end up running multiple Web sessions, but the documents within are still single-view documents.

 TIP **There is one exception I'm aware of: the InternetWorks browser.** This was designed to enable the user to open several documents in different windows and even to split a window into two or more panes. Still, this was the browser trying to make the Web easier to use—the documents were designed to be "single-view documents." In any case, InternetWorks' publisher allowed it to die when it was bought by America Online.

Some other forms of hypertext handle documents differently. They may enable the hypertext author to open secondary windows, for instance—the reader can click on a link, which opens another window showing the referenced document. The first window remains open.

This appears to be the same as Netscape's New Window With This Link command. It's not, though, because the author is determining that a new window should open, so it's the author who can determine the flow of the session. You are not opening another hypertext session, you are following the flow of the document according to the wishes of the author.

Other hypertext systems may use multiple **panes**, as well. While you may be viewing only one window, there can be two or three individual areas within the window, maybe more. One pane may contain special controls needed, another may contain a picture, another may contain a list of cross-reference links.

Well, Netscape has now introduced both of these concepts: Web authors can now create documents that open multiple panes within a Netscape window (in "Netscape-speak," they are known as **frames**), and can also tell Netscape when to open a new window.

So, what are frames used for?

The following list describes a few ways you'll see frames used:

- Authors can add banners to their documents. The banner at the top (a corporate logo, for instance) remains static while you can scroll through the contents of the document in the lower frame. Static areas such as this are known as **ledges**.

- A form in one frame may be used to accept data from you while the other frame displays the results after you've submitted the form. For instance, you might enter information you want to search for in the form, submit the form, and then view the results in the second frame.

- An author may add a control bar in one frame and the document in the other. Clicking on the control bar can take you out of the current document, into another part of the same document, or to a different framed document. This is another form of a ledge.

- A table of contents can be displayed in the left frame, with the document in the right frame. Clicking on an entry in the table of contents displays the selected document in the right frame.

- A company may choose to keeps its copyright information in a frame, as a constant reminder to the reader.

Different framed documents work in different ways. Here are a few things to look for:

- Frames may be fixed in place.

- Frames may be moveable. Point at a border between a frame; if the pointer changes to two parallel lines with two arrows (see fig. 17.1), you can drag the border to reposition it.

- Links within documents can be set up to take you away from the framed document to a completely different document, to replace the contents of the frame, or to replace the contents of one of the *other* frames in the document.

- Frames are independently scrollable; that is, you can scroll through the contents of one frame while the contents of the other frames remain static.

- Frames can even contain different documents. For instance, clicking on a link in one frame may change the contents of one of the other frames, bringing in a document from a different location entirely. Now you have two different documents displayed in the same window.

A table of contents

Figure 17.1 shows a good example of frames used to create a table of contents. This is JavaScript reference information (see chapter 16 for information about JavaScript). The left frame is the table of contents. When you click on an entry in the left frame, the referenced document appears in the right frame. Notice that the mouse pointer on the border has changed: this means you can move this border.

Fig. 17.1
The left frame provides a permanent table of contents; click on a link to change the document in the right frame.

Mouse pointer

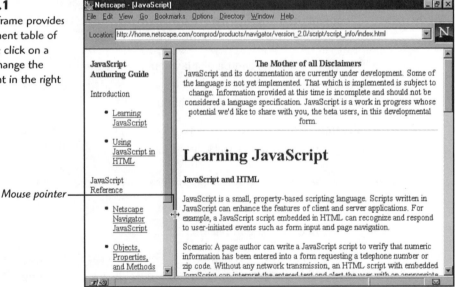

Q&A *Where can I find more framed documents?*

You can find lots of samples of framed documents from the Netscape home page. In particular, try the Companies Using Frames document (**http://home.netscape.com/comprod/products/navigator/version_2.0/frames/frame_users.html**).

A table of contents and a ledge

The Web page in figure 17.2 contains three frames: the one on the right is a table of contents, the one at the top is a "ledge" containing links to other areas of Fashionmall's Web site (**http://fashionmall.com/**), and the large area is the content area. Both the content area and the table of contents are scrollable. (Notice the mouse pointer on the horizontal border, by the way; it hasn't changed form, so these are non-adjustable borders.)

Fig. 17.2
This document has a table of contents on the right and a ledge containing other links at the top.

Mouse pointer

Input/output frames

The example in figure 17.3 shows how an author can set up one frame in which you input data and another in which you view the results. This is the Ecola Tech Directory site, where you can search for Web sites maintained by high-tech companies (**http://www.ecola.com/techcorp/frames.htm**).

Fig. 17.3
Enter your data in the top frame and see the results in the lower frame.

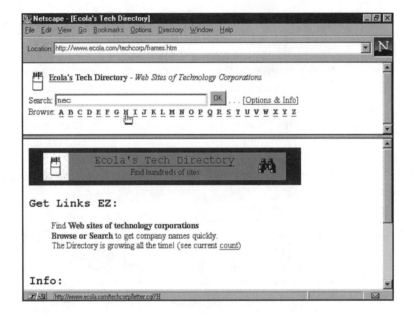

A banner (and more)

The document in figure 17.4 (**http://www.piper-studios.com/**) shows a banner at the top containing the company name. Scroll through the content area (the large frame) or choose something from the table of contents in the left frame, and the banner remains in place. There's also a ledge at the bottom of the window. (Of course, the banner is a kind of ledge, too).

Fig. 17.4
Here's an example of a frame used to place a banner at the top.

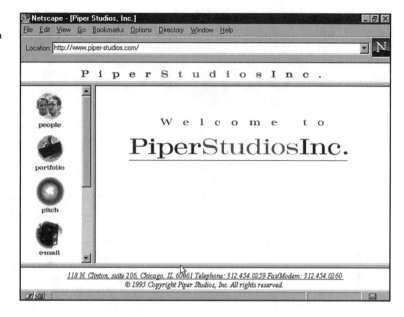

My favorite example

One of the nicest framed documents I've seen so far is actually a demo document. It's the How We See document, which you can get to from the Netscape home page (**http://home.mcom.com/comprod/products/navigator/version_2.0/frames/eye/index.html**). The largest frame contains a picture of the eye, with callouts pointing to the eye's various components. Each callout is a link; click on a callout to change the contents of the frame on the right side. The top frame is a static banner. You can see this document in figure 17.5.

Fig. 17.5
The How We See demo document, an excellent example of how frames can work.

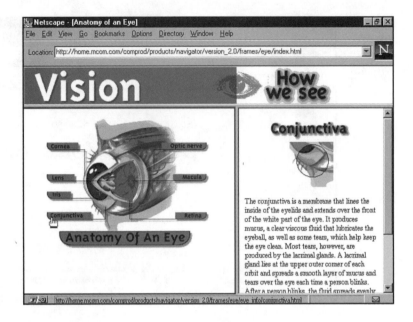

The problem with frames

Frames can sometimes be irritating, if they are not used properly. There's a tendency for many Web authors to use every neat toy that's available, without considering whether they are really appropriate. Frames can clutter up the Netscape window, especially on a small monitor.

I've run into one extremely annoying situation. I found a document with a ledge at the bottom. When I clicked on links in the main area, though—links that took me to another Web site—the frame remained in the window; the author had set up the document to change the content of the main frame but retain the frame at the bottom.

The problem with this is that Netscape assumes you are in the same document, and doesn't record your "travels" at the other site in the history list. So when you try to go back through those travels, using the history list or Back button, you can't! (Back will take you out of the framed document, back to the document you viewed immediately before viewing the framed document.)

The following list offers a few ways around this problem:

- To return to the previous document displayed in that particular frame—rather than returning all the way to the document that was displayed immediately before you entered the framed document—right-click inside the frame and choose Back. (You must use the pop-up menu; if you use the Back button in the toolbar, Alt+left arrow, or choose <u>G</u>o, <u>B</u>ack, you'll go all the way back to the document prior to the framed document.)

- Right-click on the link, and choose New Window With This Link.

- Right-click on the link to the other Web site, choose Copy This Link Location, paste the link into the Location text box, and press Enter.

Targeted windows

The other feature I mentioned earlier—allowing Web authors to automatically open another window and placing the referenced document in that window—is known as **targeted windows**. The Web author can now assign documents to windows by name. When you click on the link, Netscape looks for a window with that particular name (you can't see window names; they are hidden), and, if the window is already open, places the document in that window. If it's not open, Netscape opens another window, gives it the required name, and places the document inside.

As an example, an author may have a list of subjects in a window. When you click on a link in that window, another document may appear in another window. Clicking on another link in the first window may either open yet another window or replace the document in the second window with the new document.

Part V: Creating Web Pages with Navigator Gold

18

Creating Your Own Home Page

● **In this chapter:**

Netscape Navigator Gold helps you create Web pages, not just view them. . . . . ⊳

Publishing on the Web is surprisingly easy, and creating your own home page is probably the best first step. It's a great way to get a feel for how HTML works, and you'll produce something you can use, too. How do you go about producing a home page? Well, you can use any of several freeware, shareware, and commercial HTML authoring tools. But in this chapter, you're going to learn about one in particular: Netscape Navigator Gold.

Netscape Navigator Gold contains everything that Netscape Navigator contains, *plus* some great authoring and editing tools that help you create a Web page from scratch or take a Web page that you like and modify it. In this chapter and in chapter 19, I assume that you are working with Navigator Gold; see chapter 2 for information on obtaining it.

Your first home (page)

What is a home page? The following is a quick refresher:

- It's the page that appears when you open Netscape. (Assuming that you have the Preferences set up to display a home page, choose Options, General Preferences, then look under the Appearance tab.)

- It's the page that appears when you click on the Home toolbar button or choose Go, Home.

Netscape HTML tags

Navigator Gold creates pages using the Netscape HTML tags. Some of these are not standard tags, so not all Web browsers will be able to view the formatting that you put into your document. That doesn't matter if you are creating nothing more than a home page for your own use, but this issue should be considered if you plan to create pages and place them on the Web.

For instance, some of the special horizontal lines and text formats—the colors, and the superscript and subscript characters—are not standard. Many of the other browsers will display them, though, and in most cases, the formats don't create problems for browsers that can't use them—they're simply not visible.

As I've mentioned earlier in this book (chapter 1), there's currently some ambiguity about the term *home page*, which has come to mean two things. The original meaning is the page that appears when you open your browser or use the Home command. The new meaning is a page that you have published on the Web, a page that others on the Web can view (the Rolling Stones' home page, for example). Whenever I use the term *home page*, I mean the one that opens when you open Netscape.

Why would you want to create your own home page? The following are a few reasons:

- On the Internet, one size doesn't fit all. Everyone uses the Internet in a different way. The page provided by Netscape may be okay to start with, but it won't have all the links you want and may contain plenty that you don't want.

- The History and Bookmarks lists are very handy, but if you are going to use certain items from these lists frequently, you'll find it more convenient to have them on your home page.

- You can customize your home page with links to your favorite sites across the Internet. Or have a home page plus a series of documents on your hard drive linked to that home page: one document for work, one for music, one for newsgroups, one for whatever else. Then you can have links from the home page to those separate documents. (I'll show you how in the section called, "Creating multiple documents.")

How do you open the Editor?

Navigator Gold has an Editor window, which is shown in figure 18.1. There are two ways to open this window, as follows:

- To start a new document from scratch, choose Window, Netscape Editor. A blank Editor window opens (the browser window remains open).

- To edit a copy of the document you are currently viewing, choose File, Edit Document. The browser window is converted to the Editor window.

Why would you want to edit an existing document? Eventually, you'll want to modify documents you created earlier, of course. But editing an existing document is also a great way to create your first Web document. Find a document that you think looks good—one that you'd like to copy—and edit that document, replacing the original headings with your headings, keeping the images and links you need, and so on. Then save the modified document on your hard disk.

Fig. 18.1
The Editor window provides the tools you need to create or modify a Web page.

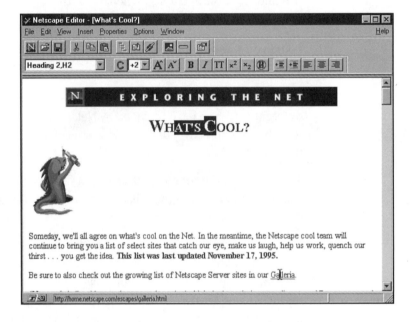

Here's a quick summary of what each button does:

 Browser. Click here to change back to the browser window.

 Open File. Click here to open a file on your hard disk.

 Save. Saves the document on your hard disk.

 Cut. Highlight text in the document and click on this button to remove the text, placing it in the Windows Clipboard.

 Copy. Copies highlighted text to the Clipboard.

 Paste. Click here to paste text from the Clipboard to the document.

Site Manager. Opens the Site Manager, which you can use to manage your Web documents—transfer them to a Web site, for instance. However, at the time of writing, this feature was not working; it should be there soon.

 Bookmarks. Opens the Bookmarks window, so that you can drag bookmarks onto your document to create links. (If you are using SmartMarks, note that this button currently doesn't open the SmartMarks window.)

 Link. Click on this button to insert a link in the document.

 Image Properties. Opens the Image Properties dialog box, which helps you insert a picture into your document. At the time of writing, though, this feature was not working.

 Horiz. Line Properties. Click here to insert a horizontal line across the document.

 Properties. Click here to open the Editor Properties dialog box.

 **Paragraph Style.** The Editor uses a system of styles, much like most good word processors. You can click on text and modify it by selecting a style.

 Numbered list. This button only appears if you select it in the Editor Preferences dialog box. Clicking on it creates a numbered list in the document.

 Bulleted list. Creates a bulleted list. Again, this button won't appear unless you select it from the Preferences dialog box.

 Font Color. Highlight text and then click here to change its color.

 Font Size. Highlight text and then choose a font size setting to make the text larger or smaller than the default for that text style.

 Increase Font Size. Highlight text and click here to increase the size one level. (There are seven sizes, from -2 to +4, with 0 being the default size.)

 Decrease Font Size. Highlight text and click here to decrease the size one level.

Bold. Highlight text and click here to make it bold.

 Italic. Highlight text and click here to make it italic (or to remove italic, if the text is already italic).

 Fixed Width. Highlight text and click here to change the text to a fixed width (monospace) font, a font in which all characters take up the same space.

 Superscript. Highlight a character and click here to raise it above the adjacent character.

 Subscript. Highlight a character and click here to lower it beneath the adjacent character.

 Clear Styles. Highlight text and click here to remove all the text styles, changing the text back to the default font for the paragraph style.

 Decrease indent. Click here to move indented text back to the left.

 Increase indent. Click here to indent text to the right.

 Align left. If a paragraph is centered or aligned to the right (right justified), click here to change it to left alignment.

 Center. Centers the selected paragraph.

 Align right. Right-justifies the selected paragraph.

Entering your text

Start creating a home page. Type the following text into the Editor window (you can see an example in fig. 18.2):

My Home Page
This is my very own home page.

Really Important Stuff
These are WWW pages I use a lot.

Not So Important Stuff
These are WWW pages I use now and again.

Not Important At All Stuff
These are WWW pages I use to waste time.

Fig. 18.2
Start typing the
headings into the
Editor; you'll find it's
just like working with a
word processor.

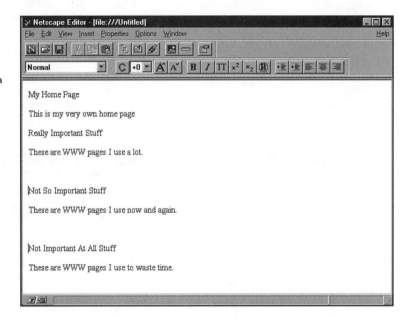

Right now, all you have is basic text; look in the Paragraph Style drop-down list box (the list box on the left side of the Format toolbar), and you'll see it shows *Normal*.

You can quickly change the paragraph styles. For instance, try the following:

1 Click in the *My Home Page* text, then select Heading 1,H1 from the Paragraph Style drop-down list box.

2 Click on the Center toolbar button.

3 Click in the *This is my very own home page* text, then click on the Center toolbar button.

4 Click in the *Really Important Stuff* text, then select Heading 2,H2 from the Paragraph Style drop-down list box.

5 Click in the *Not So Important Stuff* text, then select Heading 2,H2 from the Paragraph Style drop-down list box.

6 Click in the *Not Important At All Stuff* text, then select Heading 2,H1 from the Paragraph Style drop-down list box.

Q&A **Why do the paragraph styles have two names (Header 1 is also named H1, for instance)?**

The second names (H1, LI, DT, and so on) are the special HTML codes that are inserted into the document. If you choose View, By Document Source to see the HTML source document, you'll find these codes, not the full names, used to identify the text.

Now what have you got? Your page should look something like that in figure 18.3.

Fig. 18.3
A few mouse clicks, and you've formatted the document.

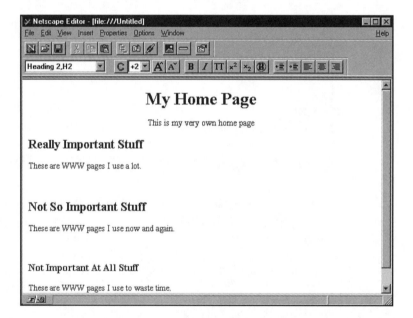

Before you go on, save what you've done: click on the Save button, type a name (**homepage**, if you wish), then click on the Save button. The Editor will save the file with an .HTM extension.

TIP **Want to see what you've just done? Choose View, By Document** Source, and you'll see the HTML source document that the Editor has created for you.

Where did my line breaks go?

Did you create multiple line breaks in your document by pressing Enter? If so, when you finally view your document in the browser window, those line breaks will be gone; the Editor doesn't like multiple line breaks.

For example, try this: Place the cursor at the end of a paragraph (a paragraph that is followed by another paragraph, not the last one in the document) and press Enter several times. Several blank lines appear. Save the document, then press Ctrl+R to reload the document from the hard disk into the Editor. You'll see that the blank lines have gone!

Why? Well, this seems to be a holdover from creating a Web document by entering the HTML codes. Web browsers ignore blank lines in the HTML document. Rather, they only move text down a line when they see a special tag: the <P> or <BR> tag. Of course, there's no reason that the Navigator Gold Editor should do the same; if you entered a blank line, you probably want it there. Nonetheless, that's the way it is.

 Q&A *I've made changes to my document, but I want to go back to the way it was the last time I saved it. How can I do that?*

Press Ctrl+R or choose <u>V</u>iew, <u>R</u>eload.

However, there is a way to add a blank line. Place the cursor at the end of line and choose <u>I</u>nsert, New <u>L</u>ine Break. A blank line appears. This time, if you save the document and then reload it, the blank line remains.

How about links?

Now you're going to get fancy by adding an **anchor**, a link to another document. For example, you may want to add a link to the Netscape home page. (On the other hand, you may not; you can always choose <u>D</u>irectory, Ne<u>t</u>scape's Home to get there, even if you are using your own home page.) Or perhaps you'd like a link to a favorite site.

 Plain English, please!

The HTML tags used to create links are often known as **anchors** because many people refer to the links themselves in the Web documents as anchors.

Click on the blank line below *These are WWW pages I use a lot*, then click on the Link button or choose <u>I</u>nsert, <u>L</u>ink. You'll see the dialog box in figure 18.4.

Fig. 18.4
Enter the text you want to see and the URL you want to link to.

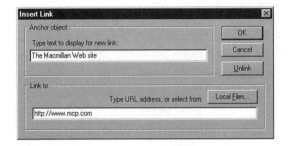

In the first text box, type the text that you want to appear in the document: the words that you will be clicking on to use that link. In the second box, type the URL of the page you want to link to.

 Q&A *Where do I get these URLs?*

You can find URLs in a number of places. You might press Alt+Tab to switch back to the browser window, then use the browser to go to the page you want and copy the URL from the Location bar. Remember also that you can right-click on a link in a Web document and choose Copy This Link Location. You can also copy URLs from desktop shortcuts (see chapter 6): right-click on the shortcut, choose Properties, click on the Internet Shortcut tab, then press Ctrl+C to copy the URL.

You can also get links from another document or elsewhere in the same document: right-click on a link in the Editor and choose <u>C</u>opy Link to copy the URL to the Clipboard.

Notice the Local <u>F</u>iles button; this lets you enter the URL of a file on your hard disk, which is very handy if you are creating a series of linked pages. And there's an <u>U</u>nlink button, too. This is only active if you click inside a link in your document and *then* open this dialog box. Clicking on the button removes the URL so that you can enter a new one, or so that you can retain the document text but remove the link from it.

 TIP **Here's another way to create a link: highlight text that you typed** into the document earlier, then click on the Link button (or right-click on the highlighted text and choose Create <u>L</u>ink Using Selected). The highlighted text will appear in the dialog box. All you need to do is enter the URL and click on OK.

More nifty link tricks

You can also create links by copying them from the browser window. Position the windows so that both are visible. Then click on a link in the browser window, but hold the mouse button down. You'll notice the link turn red. Now, with the mouse button still held down, drag the link from the browser window over to the Editor window (see fig. 18.5), move the pointer to the position you want to place it, and release the mouse button.

Fig. 18.5

You can drag links from the "What's Cool?" page (or any other Web document) into the Editor.

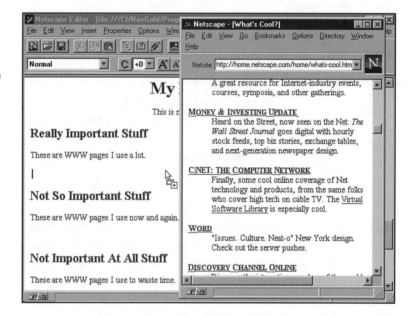

 Finally, why not grab links from your bookmarks? You've probably already created bookmarks to your favorite sites (see chapter 6), and you can quickly create links from them. Click on the Bookmarks button to open the Bookmarks window. (You'll see a message box explaining what you are about to do before the Bookmarks window opens; click on OK to remove it.)

Now you can drag bookmarks from the Bookmarks window onto your document in the Editor. As long as you don't click anywhere in the document—simply drag and release where you want the new link—the Bookmarks window remains above the Editor window.

 TIP   **To convert the Editor window back to a browser window so that** you can test the document you've created, choose File, Switch to Browser.

What about pictures?

No self-respecting Web page would be complete without a picture or two, would it? Luckily, the Editor provides a way for you to insert pictures. Or, at least, it will very soon. At the time of writing, the feature wasn't working.

 When it *is* working, you'll place the cursor where you want the picture, then choose Insert, Image, or click on the Image Properties button.

 TIP **Do you want to find some icons you can use in your documents?** Go to an **icon server:** a Web site from which you can download icons or even link your documents across the Web to a particular icon. Try the following sites:

> **http://www.bsdi.com/icons**
> **http://www-ns.rutgers.edu/doc-images**
> **http://www.di.unipi.it/iconbrowser/icons.html**
> **http://www.cit.gu.edu.au/~anthony/icons/**

Where are you going to get pictures for your documents? You can create them yourself using a graphics program that can save in a .JPG or .GIF format (many can these days). You can also grab them from the Web, remember! Find a picture you want, right-click on it, and choose Save This Image As. (Note, however, that you don't *own* the image, as it may not be in the public domain. You can use it on your own system, but don't put it on a Web site that is visible to other people unless you have permission to use it or know for sure that it's in the public domain.)

 TIP **There's a special command that makes sure that text placed after** an image appears *below* the image, not "wrapped" around it. Let's say you've aligned the picture so that the text following it appears on the right side of the picture. You can now place the cursor inside that text at, say, the end of a paragraph, and choose Insert, Break below Image(s). The text that appears after the cursor is now moved down, below the image.

Adding horizontal lines

Horizontal lines are handy. You can use them to underline headers, as dividers between blocks of text, to underline important information, and so on. And the Editor allows you to create a number of different types of lines, as you can see in figure 18.6.

To place a line across the page, place the cursor on a blank line or in a line of text after which you wish to place the line, and click on the Horiz. Line Properties button (or choose Insert, Horizontal Line) to open the dialog box that you see in figure 18.6.

Fig. 18.6
This dialog box helps you create a line; you can see examples in the Editor.

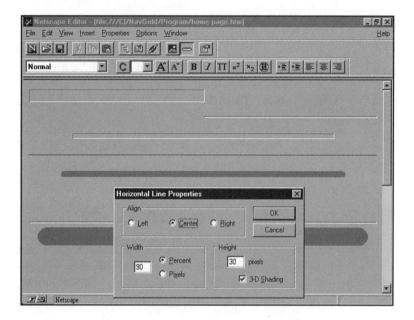

There are a variety of controls in this dialog box. First, you can tell the Editor where you want the line: aligned against the Left, in the Center, or aligned against the Right. Notice, however, that by default, the line has a Width of 100 Percent (that is, it's 100 percent of the width of the document). The alignment settings have no effect until you modify the width setting. (If a line is 100 percent, how can you center it?)

There are actually two ways that you can adjust the line's width: by Percent or by Pixels. The Percent setting refers to the width of the document (when the window is maximized). So a line that has a width of 50 percent will stretch across half of the document.

The Pixel setting is harder to predict, though. A pixel is the smallest unit that your computer monitor can display. For instance, in VGA mode, a monitor displays 640 columns and 480 rows of pixels. So if you create a line that's 60 pixels wide, it will be about 10 percent of the width of the document—in VGA mode. But what if the person viewing the document is using a different resolution—1024 by 768, for example? In such a case, the line that was 10 percent of the width in VGA is now about 5 percent of the width. Of course, this doesn't matter if you are creating a home page for your own use, but bear it in mind if you are creating documents that you plan to put out on the Web.

There are two more settings: the Height, which is measured in pixels, and 3-D Shading. The first couple of lines in figure 18.6 are 3-D shaded lines. This 3-D effect is created by using four different lines to create a "box,"—the left and top lines are dark gray, and the bottom and right lines are white. Clear the 3-D check box, and your horizontal line will be a single dark gray line.

Q&A **How do I change a line I created earlier?**

Click on the line, which places the cursor immediately before the line. Then click on the Horiz. Line Properties button, make your changes, and click on OK.

Creating multiple documents

You may want to create a hierarchy of documents. Create a home page—a page that appears when you open Netscape—with a table of contents linked to several other documents. In each of those documents, you can then have links related to a particular subject: one for business, one for music, one for your kids, and so on.

This is very simple to do. Create and save several documents in the Editor. (I suggest you put them all in the same directory, for simplicity's sake.) Each time you finish one, choose File, New Document to clear the screen so that you can create the next one. When you have all your documents completed, open your home page document again (click on the Open File button or choose File, Open File), and enter links to each page using the method previously described.

TIP **If you've worked with several documents in one editing session,** you can move back and forward through those documents. There aren't any Back or Forward commands in the Editor, but try Alt+left arrow and Alt+right arrow.

How can I use my home page?

You've created a home page; now how do you use it? Complete the following procedure:

1 Click on the Browser button, or choose File, Switch to Browser. The Netscape browser opens and displays your document.

2 Click in the Location text box, highlighting the URL.

3 Press Ctrl+C to copy the URL.

4 Choose Options, General Preferences, and click on the Appearance tab.

5 Click on the Home Page Location option button (in the Startup area).

6 Click inside the text box below this option button.

7 Press Ctrl+V to paste the URL into the text box.

8 Click on OK.

Now, the next time you start your browser, you'll see your very own home page. Simple, eh?

Here's a good one—let's change it

Navigator Gold provides a wonderful way to quickly create Web pages—by "borrowing" them from the Web and modifying them to your requirements. If you see a page you like—one that has many links that you'll need in your home page, for instance, or one that uses a particularly attractive format— you can open that page and make changes to it, then save it on your hard disk.

CAUTION Be aware that you don't own something you "borrow" from the Web. If you borrow something from the Web and simply keep it for your own use, there's no problem. But if you publish it by creating a Web site using pictures and text you grabbed from another Web site, for instance, you may be guilty of copyright infringement. If you use the borrowed stuff as a template, though, replacing everything in the page with your own stuff, there's no problem in most cases (although it's possible for a particular design to be copyrighted, too).

First, display the page you want to modify in the Netscape window. Now you have two ways to open the Editor window. You can choose File, Edit Document, which will change the browser window to the Editor window. But it's handy to have the browser window open at the same time the Editor window is open (you can then search around on the Web for other links that you need), so the following is another method:

1 Place the cursor inside the Location text box, highlighting the text, and press Ctrl+C (copying the URL to the Clipboard).

2 Choose Window, Netscape Editor. A blank Editor window opens.

3 Choose File, Open Location to open the Open Location dialog box.

4 Press Ctrl+C to paste the URL into this box, then press Enter. The Editor will load the document.

Now you have the best of both worlds: you have the document you need open in the Editor, and the browser's still open so you can move around on the Web to find things you want to add to your document.

Modifying a document

Now that you have a document that you want to modify, you can work in it as you would documents you created yourself. You can delete text and replace it with your own, and change text using the formatting tools.

How do you highlight text? The Editor window works a little like a word processor, although with some important differences. Simply click in the text to place the cursor, then use the arrow keys to move around in the text. You can also hold down the Shift key while you press the arrow keys to highlight text, though this is a little strange: Shift+up arrow highlights from the cursor point to the beginning of the line or to the same point on the line above, for example (you'll have to try this for yourself to see).

Also, you can use the mouse cursor to select text: hold down the mouse button while you drag the pointer across text to highlight it.

 TIP   **As with a word processor, you don't need to highlight text in** order to modify *paragraph* formats. If you want to change the paragraph style, indentation, or alignment, simply click once in the paragraph and then make your change.

When you've made the changes you need, click on the Save button; or choose File, Save, and you'll be able to save the document on your hard disk. (No, you can't save it to the original location even if you own that location!)

Where are the pictures?!

If you modify a document and then save it to your hard disk, you may be disappointed to find that the pictures are gone. You won't notice it right away, but press Ctrl+R to reload the document from your hard disk, and you'll find that the pictures have been replaced with the ? icon. Where have these pictures gone? Well, you've just saved the text of the document to your hard disk, not the pictures within the document.

Here's what you may want to do. Go back to the browser window and load that file again. Then save each of the pictures into the same directory where you've stored your document; you can do that by right-clicking on a picture and choosing Save Image As.

Now return to the Editor and insert the picture. (Note that later versions may handle this automatically, transferring the pictures for you.)

19

Advanced Web Authoring

In this chapter:

- **What are the other paragraph styles?**

- **How can I create lists?**

- **Aligning and indenting paragraphs**

- **Character formats: colors, sizes, superscript, and more**

- **Links within documents**

- **Relative and absolute links**

You've only learned the basics. Here are more authoring techniques you need to know . . . .

n chapter 18, you learned how to use Netscape Navigator Gold's Editor to design and produce a home page and modify an existing one. But there's more. In this chapter, you'll find out about a few more advanced features of the Editor. You may want to make your home page really cool or even use your new skills to publish your own stuff on the Web.

Q&A   *I want to publish on the Web. Once I've created my Web pages, where do I put them?*

Ask your service provider whether you can place Web pages on their server. Many allow people to set up Web pages for little or no cost. You can transfer them from your computer to your service provider's system using a program such as WS_FTP (see chapter 11 for more information). Navigator Gold should soon have a feature called Site Manager, which will help you transfer files, too.

Lots more formatting

There are a number of formatting tools that I didn't get around to describing in chapter 18. You can format a paragraph in many different ways by setting up indents and alignment, as well as by choosing a paragraph style. And you can modify particular words or individual characters, too, by changing colors and type styles.

The other paragraph styles

You've only seen a couple of paragraph styles so far, so let's take a look at the others. In figure 19.1, you can see examples of all the different *Heading* levels as well as *Normal* text, the *Address* style, and the *Formatted* style.

You can apply any of these styles by placing the cursor inside the paragraph you want to modify and then selecting the style from the drop-down list box (or by picking the style from the <u>P</u>roperties, <u>P</u>aragraph cascading menu). Note that what you see depends on how you've set up Netscape; other browsers may display these styles in a different way.

Fig. 19.1
The formatted headers
and address styles.

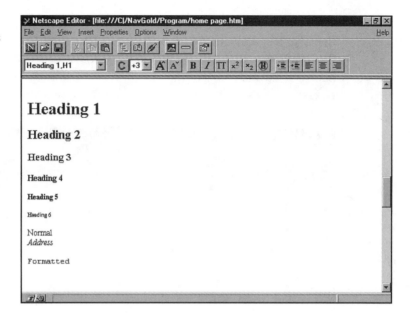

 TIP **Browsers normally remove blank lines and multiple spaces when** viewing a document. The *Formatted* style tells the browser to keep the text format as it appears in the HTML document. In fact, unless you are using the *Formatted* style, the Editor won't let you type multiple spaces into a document. Also, long lines of *Formatted* text will run off the side of the window—the text will not wrap down to the next line.

However, note that Navigator Gold currently doesn't allow you to enter multiple blank lines, even if you've selected the *Formatted* style. This is probably a bug, though, so later versions may allow multiple blank lines; try it and see.

How about creating lists?

You can also use the Paragraph Styles drop-down list box and a couple of the toolbar buttons to create lists. You can create **bulleted lists, numbered lists,** and **definition lists.**

The quickest way to create a bulleted list is to place the cursor on a blank line and then select *List Item,LI* from the Paragraph Styles drop-down list box (or click on the bulleted list button). You'll see a bullet (a black circle) appear at the beginning of the line. Type the first entry, press Enter, type the next entry, press Enter, and so on. You can see an example in figure 19.2.

Fig. 19.2
You can create lists using the paragraph styles. You can also indent these lists.

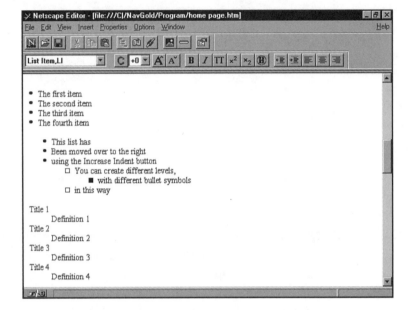

You can create a numbered list in the same way by using the numbered list button. (Or you should be able to soon; this feature was not working at the time of writing.)

Another form of list is the definition list, which you can create by alternating lines between the *Description Title,DD* and *Description Text,DT* styles, (see figure 19.2).

Q&A ***Where are the bulleted list and number list buttons? They're not on my toolbar.***

They are not displayed unless you choose them in the Editor Preferences dialog box.

Positioning paragraphs

Now, let's see how to move paragraphs around the page. You can use the five toolbar buttons on the right side of the Format toolbar to indent paragraphs, align them to the left, center them, and align them to the right. You can combine alignment settings and indentations, too. See figure 19.3 for a few examples.

Fig. 19.3
You can position paragraphs in a variety of ways.

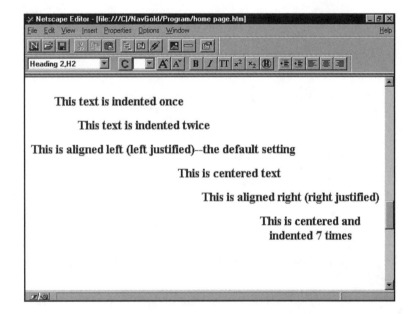

How can I modify character formats?

You have quite a bit of control over individual characters. In effect, you are telling your document to override the way in which the browser that opens your document displays the characters. A browser, for example, may have a default text color set, but you can override that color and define your own. (You looked at this and at how Netscape can be told to override this sort of overriding in chapter 3.) Figure 19.4 shows a variety of character formats.

Fig. 19.4
Highlight text and click on the appropriate button to modify it.

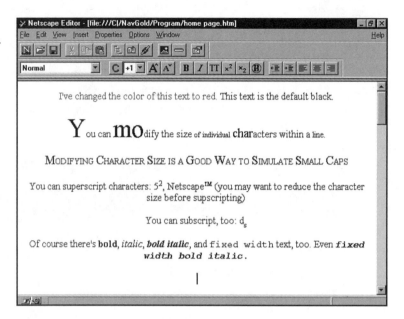

Simply highlight the characters you want to modify, then click on the appropriate button (or choose the appropriate entry from the Properties menu), as follows:

Font Color. You'll see a dialog box from which you can choose a color.

Font Size. Change a character's size, ranging from –2 to +4. (That is, from two "units" below the normal style size to four "units" above.)

Increase Font Size. Click here to increase the size one unit.

Decrease Font Size. Click here to decrease the size one unit.

Bold. This changes the character to bold (or removes bold if the text is already bold). You can combine this with italic to create bold italic.

Italic. Click here to change the text to italic (or to remove italic).

Fixed Width. This changes the text to a fixed width (monospace) font, a font in which all characters take up the same amount of space.

Superscript. This raises the character above the line of type, and is often used for the trademark symbol or an exponent in a mathematical expression, for example. You may also want to reduce the character size when using this feature.

Subscript. This lowers the character, placing it beneath the line of type.

Clear Styles. Click here to remove all the text styles, changing the text back to the default font for the paragraph style.

Relative versus absolute links

If you plan to move your Web pages onto a Web server somewhere, it's a good idea to use **relative** links. This means that a link doesn't describe the full location of the item being referenced: the image you've inserted or another document the reader can reach by clicking on a link. Instead, it describes where the item is relative to the document itself. An **absolute** link provides the full Web address of the item. For instance, the following is a URL used in an absolute link:

http://home.netscape.com/comprod/mirror/index.html

This URL provides the full Web address of the index.html document. Within the INDEX.HTML document is a picture, taken from the ONE.GIF file (INDEX.HTML is a real document at the Netscape site; you can go and take a look if you wish). But the picture is referenced using a relative link:

/comprod/mirror/images/one.gif

Notice that this URL doesn't contain **http://** or a host name. It simply tells your browser where the .GIF file is, relative to the position of the document you are viewing by giving the **path** through the computer's directory structure to the file.

So, if you tell the Editor to *Automatically adjust link references*, it makes sure that when you transfer the files to the Web server, it makes all the references to objects that are being moved— files and pictures on your hard disk—relative references, so that they will work on the other computer.

Q&A   ***Where can I learn more about creating HTML files?***

Your local bookstore has approximately eight million books on the subject. Also, go to the Netscape browser and choose <u>H</u>elp, How to <u>C</u>reate Web Services. You'll find a lot of useful links to documents that will help you get started.

Lots more to come

Netscape Navigator Gold was far from finished when this book went to print. You can expect to see many more features added over the next few versions of Navigator Gold. There will be Site Manager, a special utility that helps you manage all your HTML files and transfers them to a Web site. You'll find tools that help you create forms, tables, and JavaScripts. You'll also be able to create **imagemaps** (pictures with hotspots on them that lead to other Web documents), experiment with special characters, and add sounds and multi-media.

These features will probably begin appearing in Navigator Gold sometime in January of 1996.

Action Index

Finding and Installing Netscape

When you need information on...	You'll find help here...
Where is Netscape available?	p. 24
The different Netscape versions	p. 24
What's the Netscape Navigator LAN Edition?	p. 26
The sort of Internet connection you need	p. 27
SLIP and PPP connections	p. 27
Downloading Netscape	p. 28
The Netscape/HTML association	p. 29
Your other browser is no longer associated with HTML	p. 30
What's Windows 95 Auto-Dial?	p. 31
Network connections and Netscape	p. 33

Working on the Web

When you need information on...	You'll find help here...
How do I start the program?	p. 38
Working offline with Netscape	p. 39
The Netscape home page	p. 39
How can I define another home page?	p. 40
The Netscape components	pp. 41-43

continues

Using the Cache

When you need information on...	You'll find help here...
Using the Netscape cache	p. 65
How can I configure the cache?	p. 65
What are these files in the TEMP directory?	p. 66
When does Netscape verify a page?	p. 68
Reloading pages clears the cache	p. 68

Advanced Web

When you need information on...	You'll find help here...
How can I find things within a Web document?	p. 69
What can I do with pop-up menus?	p. 70
What are "tables?"	p. 74
Working in forms	p. 75
What's a secure site?	p. 76
Using passwords on the Web	p. 77
Why did another Browser window open automatically?	p. 77
Why is this Web page split into separate panes?	p. 78
What's a Java applet?	p. 79
Multimedia Web pages	p. 80
Why can't Netscape display this Web page very well?	p. 81
How can I view the document's information?	p. 83

The history list, bookmarks, and shortcuts

SmartMarks

When you need information on...	You'll find help here...
What are bulletins?	p. 102
Finding catalogs of useful bookmarks	p. 103
How do I know when the catalogs are updated?	p. 103

Searching for information on the Web

When you need information on...	You'll find help here...
How can I find information on the Web?	p. 108
Links from Netscape to search tools	p. 108
Using a search engine—InfoSeek	p. 109
Finding more search engines	p. 111
How can I search several engines at once?	p. 112
Using Internet directories—Yahoo	p. 112
Finding more directories	p. 114
What are robots, wanderers, and spiders?	p. 117
Your own personal agent—SmartMarks	p. 125
How do I use SmartMarks to create searches?	p. 125
How do I search sites not set up in SmartMarks?	p. 128

Saving stuff from the Web

Multimedia on the Web

continues

Connecting to non-Web sites (Gopher, FTP, etc.)

The Netscape Mail program

When you need information on...	You'll find help here...
How do I configure the e-mail system?	p. 204
The different ways to send e-mail	p. 204
The mailto: link	p. 204
How can I send this Web document to someone?	p. 211
How can I send e-mail with formatted text?	p. 212
E-mailing binary files	p. 212
MIME versus UUENCODE	p. 212
How does the address book work?	p. 214
Opening the Netscape Mail window	p. 215
How do I retrieve my e-mail?	p. 215
How do I see the full message header?	p. 216
Why can't I see the Web document in the message?	p. 216
The different ways to respond to messages	p. 217
What are message threads?	p. 217
Creating folders	p. 218
How can I move messages between folders?	p. 218
What are the flag and green-diamond columns?	p. 219

The Netscape Newsgroup program

Gopher, WAIS, finger, Chat, and Telnet

When you need information on...	You'll find help here...
Searching Gopherspace (Veronica & Jughead)	p. 244
Searching WAIS databases	p. 247
What's finger?	p. 249
Webchat	p. 250
Netscape Chat	p. 251
Connecting to Telnet and TN3270 sites	p. 251
Where can I find Telnet and TN3270 programs?	p. 253
The HYTELNET list of Telnet sites	p. 254

Security on the Web

When you need information on...	You'll find help here...
What are the dangers of Web commerce?	p. 258
Just how dangerous is it?	p. 258
What is public-key encryption?	p. 259
128- and 40-bit keys	p. 260
Carrying out secure transactions	p. 261
How do I turn off the security messages?	p. 264
What's a site certificate?	p. 265
How can I find a list of secure servers?	p. 265
Editing certificates	p. 266
Other secure transaction systems	p. 269

Java and JavaScript

When you need information on...	You'll find help here...
What is Java?	p. 272
What sorts of things can Java do?	p. 272
The dangers of Java	p. 272
Finding Java sites	p. 273
A few Java samples	p. 274
What is the Java Console?	p. 278
What is JavaScript?	p. 278
When will JavaScripts run?	p. 279

Frames, panes, and targeted windows

When you need information on...	You'll find help here...
What are frames (or panes)?	p. 282
What are targeted (or named) windows?	p. 283
The uses of frames	p. 283
Sample frame sites	p. 284
Where can I find frame sites?	p. 285
How can I go back through frames?	p. 288

Navigator Gold and HTML authoring

When you need information on...	You'll find help here...
What extra features does Navigator Gold have?	p. 294
Why not all browsers can display all the Netscape features	p. 294
Why do I want to create a home page?	p. 294
How do you open the Editor?	p. 295
Creating a Web document	p. 298
Viewing your work	p. 300
Why do line breaks disappear?	p. 301
Undoing all the changes you've made since saving	p. 301
Adding links to documents	p. 301
Inserting pictures	p. 304
Adjusting word wrap around pictures	p. 304
Creating horizontal lines	p. 304
Creating a hierarchy of linked pages	p. 306
Moving back through the pages you've created	p. 306
How can I set my page as the home page?	p. 307
Modifying a Web page you've found	p. 307
Where can I place Web pages I want to publish?	p. 312
Creating bulleted, numbered, and definition lists	p. 313
Aligning and indenting paragraphs	p. 315

continues

Index

PLUG YOURSELF INTO...

The Macmillan Information SuperLibrary™

Free information and vast computer resources from the world's leading computer book publisher—online!

FIND THE BOOKS THAT ARE RIGHT FOR YOU!
A complete online catalog, plus sample chapters and tables of contents!

- STAY INFORMED with the latest computer industry news through our online newsletter, press releases, and customized Information SuperLibrary Reports.

- GET FAST ANSWERS to your questions about Macmillan Computer Publishing books.

- VISIT our online bookstore for the latest information and editions!

- COMMUNICATE with our expert authors through e-mail and conferences.

- DOWNLOAD SOFTWARE from the immense Macmillan Computer Publishing library:
  - Source code, shareware, freeware, and demos

- DISCOVER HOT SPOTS on other parts of the Internet.

- WIN BOOKS in ongoing contests and giveaways!

TO PLUG INTO MCP:

WORLD WIDE WEB: http://www.mcp.com

FTP: ftp.mcp.com

GET CONNECTED
to the ultimate source of computer information!

The MCP Forum on CompuServe

Go online with the world's leading computer book publisher! Macmillan Computer Publishing offers everything you need for computer success!

Find the books that are right for you!
A complete online catalog, plus sample chapters and tables of contents give you an in-depth look at all our books. The best way to shop or browse!

➤ Get fast answers and technical support for MCP books and software

➤ Join discussion groups on major computer subjects

➤ Interact with our expert authors via e-mail and conferences

➤ Download software from our immense library:

   ▷ Source code from books
   ▷ Demos of hot software
   ▷ The best shareware and freeware
   ▷ Graphics files

Join now and get a free CompuServe Starter Kit!

To receive your free CompuServe Introductory Membership, call **1-800-848-8199** and ask for representative #597.

The Starter Kit includes:
➤ Personal ID number and password
➤ $15 credit on the system
➤ Subscription to *CompuServe Magazine*

Once on the CompuServe System, type:

GO MACMILLAN

for the most computer information anywhere!

MACMILLAN
COMPUTER
PUBLISHING

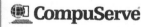

Complete and Return this Card
for a *FREE* Computer Book Catalog

Thank you for purchasing this book! You have purchased a superior computer book written expressly for your needs. To continue to provide the kind of up-to-date, pertinent coverage you've come to expect from us, we need to hear from you. Please take a minute to complete and return this self-addressed, postage-paid form. In return, we'll send you a free catalog of all our computer books on topics ranging from word processing to programming and the internet.

Mr. ☐   Mrs. ☐   Ms. ☐   Dr. ☐

Name (first) ☐☐☐☐☐☐☐☐☐☐☐☐☐☐ (M.I.) ☐ (last) ☐☐☐☐☐☐☐☐☐☐☐☐☐☐☐☐

Address ☐☐☐☐☐☐☐☐☐☐☐☐☐☐☐☐☐☐☐☐☐☐☐☐☐☐☐☐☐☐☐☐☐☐☐

☐☐☐☐☐☐☐☐☐☐☐☐☐☐☐☐☐☐☐☐☐☐☐☐☐☐☐☐☐☐☐☐☐☐☐

City ☐☐☐☐☐☐☐☐☐☐☐☐☐☐☐☐☐☐ State ☐☐ Zip ☐☐☐☐☐ ☐☐☐☐

Phone ☐☐☐ ☐☐☐☐☐☐☐☐ Fax ☐☐☐ ☐☐☐☐☐☐☐

Company Name ☐☐☐☐☐☐☐☐☐☐☐☐☐☐☐☐☐☐☐☐☐☐☐☐☐☐☐☐☐☐☐

E-mail address ☐☐☐☐☐☐☐☐☐☐☐☐☐☐☐☐☐☐☐☐☐☐☐☐☐☐☐☐☐☐☐☐☐

1. Please check at least (3) influencing factors for purchasing this book.

Front or back cover information on book .... ☐
Special approach to the content .... ☐
Completeness of content... ☐
Author's reputation .... ☐
Publisher's reputation .... ☐
Book cover design or layout .... ☐
Index or table of contents of book .... ☐
Price of book.. ☐
Special effects, graphics, illustrations .... ☐
Other (Please specify): _____ ☐

2. How did you first learn about this book?

Saw in Macmillan Computer Publishing catalog .... ☐
Recommended by store personnel .... ☐
Saw the book on bookshelf at store .... ☐
Recommended by a friend .... ☐
Received advertisement in the mail .... ☐
Saw an advertisement in: _____ ☐
Read book review in: _____ ☐
Other (Please specify): _____ ☐

3. How many computer books have you purchased in the last six months?

This book only .... ☐   3 to 5 books...................... ☐
2 books.................. ☐   More than 5 .... ☐

4. Where did you purchase this book?

Bookstore .... ☐
Computer Store .... ☐
Consumer Electronics Store .... ☐
Department Store .... ☐
Office Club .... ☐
Warehouse Club .... ☐
Mail Order .... ☐
Direct from Publisher .... ☐
Internet site .... ☐
Other (Please specify): _____ ☐

5. How long have you been using a computer?

☐ Less than 6 months   ☐ 6 months to a year
☐ 1 to 3 years   ☐ More than 3 years

6. What is your level of experience with personal computers and with the subject of this book?

	With PCs	With subject of book
New	☐	☐
Casual	☐	☐
Accomplished	☐	☐
Expert	☐	☐

Source Code ISBN: 0-7897-0728-4

7. Which of the following best describes your job title?

Administrative Assistant .... ☐
Coordinator .... ☐
Manager/Supervisor .... ☐
Director .... ☐
Vice President .... ☐
President/CEO/COO .... ☐
Lawyer/Doctor/Medical Professional .... ☐
Teacher/Educator/Trainer .... ☐
Engineer/Technician .... ☐
Consultant .... ☐
Not employed/Student/Retired .... ☐
Other (Please specify): _____ ☐

8. Which of the following best describes the area of the company your job title falls under?

Accounting .... ☐
Engineering .... ☐
Manufacturing .... ☐
Operations .... ☐
Marketing .... ☐
Sales .... ☐
Other (Please specify): _____ ☐

9. What is your age?

Under 20 .... ☐
21-29 .... ☐
30-39 .... ☐
40-49 .... ☐
50-59 .... ☐
60-over .... ☐

10. Are you:

Male .... ☐
Female .... ☐

11. Which computer publications do you read regularly? (Please list)

_____
_____
_____
_____
_____
_____
_____
_____
_____
_____

Comments: _____
_____
_____

Fold here and scotch-tape to mail.

ǁ‧ǁ‧‧ǁ‧‧ǁ‧‧ǁ‧‧‧‧ǁ‧‧ǁ‧‧ǁ‧‧‧ǁǁ‧‧‧‧ǁǁ‧‧‧‧ǁ

NO POSTAGE
NECESSARY
IF MAILED
IN THE
UNITED STATES

BUSINESS REPLY MAIL
FIRST-CLASS MAIL PERMIT NO. 9918 INDIANAPOLIS IN

POSTAGE WILL BE PAID BY THE ADDRESSEE

ATTN MARKETING
MACMILLAN COMPUTER PUBLISHING
MACMILLAN PUBLISHING USA
201 W 103RD ST
INDIANAPOLIS IN 46290-9042